Anonymous

The Catholicos of the East and his People

Anonymous

The Catholicos of the East and his People

ISBN/EAN: 9783337417901

Printed in Europe, USA, Canada, Australia, Japan

Cover: Foto ©Lupo / pixelio.de

More available books at **www.hansebooks.com**

THE CATHOLICOS OF THE EAST
AND HIS PEOPLE.

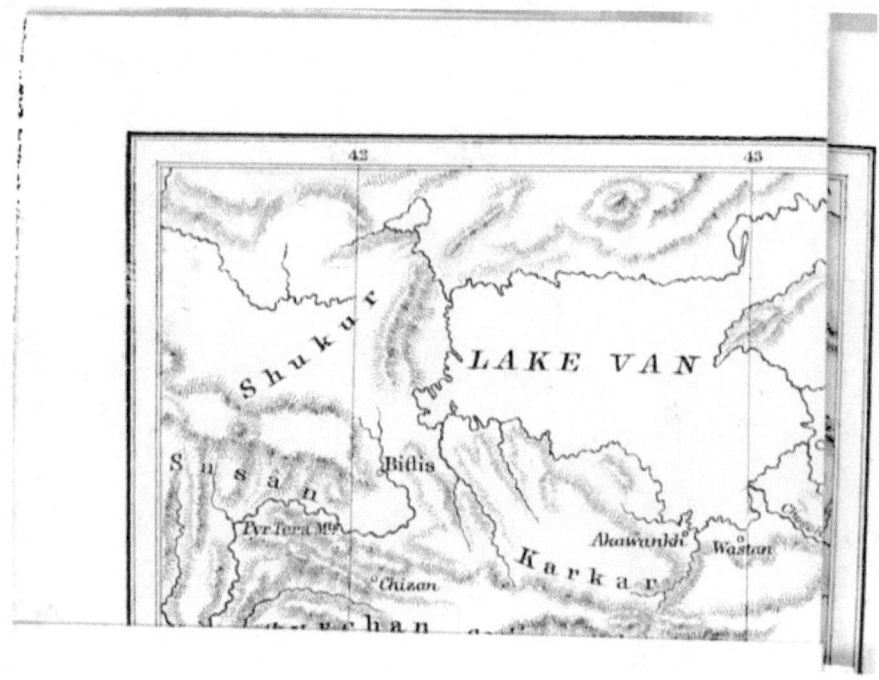

THE CATHOLICOS OF THE EAST AND HIS PEOPLE.

BEING

THE IMPRESSIONS OF FIVE YEARS' WORK IN THE
"ARCHBISHOP OF CANTERBURY'S ASSYRIAN MISSION;"

*AN ACCOUNT OF THE RELIGIOUS AND SECULAR LIFE
AND OPINIONS OF THE*

EASTERN SYRIAN CHRISTIANS OF
KURDISTAN AND NORTHERN PERSIA
(KNOWN ALSO AS NESTORIANS).

BY

ARTHUR JOHN MACLEAN, M.A.,
DEAN OF ARGYLL AND THE ISLES,
AND
WILLIAM HENRY BROWNE, LL.M.,
ST. JOHN'S COLLEGE, CAMBRIDGE.

WITH MAP.

PUBLISHED UNDER THE DIRECTION OF THE TRACT COMMITTEE.

LONDON:
SOCIETY FOR PROMOTING CHRISTIAN KNOWLEDGE,
NORTHUMBERLAND AVENUE, CHARING CROSS, W.C.
NEW YORK: E. & J. B. YOUNG AND CO.
1892.

TO HIS GRACE

THE MOST REVEREND AND RIGHT HONOURABLE FATHER IN GOD

EDWARD WHITE,

BY DIVINE PROVIDENCE

LORD ARCHBISHOP OF CANTERBURY,

PRIMATE OF ALL ENGLAND AND METROPOLITAN,

THIS RECORD OF AN ANCIENT PEOPLE,

WHO OWE SO MUCH TO HIS GRACE'S EXERTIONS ON

THEIR BEHALF,

IS,

BY PERMISSION,

RESPECTFULLY DEDICATED.

PREFACE.

WE have endeavoured in these pages to describe the life and customs, both ancient and modern, of a people who form a remarkable outpost of Christianity in the East; and we have also given an account of their services, adding some specimens from their rituals, which we have chosen as having never yet been published in English. The description of the life of this people depends on our own observation and careful questioning during some years spent in different districts of Kurdistan and Northern Persia, in the work of the "Archbishop of Canterbury's Assyrian Mission," which has been sent out by his Grace, at the repeated request of the people themselves, not to draw them away from their own old Church and customs, but to give them the means of restoring that old Church once more to a state of efficiency. But the present book is not so much a description of the Mission we have been engaged in, as of the people themselves.

In the account of the ancient customs of the people we have depended largely on the "Sunhadus," or Book of Canon Law, which is in constant use among them, and is continually consulted by their bishops in deciding cases. This is called sometimes the smaller Sunhadus, to distinguish it from the larger collection of canons and decrees of which copies are found at Mosul and elsewhere, but which is not now used by the old Syrians themselves. Reference is also frequently made in these pages to the Sunhadus found at Ashitha in Tiari. This contains, besides the usual canons, the interesting "Book of Heavenly Intelligences," attributed to Mar Shimun Bar Saba'i, and other matter.

We wish here to make clear a point on which we may be misunderstood. This book is intended to be, as far as possible, uncontroversial; and therefore we have made scarcely any reference to the Roman Catholick Mission of the Lazarist Fathers and Sisters of St. Vincent de Paul or to the American Presbyterian Mission, which both have their headquarters at Urmi. We do not wish to underrate the value of the many good works in the way of hospitals, schools, translations of the Holy Scriptures into the vernacular, and other productions of the printing press, which have been undertaken by these two Missions, or the many acts of kindness

PREFACE. ix

shown by their members to ourselves; but, as they both adopt the method of proselytizing and destroying the old "Church of the East," we have thought it better not to deal with the subject at all than to state at full length what we believe to be the harm done by their methods, and so be drawn away from our real purpose, which is to describe the life and customs of the Old Church. It will be seen also that the work of the Archbishop of Canterbury's Mission is only incidentally dealt with; we wish rather to speak of the people themselves.

We are indebted to the Rev. D. Macleane, M.A., the Rev. W. C. Bishop, M.A., and the Rev. Canon Bright, D.D., for various suggestions; to the Rev. E. Cutts, D.D., the Rev. Y. M. Neesan, and Mr. Athelstan Riley, for some of the illustrations; and to the Committee of the "Assyrian Mission" for the use of their map. It should be added that the nomenclature and orthography of this map do not agree in all cases with those adopted in this book.

NOTE ON THE PRONUNCIATION OF NAMES.

In transliterating Syriac names into English, we have adopted the continental sounds of the vowels. The letter *q* is used to represent the hard *k* sound, in order that there be no confusion between it and the soft *k*. If a word is pronounced with the hard sound when it should be pronounced with the soft, or *vice versâ*, it becomes unintelligible to a native. There are also two *t* sounds, but the exigencies of the press prevent their being distinguished in this book. *Kh* is a hard aspirate, somewhat harsher than the Scottish and German *ch*; while *ch* in this book has the same sound as in the English word "church." An apostrophe denotes a hiatus or catch in the breath, which cannot be represented by any English letter. The two Syriac *s* sounds are so little if at all distinguished in practice in the vernacular, that it is unnecessary to represent them by different signs in English. *Dh* is like *th* in "then;" *th* like *th* in "thin;" *gh* is also an aspirate. A final *w* sometimes approaches a *v* in sound.

EASTER, 1892.

CONTENTS.

CHAPTER I.

INTRODUCTORY.

Short historical account of the people—Dependence on Antioch—The Church of the Persian Empire—Tamerlane—Internal schisms—Names of the people—Their present geographical and political divisions—Ashiret and Rayat ... 3

CHAPTER II.

EVERYDAY LIFE IN THE MOUNTAINS OF KURDISTAN.

Qudshanis—The patriarchal court—Life without clocks—The patriarch's relations—His visitors—His dress—The Raban Yonan—A mediæval jester—The metropolitan—Miserable state of the Rayats—Oppressions of the people—Kurds and Turks—Miscarriages of justice 11

CHAPTER III.

THE ASHIRET COUNTRY.

The Zab—Roads—Bridges—A perilous crossing—A patriarch in difficulties—Crossing in a basket—Building fields—Disappearance of a landed property—Occupations of the Ashirets—The women—The summer encampment—Massacres by Kurds—Ashiret guns—Tiari houses—The fireplace—The roofs and mosquitoes—Vines and grapes—Types of face—Jilu and Bas—The Butterstone—Maliks—The stone of Balal the fool—The Yezidis 29

CONTENTS.

CHAPTER IV.
EVERYDAY LIFE IN PERSIA.

Rising with sun — Beds — Sleeping-erections — Sleeping in clothes — Breakfast — Syrian houses: no windows on streets — Doorways — Narrow muddy streets — Village houses — The baita — Oven — Carpets and mats — Roofs — Town houses — Christian population of Urmi — Mart Mariam and St. George's Church, Urmi — Building — Masons — Carpenters — Wet wood — Windows — Glass — Looking-glasses — Pictures — Bazaar — Modakhel — Haggling — Donkeys — Roads and bridges — Riding fast — "Drunken Europeans" — Syrian occupations — Wages and prices — Buffaloes — Ploughing — Irrigation — Wood for burning — Mills — Malaria — Vineyards — Melon fields — Booths and lodges — Watering gardens — Tobacco — Grapes — Raisins — Wine — Arrack — Threshing-floor — Winnowing — Fishing — Sheep — Description of the plains — The Sea of Urmi and its rivers — Bathing — A sheet of salt — Snow — Storks and hoopoes — Partridges — Travelling in Persia 47

CHAPTER V.
EVERYDAY LIFE IN PERSIA—(continued).

Women's occupations — Baking — Manure fuel — Masta — Honey — Dowi — Cheese — Storing — Spinning and weaving — Dress — Children little old men — Veiling — Rags — Shaving — Beards — Fair hair and blue eyes — Dying — Women's position — Kissing a woman's hand — Going to the wells at even — Hospitality — A feast — Smoking — Music — The guard and the curfew — Salutations — Presents — Coming of the Vali Ahd — The Peshwaz — "God save the Queen" — Fireworks — Letter-writing — A poem on the three birds from London 85

CHAPTER VI.
CONDITIONS OF LIFE UNDER THE PERSIAN GOVERNMENT.

Autocracy impotent to govern — Relation of master and servant — The two Jews — The landlord system — Aghas — Village tenure — Taxes — Tenure of vineyards, fields,

CONTENTS. xiii

and orchards—The kokha and malik—Oriental justice—Disabilities of Christians—Apostasy—Petty oppression—The plaintiff—Bringing up old cases—Danger of going bail—A crafty governor—A governor's account of his duties—A word worse than a blow—Testimony to a claim—One way of earning a reputation—Bribes—Intrigues—Public security—Punishing criminals—The bastinado—Frontier raids—Need of trades—Going to Russia—Usury—Earnest money—Inheritance of property—Wills 118

CHAPTER VII.

MARRIAGE CUSTOMS.

Betrothals—The parents' consent—Rebekah and Isaak—Table of affinity—A Syrian's account of the customs of his people—The wedding procession—The religious ceremony—The knitting of the bridechamber—Contributions to the marriage—Lamps—A Mussulman's wedding festivities—The dowry—Several families under one roof—A man and his daughter-in-law—Eloping—Remarriage—Divorce 142

CHAPTER VIII.

THE SYRIAN AT SCHOOL.

Intelligence of the children—Their affection for their teachers—System of schools in the Archbishop of Canterbury's Mission—The village schools—High schools—Learning by heart—"Is England in London?"—The upper school for deacons and older students—Early marriage—Trying to bribe a missionary—Mountain and plain boys—Punishments—"Pouring into prison"—Marks—Games—Writing and illumination—A "beautiful pen"—Printing Syriac—Order and method—"Fleeing"—Inquisitiveness—Inability to swallow too much—Breaking up—The girls at school—Rivalry with the boys—Learning to be good housewives—Outcome of education—Providing school-books—Bookbinding 160

CHAPTER IX.

THE EAST SYRIAN CLERGY.

The three orders and nine divisions—Comparison with the ranks of the angels—All the offices filled by our Lord—The present head of the Church of the East—His style—The succession to the Patriarchate and to the bishoprics—The old method—Mar Shimun's authority—The other Patriarchates—Independence of Seleucia—The metropolitan—The old provinces and missions of the Syrians—The bishops—Old method of election—A bishop's functions—Swearing a kind of ordeal—Fees and firstfruits—Ordinations—The parish priest—His functions and position—Dress of the clergy—The old tonsure—Election of a parish priest—Begging in Europe—The fivelegged ass—Deacons—Their duties—Minor offices—Monasteries 181

CHAPTER X.

THE DAILY SERVICES.

The semantron calls people to prayer—Houses of prayer—The evening service—Taking off shoes—The kiss of peace—"Farcing" the Lord's prayer—Congregational singing—The two choirs—The psalms and anthems—Specimen anthems—Specimen collects—The blessing—Night service—Morning service—Service on Sundays and holy-days—"Gloria in Excelsis" and "Benedicite"—The multiplicity of books—Parts of the service special to priests, and to deacons—Compline—Lights—Summer chapels—Praying towards the East—Absence of pictures—The cross—Standing and kneeling—Praying for oppressors—Devotion to the martyrs and the Blessed Virgin—Variety of the intercessions for the living and the dead—Invocations of the saints—Method of dividing the Psalter 212

CHAPTER XI.

HOLY COMMUNION.

Infrequency of the celebrations—The three liturgies—Their antiquity—The preparation of the elements—Legend of the holy leaven—Baking the holy loaves—Mixing the chalice—Description of the service—The lections and their system—Difficulty of finding places—Expulsion of catechumens, offertory, and creed—Form of Sursum Corda and cherubic hymn—Communicating the people—The children and infants—The Antidoron—Communion of the priests—Reservation—Vestments—A Syrian sermon on Holy Communion—The rest of the Takhsa—Confession—Office of absolution 243

CHAPTER XII.

BAPTISM. BURIAL OF THE DEAD.

Likeness of the Baptismal Service to the Liturgy—Description of the service—The holy oil—Invocation on the oil—Anointing the child—Confirmation by imposition of hands—Absence of kiss of peace, of communion after baptism, and of interrogations—Godparents—Swaddling clothes—Salting infants—Private baptisms not allowed—Signing a sick child—Deacons and deaconesses baptizing—Names—Surnames—Burial of the dead—The coffin—The mourning—The cemetery—The funeral procession and service at the grave—Washing after the funeral—The parting kiss of peace—Memorials—Gravestones—Rams 267

CHAPTER XIII.

THE CHURCHES OF THE EAST SYRIANS.

Description of Mar Shalita at Qudshanis—Creeping through the doorway—The metropolitan church—Great church at Mar Bishu—Reason of small doors—Entrance, feet foremost—A cave church—Churches in the mountains before Tamerlane—Hangings—The absence of outward signs of Christianity—Churches in Persia—Mart Mariam at Urmi—The tomb of the Magi—Shimun Safa at Mosul—Mar Sergis—Dedications—Consecration of a church—Restoring old churches 290

CHAPTER XIV.

EAST SYRIAN IDEAS, THEOLOGY, LANGUAGE, AND CHARACTER.

Nestorianism—Relation of the Syrians to that heresy—Their unorthodox language—Their agreement with the

Catholick faith when expressed in untechnical language
—Their statements contradicting Nestorianism—The
schism from the rest of Christendom—Hopes of conciliatory explanation—Ceremonial defilement—Dogs—Shell-
fish—An experiment in lobster salad—The tortoise's
freedom from house tax—Mosaic law—Asceticism—
Externals in religion—Use of God's name—Punishing
whole families for one man's fault—Parables—The deaf
man—Open Sesame—Riddles—The Bible—Uncertainty
as to the Syrian Canon—Charms—The Syriac language
—Their idioms—Note on falsehood 305

CHAPTER XV.

THE KALENDAR. FASTS AND FESTIVALS. SUNDAYS.

Beginning of the year—The Era—Blessing the months—
Shwat, or February—Easter—Shawu'i—Vigils—A festi-
val of our Lord—Village festivals—Dancing—Sacrifices
—Epiphany—Mart Mariam, Urmi—Ascension Day—
Holy Cross Day—Veneration of the Cross—Saints' days
—Legend concerning St. George's martyrdom—Sundays
—How reckoned—Sunday bathing forbidden—Fasts—
Sunday fasting—Animal food forbidden—Wednesdays
and Fridays—Fasting Communion—Soma—Table of
holy-days and Sundays, with some account of saints
commemorated—How to find Easter 328

6   B

THE PATRIARCH MAR SHIMUN, CATHOLICOS OF THE EAST.
From a photograph by Mr. Athelstan Riley.

THE CATHOLICOS OF THE EAST AND HIS PEOPLE.

CHAPTER I.

INTRODUCTORY.

Short historical account of the people—Dependence on Antioch—The Church of the Persian Empire—Tamerlane—Internal schisms—Names of the people—Their present geographical and political divisions—Ashiret and Rayat.

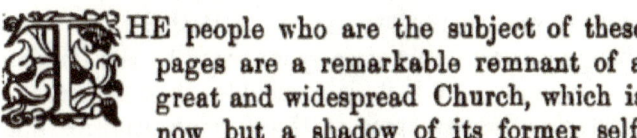HE people who are the subject of these pages are a remarkable remnant of a great and widespread Church, which is now but a shadow of its former self. The great Christian body which was founded, as it is believed, by St. Thomas the Apostle, in conjunction with St. Adai,[1] one of the Seventy, and St. Mari, his

[1] This name is usually spelt in England "Addai," as the *d* is "virtually doubled." But the Eastern Syrians dislike doubling letters, even virtually, and consequently, when they read classical Syriac, and in speaking the vernacular, the short *a* is constantly pronounced broad. When they do double letters, they pronounce them both distinctly. The present writer produced roars of laughter when he directed a servant to put some hay into the *mul-la* (mollah, Mohammedan minister of religion) instead of into the *mula* (store-room).

disciple, and which in the Middle Ages spread over the whole of Central Asia and gave to Europe the story of Prester John—is now represented by a small and persecuted body of not more than two hundred thousand souls.

In the early ages the "Church of the East," as it calls itself, was a dependency on the Patriarchate of Antioch. To this fact its own histories testify. It was founded in the district east of the Roman Empire, with its head-quarters at Seleucia-Ctesiphon, the twin capital of Persia. Its bishops were subject to Antioch; but before many ages had elapsed it was found that the political separation made an ecclesiastical union impossible. The difficulty of sending the metropolitan elect to be consecrated, as the usage of the times required, at the patriarchal city on the banks of the Orontes, caused the gift of a certain independence to Seleucia, and its metropolitan was thereafter known as Catholicos.[1] The change was no doubt greatly favoured by the Persian Government; and it is probable that when the Nestorian heresy arose in the Roman Empire, and Nestorius, the Patriarch of Constantinople, was excommunicated by the Council of Ephesus, A.D. 431, the opportunity was gladly seized by the Persians to persuade the Christians under their rule to cut themselves off from the communion of their fellow-religionists to the west of them. But whatever was the reason, the see of Seleucia definitely adhered to the side of Nestorius, and refused to accept the council which condemned him. At the same time, or soon after, the Catholicos assumed the title of Patriarch.

[1] For the Syrian account of the change, see below, chap. ix.

INTRODUCTORY.

From this time forward this body of Christians had an isolated existence. They did not at once diminish in numbers. On the contrary, they were reinforced, first by refugees from the Roman Empire, who brought them a fund of Nestorian learning, and later by the converts whom their zeal made in China, India, Central Asia, and other countries of the East, so that they became the most numerous body who professed the religion of our Saviour. But in the fourteenth century a terrible disaster fell on them at the hands of Tamerlane, or Timur. They had indeed often suffered severe persecutions at the hands of their former rulers, who seem to have patronized and oppressed them in turns; but these were as nothing when compared with this later scourge. Whether their numbers shrank suddenly or by degrees is not known, but the result was that only a handful was left to bear witness to the history of the past. Even then their small body was rent by faction. A disputed succession to the patriarchate divided them into two parts in the sixteenth century. Of these the larger portion, who live in Kurdistan and North-West Persia, obey the rule of Mar Shïmûn, who is styled the "Patriarch of the East;" and the smaller portion, who live in the plain of Mosul and the neighbouring hills, obey the rule of Mar Elia, called the "Patriarch of Babylon." This last body, after many fluctuations, has allied itself with the Church of Rome, and is known as the "Uniat Chaldean Church."

In these pages it is proposed only to follow the fortunes and to describe the life of the former of these two bodies, the adherents of Mar Shimūn; and, in order to avoid confusion, it may be as well to explain the names by which they are known. They habitually speak of themselves as Syrians—*Suriayi*, or more commonly *Surayi*. More rarely they call themselves Nestorians; but if this is given them as a nickname, as is commonly done by other nations, they often resent it. The name, however, which they adopt in formal documents, and which their old books uniformly give them, is "The Church of the East;" and the books even say simply "The Easterns" when they wish to make a contrast with the Jacobites, Greeks, Latins, and others, whom they join under the one name of "Westerns." In England the fashion has arisen of late years of using the name "Assyrian," partly from a desire to distinguish these Christians from the Jacobites, to whom the name Syrian is more commonly given in the West, and partly from a supposition that they are descendants of the old subjects of Shalmaneser and Sardanapalus. Lastly, the name "Chaldeans" has also been applied to them, for the same reason; but this name they themselves give in their old books to the astrologers, against whom they had an old emnity, though they now occasionally apply it to themselves in formal documents.

In choosing a name to distinguish these Christians by, it would seem *à priori* to be desirable to call them by the appellation which they themselves use. The name "Syrians" is now of universal and constant employment among the people, but it is not altogether easy to account for it. It seems to be the name of all Christians, of whatever nationality, of the old Patriarchate of Antioch.[1] Syria, indeed, in its strictest sense, means the country round Antioch, but the name is also applied to all the country eastward to the Tigris, at least, and perhaps further;[2] and thus St. Ephrem, who lived at Edessa and Nisibis, is called "the Syrian;" and in the office books of this people the festival of the "Syrian Doctors" commemorates the teachers of the Church of the East as opposed to Nestorius, Theodore, and others who are classed among the Greek doctors. So Ebedjesus (Audishu), Metropolitan of Armenia and Nisibis, calls the Greek and other fathers the "Westerns," but those of his own far east "The Syrian Fathers" (A.D. 1298).[3] And the same thing is seen in the diptychs of the patriarchal church of Kuki (Seleucia) found in a very rare manuscript. But this is not the most ancient name of the people; for in the Sunhadus they are only called "The Easterns" or "The Church of the East." There is no reason to suppose that "Syrian" is a name marking race or nationality, but rather it is probable that it is the religious name common to themselves and the Jacobites. Names do not always or generally denote race. The English nation, for instance, does not draw all its blood from the Angles.

Dr. Badger seems certainly to be right in say-

[1] In some parts of Kurdistan the people will even call all Christians "Syrians." They say, "There are twelve nations of Syrians, but only two of Mussulmans." But usually the name Syrians is only applied by them to themselves and the Jacobites.

[2] *e.g.* Gen. xxxv. 9 (LXX.) and (in Christian times) explicitly in the "Book of Kaldayntha," or Chaldeo Astrology (Qudshanis MS).

[3] See his Catalogue of Syrian books, part iv. in Badger, vol. ii.

ing[1] that until Latin missionaries came to Mosul the name "Chaldean" was never given to this people. The Latins gave it them to distinguish them from their Jacobite converts, whom they called "Syrians." Before that time the name was given by the people themselves, as has been said, to the astrologers.[2] Thus, however appropriately the name "Chaldean" may be thought to apply to the Roman Catholic Uniats of Mosul, it would seem not to be properly applicable to the people of Mar Shimun.

To adopt the name "Assyrian," as has been often done of late years in England, is perhaps undesirable, as asserting a theory which cannot be proved, that these Christians are descended from the people of the old empire of Nineveh, and indeed are their sole representatives. It is probable that some, and even much, of their lineage is to be traced to the old Assyrians; but most likely they are a mixture of races—of those who fled from all the surrounding countries in times of persecution, with perhaps the primitive inhabitants of the Kurdish mountains. Also it must be remembered that they were not merely the Church of Assyria, but the Church of Seleucia and Ctesiphon, in which Assyria was only a province.[3] It seems unsafe, therefore, to call them by a name which they themselves have never used, and which depends on an unproved theory, however probable it may be thought by some to be. Gibbon says that the

[1] "Nestorians and their Rituals," vol. i. pp. 177-181.
[2] Cf. Audishu's "Catalogue," part iv. Layard refers to an old book of the Gospels of A.D. 1241 as applying the name to the Syrians in the subscription; but it does not appear if the subscription is of that date ("Nineveh," p. 199).
[3] Some of the patriarchal race claim to be Babylonians.

INTRODUCTORY.

"Nestorians, . . . under the name of Chaldeans or Assyrians, are confounded with the most learned or the most powerful nation of Eastern antiquity."[1]

It is also worth noticing that no part of the country now inhabited by Mar Shimun's people can properly be called Assyria. The Persian plains are beyond question not Assyria; and even the Kurdish mountains, which in some of our maps are assigned to Assyria, were not really a part of the country. Sennacherib's sons escaped to them ("into the land of Ararat") after killing their father.[2]

In these pages the people are called by the name by which they call themselves, "Syrians;" but as confusion may occur between them and the Jacobites, who are the Western Syrians, the other name used by the people is, when necessary, added; and they are then called "Eastern Syrians." This combination is occasionally used by the people themselves when they wish to distinguish themselves from the Jacobites.

In order to make the following pages intelligible, it is necessary to explain that the Eastern Syrians —those who obey the rule of Mar Shimun—are divided into two portions, those who live in Turkey, and those who live in the province of Azerbaijan, in North-West Persia. The life of the two portions is very different, and we will therefore describe the customs of their everyday life in separate chapters. These will be followed by descriptions of the ecclesiastical organization and services of the whole

---

[1] "Decline and Fall," chap. xlvii.
[2] 2 Kings xix. 37, margin. See Smith, "Dictionary of the Bible, *s.v.* "Assyria."

nation together. The Azerbaijan Syrians live chiefly in the plains bordering the Sea of Urmi,[1] but also in the hill country between the plains and the Turco-Persian frontier. The part of the nation under the rule of the Sultan of Turkey live in Kurdistan, and chiefly in the district, or *sanjak*, of Hakkiari, in the vilayet of Van. These again are divided into *Ashiret*, or tribal Syrians, and *Rayat*, or subjects. The former are half independent of Turkish rule, live in the mountain fastnesses of Tiari, Tkhuma, and neighbouring districts, and only pay tribute irregularly. The Turks have but little hold on them, except through Mar Shimun, or unless they leave their homes to buy wheat, and for other reasons. They are very warlike, and are often a match for the Kurds, unless the latter bring an overwhelming force against them, as when Bedr Khan Beg massacred so many of them in 1843. The Turkish soldiers do not penetrate their country except with their good will. The Rayats, on the other hand, who live in the more open country, which is directly ruled by the Turks, have a most miserable life, being at the mercy not only of the Kurds, but of every rapacious Turkish official who wishes to make money by fair means or foul. Both the patriarch, Mar Shimun, and the metropolitan, Mar Khnanishu, live in the Rayat country, though the village of the former, Qudshanis or Kochanis, is reckoned Ashiret. With these few words of explanation we may proceed to describe the life of the Syrians in Turkish territory.

[1] This is the Syrian name. The Mussulmans say Urumi. European forms of the name are Urmia and Urumia (Oroomiah).

CHAPTER II.

EVERYDAY LIFE IN THE MOUNTAINS OF KURDISTAN.

Qudshanis—The patriarchal court—Life without clocks—The patriarch's relations—His visitors—His dress—The Raban Yonan—A mediæval jester—The metropolitan—Miserable state of the Rayats—Oppressions of the people—Kurds and Turks—Miscarriages of justice.

IN describing the mountaineers' everyday life, it is only fitting that we should begin with Qudshanis and the patriarchal court. This village is perched on a high triangular alp or pasture, some 7000 feet above the level of the sea, and is shut in on two sides by deep ravines, at the bottom of which mountain torrents hurry down, to meet just below the village and to flow together to the greater Zab, or Zawa, which the Syrians identify with the Pison of Genesis. The third or upper side of the alp is shut in by precipitous mountains; other mountains rise on the far sides of the ravines, and the situation is thus beautiful in the extreme. On a rock at the lower end of the village rises the patriarchal church of Mar Shalita, round which are laid the dead of all ages. Another church, dedicated to Mar Mushi (Moses) stands, in ruins, about a mile up the plateau.

In the village the rude patriarchal house, or cell as it is called (*qilaita*), is marked by a tower. Here the patriarch lives, not in pomp and circumstance as we understand the words, but in quiet dignity, and highly reverenced by all his people. Here he is usually to be found at home, to receive his many

THE PATRIARCHAL CHURCH, QUDSHANIS.
From a photograph by the Rev. Dr. Cutts.

visitors from all parts of the country. Sometimes, indeed, he takes a walk, or goes over the mountain to Julamerk, the seat of the Turkish Government, or makes a tour in his diocese. But usually he sits in his room all day. He will often have twenty or more visitors to entertain: Ashirets, with flint locks, scimitars, and shields; or Rayats who have managed to escape robbery on the way; or bishops and others from Persia who have not been turned back by

Government officials or hindered by the dangers of the road. Some have come to bring him dues or presents; some seek to be made *maliks* (lay chiefs) or *qankayas* (sacristans) or *sirdars* (churchwardens) of churches in the mountains which are endowed with land. Some have come to the head of the Church and "Nation" with matters of canon and customary law for settlement. Some Ashirets have come to ask the patriarch to speak to the Government about depredations or murder or rapine by their Kurdish neighbours. Or Rayats have come to complain that they cannot live in their villages because the Kurd, Hipzillah Beg, is oppressing them so severely, taking away or destroying their corn or cattle, and not allowing their priest to marry them nor to visit their sick; or because another Kurd, Shian Agha, is threatening to fine them for letting Turkish soldiers lodge in their village on their way to make a feint of arresting him. Or five wedding guests have come, clothed only in turbanless hats and cotton drawers and shirts, to beg the patriarch to inform the Government at Julamerk of their having been stripped of all else by Kurds on the road from the wedding. Or gendarmes or Government officials have come to spend half the day and the night on their journey to some other place. Or Kurds have come to try to trap Mar Shimun into placing himself at their head in resisting the edict from Constantinople for a new census, which if he will do all the Kurds will be his devoted servants (until the wind changes). His holiness (and everybody else who knows of these things) become thoroughly cast down at the almost daily recurring tales of oppression and wrong, which he is powerless to remedy. It is not to be wondered at if high ideals should be crushed by the weight of such experiences; and it must seem hard that Western missionaries should ask him to risk the anger of the Government, when the powerful British and other European nations do nothing of any service for him or his people in the matter of their secular troubles.

Westerns, who think themselves superior to Orientals, might learn from the Syrians a lesson of childlike faith and submissiveness to the Divine Father and King. Sometimes they say, "God is angry with us for our sins, and therefore lets us suffer so;" but the usual comment is, "It is the Lord's will: glory be to His Name." At the same time they will be fierce against the human wrong-doers, and impatient with the negligence of those who might interfere on their behalf and do not, especially the Turkish rulers.

Mar Shimun is very shrewd, and quickly takes the measure of Turks, Kurds, and Christians with whom he has to do. His surroundings are not calculated to encourage optimism nor unsuspiciousness; but when he is not depressed with tales of wrongdoing, he is lively and pleasant in conversation, and he takes an intelligent interest in all that he hears, whether it be of some intrigue in Turkey or of inventions in Europe, and he is very quick to understand or appreciate whatever is being laid before him.

Every guest on arriving kisses the patriarch's hand, most of them kneeling to do so. Some take his hand in theirs; others of lower rank do not touch his hand except with their lips.

He dresses in wide trousers and short jacket of very dark blue. His waistcoat is gayer, and his cincture is of many-coloured silk. Though his beard is almost entirely black, his hair is quite white; but except in the church this is covered by his fez and turban of black silk. He is very neat in his dress and natty with his fingers; and he often calls his servant to remove a piece of fluff or other "matter out of place" from the carpet. He sits on a rug on the floor, not cross-legged, but in the Persian fashion, with his knees doubled under him, so that he is sitting on his feet. Two or three chairs are placed for European guests or Turkish officials. Kurds and common soldiers take precedence of Christians, except of the patriarch's relatives. Mar Shimun can understand Kurdish, but does not speak it. But he knows Turkish well. He can read both old and modern Syriac fluently, and can write a beautiful hand; but all his letters are written by a scribe, for it would seem to be *infra dignitatem* for a great man to write with his own hand. He seems to know his service books well, and he is always up early for his morning prayers, and equally punctual in saying evensong. He and one or two with him remain in the baptistery during the Liturgy, and receive communion at the doorway between the baptistery and the sanctuary.

Hard by the patriarch's house live his relations, who make a sort of informal council—his half-brother, Ishai (Jesse), and his cousins, Mar Aúraham, the patriarch designate,[1] Awisháluin (Absalom), Nimrod, Shmuel (Samuel), and Shlímun (Solomon), with their wives and families. It is curious to see how strictly etiquette is observed in the patriarchal circle. Each sits in his proper place, according to his precedence, on the strips of felt which are spread along the sides of the patriarch's room; while Mar Shimun himself sits generally on a rug at the top. The members of the council give their advice when desired on whatever business may be on hand; they are also commissioned to go to the various villages or districts to transact patriarchal business, to settle disputes, or hear complaints, or collect the dues. One of them, Shámasha (deacon) Nimrod, is a member of the Turkish mutaserrif's council at the neighbouring town of Julamerk, and is entrusted with much of the civil work of the patriarchate.

Let us consider how the Qudshánis people spend their day from the time they get up till bedtime, and give the impressions of a European visitor about their ordinary life. One of the things most trying to the Western newly arrived in Kurdistan is that life is carried on without clocks. When the sun is shining appointments can be kept. In time of rain the sun's position can be approximately made out by people who have not the privilege of London fogs. But who is to tell the time at night,

[1] Mar Auraham has been designated successor to the patriarchate, but whether he will actually succeed or not cannot be foretold. He is a pious and good man. Shamasha Nimrod is a most able man, who is of great service to the patriarch, to the Syrian nation, and to the Government, and could do much more good if he were unhampered and had full play for his ability.

seeing that the perfidious moon daily alters her position? The time of morning service at Qudshanis is so irregular in summer as to have suggested to the Mission priest with two bumps of causativeness and a congenital affinity to the word "Why?" the theory that it varied inversely with the wholesomeness of the supper partaken of by the village priest. Despairing of finding a working formula which would secure his being present at the daily morning service, the English clergyman fell back upon the Western custom of governing himself by the clock, except on mornings when the Liturgy was celebrated; so that on ordinary days he was sometimes only in time to see the morning *levée*. After service the chief men of the village and any strangers who may be Mar Shimun's guests go to the patriarch's room, and there drink coffee and smoke their pipes or cigarettes for a while, and then, if it is a working day, go to their work. About nine o'clock is the time of the "breakfast of working men," and the midday meal is usually eaten long after the middle of the day. Men work till near sunset, when the devout will go to church, and those who stay away will say some prayers in their houses, having previously washed their faces and hands, not merely to make them clean, but as a ceremonial act. Curiously enough, combing the hair is often carried on while they are praying. Supper is commonly served after the lamps are lit; but in the Ashiret districts, in the summer, it is often hurried forward into the twilight or earlier.

Drinking tea and coffee has become a part of the

daily life of the patriarch and his relations, and some few chief men among the Rayats can indulge a guest with these luxuries. There seems to be reason to fear that the beverage, which boasts that it cheers but does not inebriate, is already beginning to do considerable injury to the young people of the most exalted families, as it does with so many people in England.

The patriarch's brother and cousins are too highly placed to work, but they sometimes are occupied with ecclesiastical or secular affairs of importance. Now and then they go to shoot a bear or catch partridges, or to ride; but they do not even amuse themselves with any vigour.

Sometimes, however, they perform equestrian feats in the open fields above the village. On one occasion, when we were staying with Mar Shimun, a large number of Syrians from Sŭrad'Mamidayi, a village in the neighbourhood of Van, arrived to visit the head of their nation. Apparently they were well-to-do, or at least they were gorgeously dressed with turbans and embroidered suits. They entertained the village with all sorts of riding, just like a mediæval tournament. They had spears, twelve feet long, with which they rushed at each other, and tried to take off one another's turbans. Many of these mountaineers, like the Kurds, are excellent riders, and can balance themselves in almost any position on a horse, and shoot off their guns the while. But the Ashirets do not ride much; their country is not suited to equestrian exercise.

Among the Qudshanis amusements, we must not

omit chess. All the patriarchal household play well; Mar Shimun, Mar Auraham, and Shamasha Shlimun are *facile principes*. The rules are the same as with us. Many of the chess names which we use are also employed by the Syrians, such as *check, mate, rook*. M. Huc, in his "Travels in Tartary, Thibet, and China," says this is so also in those countries; but the Tartars and Thibetans play like us, while the Chinese have quite different rules (vol. ii. chap. viii.).

There was one at Qudshanis who was constantly appealed to for advice in all matters ecclesiastical, who has now passed to his rest. Raban Yonan, (Monk Jonah) lived in a little chamber off the patriarchal church of Mar Shalita, and was one of the few monks remaining. A little man, with grizzled hair, surmounted by a high conical hat and black turban, he had a singularly pleasant smile and beautiful expression, which commanded love and reverence from all who saw him. He spent most of his time copying the service books and the other old works of his nation; indeed, he lived among books, and was quite the most learned man the Syrians had. Many had been his scholars, and we have often been struck on hearing some beautiful or curious comment on Holy Scripture by being told, "I learnt that from Raban Yonan." Every one paid the greatest respect to him, and he took a sort of honorary precedence of all but the patriarch; wherever there are Syrians, his name is held in honour and love. He was referred to on all points of learning; and it was rather remarkable sometimes to see the priests stop in the middle of a service, to have a consultation with the good old man as to what should be done next.

He was suddenly called to his rest while bathing in a mineral spring at a distance from Qudshanis, for a rheumatic affection; he seems to have had a fit in the water. Perhaps he had a warning of his end, for he came to our tents just before starting for the spring—we happened to be staying at Qudshanis at the time—and bade us a solemn farewell. We little thought it was the last. The funeral took place the next day, in the graveyard of the patriarchal church, and was attended by all the villagers, who mourned loud and long for their departed friend.

We must not leave Qudshanis without noticing a very important personage—Shlimun, the patriarch's jester and general man-of-all-work. Like his predecessors in the Middle Ages, he is privileged to play his pranks on all, but, also like them, is the butt of every one else. He serves to keep the village lively, and would be sincerely mourned if taken from it.

The metropolitan, or matran, Mar Khnanishu (Mercy of Jesus), lives in one of the most beautiful places in Kurdistan, on the side of a very steep slope, at the bottom of which, far below, runs a stream which flows south, to meet the Zab a long way down its course. There is no proper village, but merely the walled enclosure containing the matran's house (an old monastery) and church, dedicated to Mar Ishu (Jesus, or Joshua); one or two shepherds' houses and sheepcots are close by. The slopes are fairly well covered with trees—amongst others large walnuts, and mulberry trees whose white fruit is rather tasteless. This is in the district of Shamsdin, in the Rayat country, and the metropolitan has the perpetual sorrow of seeing his people robbed and even murdered by the Kurds. Even his own sheep are often carried off; and it is easy for the marauders to escape from justice, if they should be sought for, by crossing the Persian frontier. This district is dominated by the son of the late Sheikh Obeidullah, who invaded Persia in 1880; and between this Kurd and the nomad Herki Kurds the matran and his diocese have such a bad time of it, that he has repeatedly been advised to follow some of his flock who have fled to Persia.

The frontier is the cause of endless trouble to the Christian villages which are near to it on either side. A village in Turkey is robbed of its sheep by Kurds from Persia, and a village in Persia by those in Turkey. There are then negotiations between the two Governments if pressure is put on them by the consuls; but often nothing comes of it. The jealousy between Persians and Turks disinclines the officials to take action; and after all, they say, it is only some Christians who suffer. On the whole the Persians are more ready than the Turks to make the Kurds give back the sheep; but then it is easier for them to do so from the less difficult nature of the country. The Persians often say to the Turks, "We will not compel restitution of your sheep unless you compel restitution of ours." And as the Turks either cannot get at the Kurds on their side, or if they can are often too corrupt to do so, things usually remain as they are, and the Christians suffer all round. It must, however, in fairness be stated that, at least in one case, some Christians on one side of the frontier who had been robbed by Kurds on the other, helped to rob another Christian village across the frontier. It is, of course, to the advantage of the Turkish Government that the Syrians should keep as many sheep as possible, as each head of sheep is taxed. The Christians suffer most in the spring and autumn, when the nomad Kurds are moving to and from their summer pasturages.

The poverty of the Rayats is very great. At one large village not far from Qudshanis we wished to buy a chicken, or an egg, or anything we could get to eat. But one of the women said plaintively, "The Kurds and the Turks between them have taken from us everything we have; we have nothing to eat ourselves, far less to sell." What the robbers had left the soldiers had seized.

The matran is a tall, good-looking man, with a large jet-black beard, and is most gracious as well as dignified. He has shown himself warm-hearted. He is pious and zealous for his church and for religion. He would not hesitate to break off friendship from those whom he suspected of undermining the faith; and his friendship for the English Mission carries great weight with all the religious people. He is very strict in the matter of fasting and all ecclesiastical duties; and this is no pharisaism, for as far as man can judge he is devout and is trying to serve God. The tone and atmosphere of his house are such as are becoming to the *entourage* of a man of God. The very servants are grave, and speak as if they recollected the presence of God.

Conditions of Life in Kurdistan under the Turkish Government.

Before passing from the Rayat to the Ashiret Christians it will be as well to make some remarks on the condition of the people under Turkish rule; these naturally apply more to the Rayats than to the Ashirets, who are comparatively independent of both Turks and Kurds.

The relations between Turkey and her Christian subjects have unhappily become the sport of political disputants. One set of people speak of the Turks as unspeakably bad, and impute to them the worst and only the worst motives. Another set seem to be guided by nothing but opposition to the former. Some people who are sane on other points are so disgusted by prejudiced and unfair attacks on the Turks, that they become fanatical on the other side, will not listen to nor weigh any tale of injustice, and sometimes appear not only to be anxious to defend the aggressors, but even to delight in damaging the case and the characters of the Christians of Turkey.

Protesting against the levity and the rash judgments on either side, we will not seek to pit Mussulman and Christian one against the other, but will give some account of the life of the Syrians in Turkey. It must be stated that the present *vali*, or governor-general, of Van, Halil Pasha, since Hakkiari was added to his government in 1888, and the three *mutaserifs* (governors) who have been stationed at Julamerk[1] since it was raised to be a mutaserifship, have to some extent supported

[1] A small town close to Qudshania.

their professions that they desired to govern well by the evidence of their actions. These leave much still to be desired; but some allowance must be made for local difficulties; and the governors would appear to be most seriously hindered by their not being properly supported by the central Government at Constantinople against intrigues for their removal, by the inadequacy of their force of soldiers, and by the corruption of many of the officials, some of whom are hand in glove with wrongdoers. Still, great improvement in many respects is to be noted since the days when the Kurd, Fikri Pasha, was vali at Bash-qal'a,[1] and the malicious *qaimaqam* (deputy-governor), Ahmed Beg, and his council of Kurds ruled and misruled at Julamerk. It is because these improvements have not sufficiently extended through the Sanjak[2] of Hakkiari, and because the Kurds have increasingly adopted the idea that whatever they do they will not be interfered with, that the position of the Christians in some parts is more miserable and more hopeless than before. The cry everywhere is for government. Many Kurds as well as Christians wish that any Government—whether European or Turkish reinvigorated—would take the country in hand. Some districts were better off in the days when they were under the rule of the Kurdish mira[3] and other chiefs, who, if they themselves fleeced now this village and now that, yet protected their subjects from others. Some districts and villages,

---

[1] He was dismissed in 1888, and died soon after. Bash-qal'a was the seat of government when Hakkiari was a vilayet.

[2] The subdivision of a vilayet or province.

[3] This was the name of the Kurdish ruler before the Turks took the direct government of the country.

on the other hand, have gained by the Turks ousting the Kurdish mira. Every one says that when the Turks first became direct rulers of the country they governed well, and things were comparatively prosperous, but that since the last war with Russia matters have gone from bad to worse, and especially in the last three or four years. The state of things gives colour to the notion which has been expressed by some travellers, and which is held by Syrians and most Kurds, that the policy of the Porte is to allow the Christians to be impoverished and exterminated by the Kurds, provided that this is done so covertly that Europe shall not be aware of it. This, probably, is the intention of some officials; but it would be wrong to ascribe this policy to the Sultan and his Government, or to many of the officials who often have shown mercy, kindness, and patience to the poor people.

One cause of suffering is in the Syrians themselves —that they do not know how to conduct their cases in courts of law or before the governor's councils, and Mar Shimun and his cousin, Shámasha Nimrod, who is often deputed to look after such matters, are not able to see to every case. Another cause is in a good law being adopted without the complement which would make it efficient. For instance, a man complains that so and so robbed him on the road or burnt his corn. He is met with the reply, "Where are your witnesses?" And as robbery and arson are not usually committed in the presence of witnesses, and as there is no policeman to look for other evidence, the complainant feels that he is being mocked. These technical difficulties could be obviated by officials who were seriously bent on doing justice; but too often they are not.

Gross miscarriages of justice are frequent. Thus a notorious oppressor, the Kurd Hipzillah Beg, was called by the mutaserif's orders to Julamerk, to answer complaints against him. But, as the *qadi*, or judge, openly made him a present, the poor Syrians dared not prosecute, and begged Mar Shimun to make their peace with the Kurdish oppressor. In another case, a carpet stolen by the Kurds from a Syrian priest was found decorating the apartment of the chief of the *zaptiehs*, or gendarmes, in Diza. He ought to have arrested the thief, but was found himself to have received the spoils, and so the thief was not caught.

In another case, a Kurd named Abdurrahman, who had killed a Syrian in cold blood for refusing to pay blackmail, after a brief flight to Persia, was allowed to live in peace close to a garrison town for a couple of years, and being taken prisoner after some fresh marauding, was released the following morning. The vali's endeavours in 1890 to catch or kill this man were thwarted by the colonel in command of the troops in Gawar. He paid the penalty of his crimes last year. It must be added that the vali also tried to capture Hipzillah Beg in 1890, and was thwarted by the treachery of a Syrian.

In a late case judgment was given, since acknowledged in an official document to be false, the purport of which was to alienate the ownership of the land of two villages and part of a third, not far from Qudshanis, from the peasant proprietors, who can hardly pay their taxes as it is, to a Kurd whose father had been allotted the taxes thereof for two years only, in the days of the mira.

Acts of transparent injustice, of corruption, and refusal to do justice, of which these are samples taken at random, are frequent; and they and the cheating in courts of law and by Government officials not only depress the spirits of the people, but actively aid in reducing them to poverty. It must be said that the Kurds who rob on the highway, and those who openly levy blackmail on the villages, as if they had a claim on them, are many and powerful and revengeful, able to burn corn or haystacks, and to cripple or kill men. They demand, for instance, a ewe and a lamb in May and a ewe and a goat in August from every house in one village, or requisition corn or the use of land for sowing corn in another, or absolutely claim to be landlords of a third, in spite of having been sent to prison in former years for trying to enforce this groundless claim, or carry off firewood from a fourth and hay from a fifth. But if there were honest officials, the soldiers who have been drafted into Hakkiari could keep them in order after a few months proof of a new *régime*.

Taxes are very heavy, and sometimes all beatings and quarterings of gendarmes on the villagers cannot get the full amount. But heavier taxes could be paid in many parts if the villagers might use all their resources and keep what they own. As it is, fields are out of cultivation because some of the bulls or buffaloes which should plough them have been taken by Kurds or sold to pay taxes, or because the owners have fled to Persia or Russia, being unable to live in Turkey. One whole plain, which contained seven villages when protected by Sheikh Obeidullah, has now no inhabitant. All fled from fear of the nomad Herki Kurds, and their taxes are lost to the Government. So, too, villages which owned a thousand head of sheep now own but a few score. And the nomad Artushi Kurds who carried them off do not reimburse the Government the sheep tax and the grass tax which used to be paid. The present vali's checking the lawlessness of these nomad Artushi Kurds is one of the most notable of his acts. It is to be hoped he may have sufficient soldiery to follow his own precedent with the Herki nomads.

CHAPTER III.

THE ASHIRET COUNTRY.

The Zab—Roads—Bridges—A perilous crossing—A patriarch in difficulties--Crossing in a basket—Building fields—Disappearance of a landed property—Occupations of the Ashirets—The women—The summer encampment—Massacres by Kurds—Ashiret guns—Tiari houses—The fireplace—The roofs and mosquitoes—Vines and grapes—Types of face—Jilu and Bas—The Butterstone—Maliks—The stone of Balal the fool—The Yezidis.

LET us now descend the course of the Zab from Qudshanis to the Ashiret country, which comprises the districts of Tiari, Tkhuma, Diz, Waltu, Tal, Bas, and Jilu. The first thing that will strike the stranger is the clannishness of the people. The tribes not unfrequently fight one another, and in times past some have even helped the Kurds against another tribe. It is this want of unity which has made massacres in the past possible. Let us hope the Syrians have now learnt wisdom. It is a matter of common experience to be told by a local guide that he cannot go further than a certain place, because there is enmity between his village and that which the traveller is approaching

Through these districts a traveller—there are *very* few of them—will do well to take a letter from the patriarch if he can obtain one. It will be of more use to him than any documents or guards which the Government can provide. As he goes along the rough roads his " peace " is replied to with " In peace, a hundred peaces," or " In peace, in goodness " (*sc.* "you have come "), which are the words of welcome. The traveller will probably find his way to the house of the malik, or temporal chief of the district, to whom he will make a present of a knife, or some such thing, and who, if his credentials are right, will receive him hospitably.

These Ashiret districts are in the valley of the Greater Zab, which in Tiari is some three thousand feet above the sea-level, or fifteen hundred feet lower than the Urmi plain, four thousand feet lower than Qudshanis; and also in the cross valleys down which torrents run into the Zab. The roads running along the streams are rough in the extreme, and are almost impassable for horses. Mules with difficulty pick their way along them. The roads often climb up the steep sides of the mountain to avoid a precipice which comes sheer down into the river; and they are generally so narrow that they look, at a distance, as if no animal could possibly pass over them without falling over the precipice. In many places these roads are built out into the river, and are swept away by the floods caused in the spring by melting snow; they then have to be reconstructed, at the cost of an infinite amount of labour, by the villagers. The scenery, however, is most beautiful. The mountains tower above the valleys, and are of all shapes and heights; those of Jilu reaching fifteen hundred feet or more.

Over the foaming Zab, which in most places in the Ashiret country is quite unfordable even in summer, are thrown wicker bridges. One of these at the northern entrance to Upper Tiari, is a substantial structure, which mules can cross, though the great oscillation would make it unpleasant to ride over it. Other bridges are much slighter, and are only available for pedestrians. The site of a bridge will be selected for its proximity to an important village, due regard being paid to its approaches not encroaching on the scanty arable land. On one side of the river is, if possible, an *isára*, or cliff-like rock, which will do for the abutment of the bridge. On the opposite side a pier has to be built on the shore; and perhaps another a little way into the river. These often get washed away in the spring floods. To construct them large stones are brought down to the river's edge on little sledges over the hard smooth snow. Seldom can the expense of gypsum and of hiring skilled workmen be afforded,[1] and the building is generally very rough. On the natural pier of the cliff and on the newly built piers three parallel poles of poplar are laid, their landward ends being well built into the stone and their other ends projecting a little over the river. On each another pole is fastened which projects still further over the river, and over these is another set of three. The inner ends of the topmost layers of poles are now so

[1] The Bas men are the best masons, having learnt their trade in Mosul, and other places.

far projecting that three long poles can reach from one set to the other; and thus the river is spanned. Upon the poles osier-work hurdles or pieces of flat basket-work, some six feet long by three feet wide, are laid and secured. Large flat stones are placed on many of them, especially where pieces of the osier-work have worn or broken through. The dancing of such a bridge when it is walked upon, and the roaring of the foaming torrent which, so many feet below, battles angrily with the boulders it cannot carry away, cause a stranger, and even some of the natives, to accept the helping hand of others, and so they experience more shaking than they would if they traversed the bridge alone.

Sometimes the bridges sag, not only lengthways, but also sideways, in the middle, so that the south side is lower than the north, and if, in addition, the felt sandal of the passenger catches for a moment in a hole where the osier has broken, it makes the passage very difficult and even hazardous. Other streams are crossed by still slighter bridges, some even by two poles, which are parallel but of different elasticity. They could not be crossed in shoes.

In the latter part of the summer little bridges a foot wide, and a foot or so above the water, are built from rock to rock for the sheep to cross by. These are sometimes wattled and sometimes have stones for the roadway upon the pair of poles which form each span.

In the end of the winter, before the river has risen much, men coming up from Tiari by the river

THE ASHIRET COUNTRY. 33

route to Julamerk have to ford the Zab. You may be carried across by a strong man. You take off your felt sandals—for if they get wet they are liable to be torn by the stones when you resume your walk—and sit as high as you can in hope and fear and great anxiety as the porter stumbles on the slippery stones, and the water creeps higher and higher up his legs.

It is said that the Mar Shimun who preceded the present patriarch, was once being carried across a ford, when his subject alarmed him by telling him he would now drop him unless he would give him a *vivâ voce* dispensation to smoke his pipe even in the mornings during Lent. Needless to say the patriarch recognized the straits he was in as amounting to "necessity." The martyrs' spirit has vanquished fire; but how if they had been threatened with having their great toes and then the tickly part of the soles of their feet slowly let down into snow water?

When there is no bridge, sheep and men are ferried across in a basket, carried along ropes fixed to either side. This is a fearsome, and even (at any rate for sheep, who have not the sense to guide the basket) a dangerous method of crossing. The ropes are made of goats' hair. On these is an iron ring, from which the deep basket depends by four cords, so that two sheep or one man can be transported at one time. The launching of the basket calls for skill on the part of the launchers; and where there are knots joining the short ropes together, it is advisable for the passenger to pull the rope downwards that the ring may easily pass

D

over them. Even some of the Tiari men decline thus to travel in mid air; and accidents have been known to happen through the rope breaking.

Higher up the Zab, not in the Ashiret country, at a place called Kermi, is a natural bridge formed by two great masses of rock having fallen together. In summer and autumn the river is fordable near Qudshanis and also below Tiari.

In the valleys of the tribal districts the only possible places for fields or villages are where there is an occasional widening of the gorge. In many places there is only just room for the roaring river, which makes noise enough to drown any ordinary voice, and to make the people shout as a habit. In other places it is possible to *build up* artificially a small field by the side of the river, the whole side which faces the stream being constructed of stones. As these fields have a plentiful supply of water, which is ingeniously carried along the mountain sides from a higher level of the river by little streams often cut out of the face of the rock, the soil is very fertile. Two kinds of millet are grown, and rice; and the river sides thus show a bright green which is very refreshing. Wheat is not grown, and has to be brought from the Rayat districts. In Tiari there are two harvests in a year.

These fields are often swept away, like the roads and bridges, by the spring floods. At Ashitha, a village at a considerable height above the Zab, at the top of a cross valley, a hundred and thirty-two fields were swept away in the spring of 1887, and two houses. It is indeed hard for a man to wake up one morning and to find that the whole of his landed property has disappeared. The greater part of the fields in Tiari in the valley of Zab, and of the fields in Tkhuma and Salabekan valleys, have been carried away and still remain fields of boulders.

The work of the men of Tiari consists almost entirely in tending the sheep and in ploughing, sowing, and reaping. Many of them also weave the woollen threads the women have spun into material for trousers and overshirts; they also tend vines and make wine, and all have to cut down small branches from the trees—a kind of oak—and stack them on the hills, from whence in time of snow they with great labour bring them down, a backload at a time, for the sheep to eat the leaves off instead of hay. The twigs or little branches which have thus been stripped of their leaves are used for making a blaze in the fire. In some parts of Tiari wood is not so plentiful, and the bulk of the sheep of the village are kept up at a higher situated village where there is hay.

In the villages the women and girls of course do all the household work, cleansing the rice, millet, and other seeds used for food, and separating from them stones and earth and uneatable seeds; and pounding and grinding such grain takes up a good deal of their time. And as most of the cooking, whether of cereals or of beans or of meat, is not roasting, but boiling or stewing, it requires the perpetual presence of some one to stir, skim, add fresh water, and do other acts and deeds pertaining to the mystery and art of a mountaineer cook and baker of bread. Walnuts have to be shelled, and oil expressed from some of them, and various other articles of food prepared. Sheep-skins have to be cleansed and made fit to receive flour or *masta* (curdled milk). Clothes are washed and persons bathed in hot water every week; and the hair of men and women must be combed and plaited again.

LADIES AT QUDSHANIS.
From a photograph by the Rev. Dr. Cutts.

Clothes—but especially socks—are patched and darned almost *ad infinitum;* and, when babies and all things else have been attended to, the women's well-earned leisure is swallowed up in the alternatives of knitting socks (some of the Tiari particoloured socks are really beautiful works of art), and of spinning with the distaff and spindle, which are never out of hands not otherwise occupied, except on Sundays and holidays and at bedtime. A couple of "needles of England," with a reel or two of glacé thread, form a most grateful and valued addition to the few yards of coloured calico with which a stranger testifies his good will and appreciation of the trouble taken on his behalf by the lady of the house; and most of them are real ladies by lineage and in manner and feeling, and are much more like Blessed Mary and the women of the Bible than many of their sisters of England and America. The coloured material which she makes may go to her husband or children; the white calico certainly will go for his shirt or drawers, but the European needle and thread will save her fingers and her patience and enable her to sew the seams in a way that will do her credit.

But the chief occupations of the Ashirets are pastoral. The name Tiari means "the sheepfolds" in classical Syriac. But as there is not enough pasture for the sheep near home, the shepherds have to take their flocks to a distance, and so often fall into the hands of the Kurds. The valleys are intolerably hot in the summer, and the people form an encampment on the hills called *zuhma* from a word meaning "to make butter." The place of camping is called by a Kurdish word, *zozan*. Here they live in booths or occasionally in tents, and lead a thoroughly pastoral life during the whole of the hot weather. The women milk the sheep and goats, and make the cheese and *masta*, which are sent down to the village on the backs of mules or of women. The men meanwhile are often occupied in agriculture down in the valleys. These encampments are sometimes attacked in a terrible way by the Kurds. On July 31, 1888, a *zuhma* near Ashitha was overpowered by a band of Kurds, who killed the few men who were there and ravished the women. This nearly led to a general massacre of the Christians by the Kurds, who were assembled in great numbers, which even the Turkish officials stated as 8000. The ravishing of the women was a proof that it was not merely a raid, but the beginning of a war of massacre. A disaster was only averted by the energetic action of the consuls, which compelled the Turks to take immediate steps to check the Kurds.

It must be stated that the warlike Ashirets sometimes take revenge. But they are vastly inferior in numbers to the Kurds, and have no chance against them out of their own country. Moreover, they have only their ancient matchlocks against the modern rifles of the Kurds, who received these weapons in the Russo-Turkish war and at other times, and calmly appropriated them. They have a large number of Martini-Henrys among their different tribes. Most of the Syrians, indeed, believe that the Turks deliberately arm the Kurds in order to exterminate the Christians. The Kurds do not bring their Martini-Henrys to government villages, but they are allowed to have chassepôts. If a Christian is found with one of these it is taken from him by the zaptiehs or Turkish soldiers.

In Tiari and most of the Ashiret districts the houses are built of stone. Tiari itself may be said

THE ASHIRET COUNTRY.

to be made of stone, with comparatively and absolutely very little earth to afford root space for trees and grass, and indeed, it is wonderful in what scanty soil trees grow. Frosts split off and avalanches and torrents carry down from the craggy mountain tops an abundance of stones of all sizes. Of these stones four walls of two feet or more in thickness are built up as high as a man can reach with his uplifted hand, and on the top of these walls beams (of poplar, in Tiari) are placed at spaces of two feet from one another. From one beam to another are placed thick and rough laths of small or of split branches of the poplar. Over these are laid twigs, which in turn support thin flat stones. Above all mud is put and trodden hard, and then more wet earth is laid and trodden or rolled. There will have been left space for a door some five feet high by three or more wide, and two or three holes of twelve or fifteen by six or nine inches to admit light and to allow smoke to escape. The room thus built is the *baisha* (as the Tiari people call *baita*) or "house" which is such a great feature in Eastern houses. It is only lived in in the depth of winter, which in the valleys in ordinary years would be from near the beginning of December to the beginning of February. Mud ought to be used for mortar between the stones and the interior faces of the walls, and the floor will be coated with a special kind of clay which women rub with a round stone until it is hard and smooth, and has a certain polish. In one part of the *baita* there will be a circular platform of clay, rising an inch or so above the floor on which the fire is laid. The fire consists of a log (which is never extinguished the whole winter through, but slowly burns as it is pushed into the red embers, until it is consumed and makes way for its successor) and *siryuki*, i.e. thin branches of trees, mostly a kind of oak, from which the sheep in the course of the preceding day have eaten the leaves, of which their only food in the time of snow consists, because there is hardly any grass for hay, and what there is is wanted for the mule and the bull. These *siryuki* burn rapidly, and give out great heat and some light; the smoke is carried up over the heads of the men who sit round the fire to the roof, along which it makes its way to the window-holes, and into the eyes of any visitor who is walking in upright. Over the fire near meal-times a woman or girl will place a *digdin* or three-legged stand on which to set the pot in which the rice or other food is to be cooked. On the *digdin*, too, can be laid the thin slightly convex iron shield on which is spread sheets of dough when wheaten bread is to be provided for a guest of consequence or dignity.

Ordinarily, cakes of millet bread six or eight inches in diameter and about three-quarters of an inch thick, or in well-to-do houses, on some occasions, wheaten cakes of the same size, are baked in another contrivance. On a base formed by the space between two concentric circles about six or eight inches apart, or rather on what remains of such a ring-space, when about a quarter or a sixth of it has been subtracted, a wall is built curving inwards as it rises, so that it tends to form a hollow cone, except that a quarter of its front side has been cut away, until the (incomplete) ring measures only about a foot across internally.

On the floor enclosed by this truncated hollow cone of solid clay a fire is made, and the heat is further confined by the top being almost closed by a sherd of an old cooking-pot, in which at the same time seeds are being roasted. Presently the pot is taken from the top, the fire is swept away, and a broom dipped in water is used to clean the interior of the oven of all dust and smoke. Then the dough cakes are forcibly slapped against the side of the oven to which they adhere until they are baked. Sometimes it is necessary to put the embers back into the oven to bake the bread thoroughly. There are not in Tiari (except in a very few instances) *tanuri* or ovens built down into the ground underneath the house, such as are always found in the Rayat country and in Persia. Apropos of this fact it is related that one winter's day some Tiari men, dripping with perspiration and melting snow, arrived at the unfortunate village of Khananis, near Julamerk. Entering a house, they were bidden to "enter" under the *kursi* (a raised platform over the *tanura* over which carpets are spread) so that they might sit or recline with their feet on the edge of the tanura and dry themselves and their clothes under the carpets, which would reach to their necks and convey to them the grateful warmth. The bold mountaineers, who had never seen such a method of avoiding the pleurisy from which so many of them suffer at home, began to crawl in head first! They were only recalled by the laughter of their hosts.

The baita may be divided into two parts by a wall, and then the inner one will be a storeroom or sleeping apartment for the family. But all apartments are used to store things in; for the corn or *masta* (curdled milk) sheepskins, which have been stripped off the sheep like a glove, are kept in abundance. Above the *baita* there will be built one or more *bi'lawatha* or upper rooms, which resemble the baita in every respect except that they are, as a rule, loftier, and that the greater part of one side or parts of two sides are open—like a Regent's Street shop front without the plate glass. In these rooms the people live during the greater part of the year. Tiari men are different from all other Syrians, in that they never sit on the ground if they can help it. They have little wooden stools about six inches high. It is most amusing to see how, when one man leaves, another who has been on the floor or on a felt seizes the vacant stool and puts it under him. The roof of the house itself makes practically a third storey. On it are often erected high sleeping-places, formed by four poles placed upright and bound together by a flooring at the top, and by another nearly at the bottom. This gives two sleeping-places. In some places, to avoid mosquitoes, people make a sort of pier of wood, projecting out into the river, and covered with matting from the banks; they thus sleep over the water. These sleeping-places look not unlike lobster nets. Occasionally a man makes his bed on a huge boulder out in the river itself. Another method of getting rid of mosquitoes is to put a sort of thyme on one's pillow. It is called *rikhána*, i.e. the "smelling" flower.

As the floors in Tiari and some other districts are made of a hard clay which, when set, is perfectly firm and makes a very clean floor, it is not necessary, as with the mud floors of other districts, to spread mats first and then carpets. The beautifully clean and white felts, which are one of the best household things the Tiari men have, are put directly on the floor. But except to lay bedding upon, even this is not necessary, and most of the floor is quite uncarpeted. The great merit of this cemented floor is that it does not harbour fleas. Ordinarily, felts and quilts abound with these most annoying little insects, which make life a burden in some places in summer; but one is as free from them in Tiari as in England.

The vines are often beautifully twined on houses and up trees, as in Italy. There is nothing like this in the Persian plains, where the vines only grow in the vineyards. In fact, a Tiari or Tkhuma house is picturesque; an Urmi house, especially in the villages, unspeakably ugly. The Tiari grapes are of various sizes. The very small ones, which are usually a dark purple and extremely sweet, are most used for wine-making. In these districts also, unlike any other part of the Syrians' country, a very small fig is grown. Gourds are greatly cultivated. The outside shell is used for drinking-cups and as vessels for holding water. Those who have experienced the terrible heat of these valleys in the summer will sympathise with Jonah for the loss of his gourd; the least shade is eagerly sought after. Melons also are grown, but are inferior to those of Persia. Blackberries abound, but the people do not seem greatly to care for them.

Tiari people, and, indeed, almost all the mountaineers, differ from the Urmi folk, in that they always eat with spoons, wooden spoons carefully cut out of a white, hard wood, which gradually becomes almost red.

Many of the Ashiret men go down to the plain of Mosul to work, especially those of Jilu and Bas and Tal, but not now those of Tiari. Readers of Sir Henry Layard's book on Nineveh will remember that many of these tribesmen worked at his excavations. The Jilu men have a rather bad reputation for "going to countries," as they say, or "to the other side," as they often euphemistically put it, to beg; and religion is at rather a low ebb among them. They are many of them, unlike the other Syrians, of a very Jewish type of face. It may here be necessary to remark that Syrians are not "black men," as many suppose. They have usually very black hair, but their complexions are as fair as ours, and sometimes they have fair hair and blue eyes. The types of face vary very much; but most of them are very European and un-Jewish. There are, however, some exceptions. In this district, over which Mar Sergis rules, there is a famous church called The Hundred Courses (of stones?), dedicated to Mar Zaya; with whom is also connected the "Butter Stone," on the heights above the district of Bas, on which the women sprinkle the first clarified butter (*mishkha*) of the season.

THE ASHIRET COUNTRY. 45

The temporal rulers of these districts, appointed by Mar Shimun, are called *maliks*; though in some villages, like Ashitha, in Tiari, there is a head called a *reis*. A malik spends his day just as any owner of property does, working on it to some extent himself. But he will often have to give directions about tribal concerns, and frequently he has to settle disputes between his own subjects. He may receive embassies from Kurdish chiefs who want his friendship, and he may have before him matters of *la haute politique* with reference to other maliks or to Kurds, or to the government at Julamerk or even at Van or Mosul. In the evening, after work is over, men of his village will gather and form his court. This assembling round Mar Shimun, or round a malik or a reis, is a way of showing respect and loyalty. If we had the same notions about this sort of thing at home, our people would better understand the duty of coming into God's courts, and would feel the force of the warning not to "forsake the assembling of yourselves together."

To the south of Tiari are the Rayat districts of Berwer (which we may call Southern Berwer, to distinguish it from a district of the same name near Qudshanis) and the Supna. In the latter, the Christians partly adhere to Mar Shimun, and partly are Roman Catholic Uniats. In the former there are two bishops, both of whom are miserably poor —Mar Ishuyáw (Jesus gave) at Duri, and Mar Yonan (Jonah) at Ukri. There were once three bishops over these few villages; for when the late bishop at Duri died, there were two "successors," and as there was some dispute which should be made bishop, both were consecrated, and lived in the same house. One was the present Mar Ishuyáw, the other Mar Yawálaha (God gave). The latter is now dead.

In the valley of the Supna, which is mostly inhabited by Kurds, but has a few poor Syrian villages, is the natural fortress of Amadia, one of the most fever-stricken places of Kurdistan. On the pass leading to this from Berwer is a celebrated monolith called "the stone of Balal the Fool." Balal was a famous Kurdish jester. The story is that a certain Kurdish chief besieged Amadia and vowed not to return home till he had taken it. Finding after seven years that it was useless to go on, he agreed to raise the siege on condition that the governor would allow him to march through the town with his army, so as to keep his oath. Afterwards, coming to this stone, he composed a poem in which he described himself as Balal the Fool.

Here is the present southern limit of Mar Shimun's people. Between them and the plain of Mosul is the head-quarters of the Yezidis or so-called Devil-worshippers—Devil-propitiators would be a better name—the spire of whose temple of Sheikh Adai rises in a picturesque valley like that of an English village church. They accord very well with the Christians, who have, with them, a common antipathy to the Kurds. Their religious head, the Sheikh Nazar, who is described in Layard's "Nineveh" and Badger's "Nestorians and their Rituals," was still alive in 1887, and full of friendly reminiscences of the English. The Syrians say that his temple of Sheikh Adai was once one of their churches, dedicated to their apostle, Mar Adai.

CHAPTER IV.

EVERYDAY LIFE IN PERSIA.

Rising with sun—Beds—Sleeping-erections—Sleeping in clothes—Breakfast—Syrian houses: no windows on streets—Doorways—Narrow muddy streets—Village houses—The baita—Oven—Carpets and mats—Roofs—Town houses—Christian population of Urmi—Mart Mariam and St. George's Church, Urmi—Building—Masons—Carpenters—Wet wood—Windows—Glass—Looking-glasses—Pictures—Bazaar—Modakhel—Haggling—Donkeys—Roads and bridges—Riding fast—"Drunken Europeans"—Syrian occupations—Wages and prices—Buffaloes—Ploughing—Irrigation—Wood for burning—Mills—Malaria—Vineyards—Melon fields—Booths and lodges—Watering gardens—Tobacco—Grapes—Raisins—Wine—Arrack—Threshing-floor—Winnowing—Fishing—Sheep—Description of the plains—The Sea of Urmi and its rivers—Bathing—A sheet of salt—Snow—Storks and hoopoes—Partridges—Travelling in Persia.

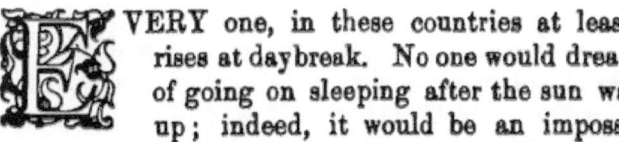VERY one, in these countries at least, rises at daybreak. No one would dream of going on sleeping after the sun was up; indeed, it would be an impossibility to do so when one's bed is in the open air, and a summer sun is streaming down its scorching rays even at 5 a.m. And in winter, also, if a man gets up before sunrise, it may be the middle of the night for all he knows. For watches and clocks

are not part of his regular belongings. Accordingly, when the sun rises, every one rises also, "takes up his bed," like the paralytic (St. Matt. ix. 6) from the floor where it had been spread, neatly folds up the quilts, mattress, and (if he has them) sheets, in an outer cover, and places them against the wall, where they make a convenient rest to any one sitting on the floor. Bedsteads are scarcely ever used either among the Syrians in Persia or among the Mussulmans, even among the rich; and to express them they have to borrow a Greek word through the Russian [1];—their own old word for it, owing to its proper meaning not being wanted, now expresses but a dead man's bedstead, a bier. In this, however, the Syrians in Persia differ from their mountain brethren, among whom bedsteads are much more common.

When, as in summer, people sleep on the flat roofs of the houses, a mat or a carpet is spread and the mattress and bed-clothes are placed on it; but occasionally, especially in villages near mountains, where there is danger of an incursion of wolves, wooden sleeping erections, ten to fifteen feet high, are made on the top of the roofs, to which it requires a steady head to ascend. But the people run up and down the shaking ladders which lead to them with the ease that comes by practice. The fear of wolves is no vain one, for a case is reported in which a wolf carried off a child placed for security between its parents, and the latter did not discover their loss till the morning. Only a year or two back wolves entered the city of Urmi at night

[1] Karabat. κρεββάτι in modern Greek = κράββατος, grabatus.

through a breach in the walls, and dug up and devoured a Mussulman who had just been buried.

The first thing the Syrians do on rising is to shake together their garments—in which they usually sleep, especially in winter, doffing only their shoes, hat, belt, and outer coat—and to go to the stream which flows through most of the courtyards for a wash and comb. Soap, towels, and brushes do not form part of the toilet. They are then ready for their morning prayers in the church. They have yet to learn to say private morning and evening prayers; but on the other hand many attend the daily public service, if not twice, at any rate once. After this the more well-to-do drink tea, but do not often eat much till midday. Their breakfast is called a "taste," and it is literally no more. Indeed, in part of the mountain districts the midday meal is called "breakfast," and if a man takes one or two small meals before it these are called "a taste" and "a little taste" respectively; *t'ama* and *t'amta*. But Syrians are not very regular about their meal-times; as they say themselves, "It is better for a man to eat when he is hungry."

While our Syrian is thus engaged let us look at the house he lives in. Looked at from the outside it is not prepossessing; for one can only see an expanse of mud, without windows—or at the best with only one or two tiny slits high up above the ground. The Persian has a horror of the idea of any one being able to look into his house; he loves privacy, especially, of course, in the women's apartments, and therefore all his windows look out on his courtyard. This is perhaps now kept up in Chris-

E

tian houses chiefly on account of Mohammedan influence. The Sunhadus says that houses may have doors, windows, and water-spouts in the streets. (book iv. § 14). For the same reason no one is allowed to build his house, except by special private arrangement, so that any of the windows look over his neighbour's courtyard, and therefore all houses built round the courtyard have to be but one room thick. It is also the height of bad manners when one goes up on to the roof to look over into a neighbour's domain.

The only striking object in the streets, except in the bazaars, where of course the shops or booths are open to the streets, and except the mosques with their great windows on the outside, are the large doorways. The larger the doorway the richer the man. And there is an old law, not now enforced in Urmi, that no Christian may have a higher doorway than a Mussulman neighbour. But, apart from the doorway, the entrance even to the best houses is often mean in the extreme, passing by stables and offices, or through very narrow lanes. It is seldom an index to the richness or poverty of the interior; and this is only one out of many instances of the struggle between a love of display and a fear of being the prey to an extortionate government. A man has been known to be "squeezed" simply because he rebuilt his doorway on a larger scale than before. A man known to be prosperous is a natural prey to officials, especially if he happens to be a Christian. But here, as in many cases, the protecting influence of European residents is felt. The streets themselves are usually narrow, a sea of mud, or obstructed in winter with piled-up snow, thrown from the roofs; sometimes in the villages quite impassable for pedestrians and difficult even for riders. The Sunhadus (book iv. § 14) says the streets are to be twelve, the lanes six feet wide, and they are often not more.

In the villages[1] the houses seldom cost more than £35. They are generally built of mud in layers. Each layer is about eighteen inches high, and after being built is left to dry in the sun for several days. When it is quite dry, another layer is placed on the top of it, and so on until all the wall is built. Walls built thus have to be very thick, especially at the bottom; but they become thinner towards the top. The better village houses are, however, made of sun-dried bricks, which are simply squares of mud baked in the sun. Burnt bricks are very seldom used in the villages, even for the house of the agha (landlord). Most of the villagers have small courtyards, with stable, granary, and store-rooms attached. But the great feature of every dwelling is what is called emphatically "the house" (*baita*). This is always on the ground floor, and must necessarily have no second storey on the top of it, as it has its only outlet, save the door, in the roof. It has no windows. In the floor is dug an oven some two or three feet deep, which is cased with clay, and is used for baking the flat wafer-like bread of the country as well as for all other culinary purposes. For cooking meat and other things, large cauldrons are placed on the top of this oven.

[1] The vernacular Syriac for a village is *matha*, a word rarely used in classical Syriac, probably meaning "a hundred houses."

When nothing is being cooked, a carpet or low table is often put over the top, and people keep themselves warm by sitting round it with their legs dangling down. The children may nearly always be seen amusing themselves in this way.

In these "houses" the family generally live, the women do their spinning, the men smoke their waterpipes (qalyuns) or chubuqs; and at night the beds (which in the daytime are rolled up and put away) are spread.[1] The floor is always of earth; on this are placed mats made of rushes, and carpets often cover the mats. As every one eats, sits, and sleeps on the floor, carpets are more necessary than in Europe. Some of these are very good, and one is often astonished to find in quite a poor house a fine Persian carpet which would fetch a high price in Europe. The better kind of carpet is called *khali* (Turkish *qali*); but the new ones are seldom so good as the old, on account of the introduction of aniline dyes. Hence it is often better to buy a second-hand carpet than a new one. There is an inferior kind called *prista* (Turkish *kilim*); and felts are also much used, especially along the sides of a room. Those made of camel's hair are the best, but they are expensive; and all felts foster vermin, the plague of the East. To protect carpets druggets are often used; and of course no Eastern thinks of walking over them in his shoes.

Besides a "house," most dwellings have one or more "rooms." These are also used for living in, especially on state occasions. They are generally whitewashed, and in the walls are a large number of

---

[1] The Syriac for bedding is "that which is spread."

recesses, which serve the purpose of cupboards. Wall paper is almost unknown. These rooms are warmed either by an open fire-place or by iron stoves, in which wood only is burnt. The floors of these rooms are made of earth, but on the top of the earth is laid a plaster of gypsum and mud which makes a hard flooring. Wooden floors are not found even in the best houses.

The great thing in a house is to have a good room to receive one's guests in, with suitable carpets. A man will often himself live in great discomfort (as we should think) and yet have a good sitting-room to entertain his friends in. This is especially the case with the Urmi Mussulmans, even with those of a better class than the general run. They infinitely prefer show to comfort.

A room on the first floor is called a *balakhána*, a name which is said to be the origin of our balcony. If so, it is curious that the word has travelled back in its modified form from Europe to the East, to denote what we mean by a balcony. This is called by the Syrians a *bálqán*.

In the summer every one sleeps on the roofs, which are of course flat, and are approached by an inside staircase or by an outside ladder. Native houses are seldom or never built in more than two storeys. These roofs are made curiously. The timbers are first firmly fixed into the walls, and are covered by transverse laths, and these again by mats. On the mats is placed a layer of hay, and on the hay a great quantity of earth; the whole is then plaistered down with a composition made of mud and chopped straw (Exod. v. 7). The roof is made to slant very slightly, so that the water may run off, and spouts are placed at intervals for this purpose. In winter it is of the utmost importance that the snow should be cleared off as soon as it falls, or the roofs will be utterly spoilt. In the villages the roofs generally run continuously from one to another, and one may walk over most of the village on the housetops. The first impression of a stranger

MISSION HOUSE, URMI.
From the authors' photograph.

arriving is of a mass of red, white, and blue, from the dresses of the people on the roof. The housetop is the general place of meeting, where things heard "in the ear" are proclaimed publicly (St. Matt. x. 27; St. Luke xii. 3). In time of persecution a man might run along the housetops to the outskirts of the village without waiting to go down into his own house (St. Matt. xxiv. 17). These roofs are often in spring quite green with "grass upon the housetops," which, however, in a comparatively cool country like Persia, does not wither "afore it groweth up" (Ps. cxxix. 6, A.V.), but has to be eradicated with salt.

In the town of Urmi the houses are much larger and better built, being generally faced with red bricks, which are from six to seven times as expensive as the sun-dried kind. These town houses are freehold; that is, the land belongs to the tenant, who pays no tax for it to an agha, and the courtyards are also very much larger. Thus the houses in Urmi are much more expensive than those in the villages; a good one, suitable for a European family, will cost from £100 to £300. The courtyards in the town are generally laid out as gardens, and have streams running through them, with pools for washing; for Urmi is one of the few Persian towns that have a plentiful supply of water. Frequently also there are tall plane and other trees, which tower above the two-storeyed houses. These give the town, seen from a distance, the appearance of a great walled garden. Most of the Christian inhabitants of the town are well-to-do settlers who have come in from the villages to practise a trade; and the Christian town population is not very great. It must, however, at one time have been greater, for there were at least two churches in the town, one of which is now a mosque, and the other, Mart Mariam (St. Mary) remains in the hands of the Christians. It professes to be the oldest church of the world, and to have been built by the Magi, one of whom is buried there.

The first thing to do in building the more substantial houses, such as those in the city of Urmi, is to lay a deep foundation of stones, digging until the earth is very firm. There will generally be three or four layers of large stones below the surface. The stones are brought from the quarry on donkeys' backs, two or three going to a load. They are built up with mud and water in which straw is mixed (lime being only rarely used, as when a watercourse passes underneath) to a little above the level of the inside, which, to prevent damp in a living room, should be two or three feet above the outside level. This foundation of stones is very expensive in Urmi, and costs almost as much as all the bricks which are to be placed on the top of it. The stones finished, the bricks are built up to the required level; and it will be lucky if some room is not built without windows, or doors, or if the staircase is not forgotten, for the mason and the owner are the only architects the house is likely to have. The staircase difficulty, however, is sometimes met, especially in the villages, by the use of very rickety ladders, which the people themselves run up and down easily, but which are a source of some anxiety to the inexperienced European. To build a house three or four masons will usually be employed; these do the edges of the walls and all the difficult work, and receive as wages 1s. 6d. a day; the middle part of the wall is then filled up by the boys, of whom each mason has several, and who get about 4d. a day. One boy brings the mortar, one the bricks, one lays the middle bricks (this will usually be an apprentice), and so forth. The old custom is for the masons and boys to keep up a recitative the whole time to the effect of, "My son, give me a brick," "My father, behold the mud," and so on; but this is dying out, which is to be regretted, as it is a delightful feature of Persian building. Besides these there are several workmen employed, who get about 7*d.* a day, to cast away earth and make mortar; also one or two jobbing carpenters who get 1*s.* a day, and a few others. But these prices are lower for Mussulman workmen in Ramazan, the month of abstinence, as they then only work till midday; longer hours being impossible, as they may not eat or drink from sunrise to sunset.

The thickness of the walls (nearly one yard) which is necessitated by the crumbling nature of the sun-dried bricks, has the good effect of keeping the house cool in summer and warm in winter. And if the wood used for doors and windows were dry and did not warp so that no door or window fits, the houses could be kept very comfortable in the cold weather. As it is, the draughts are terrible. Buttresses are hardly ever used. There are very small ones, half a brick thick; but these are more for ornament than anything else. The sun-dried bricks used in building the houses are usually made in the courtyard as the building is going on. It is no wonder that the greater part of old cities like Nineveh has entirely vanished when we consider that they were built of this material.

The doors of all the rooms are made double, meeting in the middle, so that the weight of a broad door may not hang on hinges fixed in wet wood. They are closed with iron chains and staples; the ordinary European locks, latches, and door-handles are very seldom used, padlocks being substituted. The outer doors are secured by a large bar, and have wooden locks and keys, which a European finds very difficult to open and shut.

A great feature of the better houses is the windows, which often take up the whole side of a room; in which case the weight of the wall above is supported by a great beam on the top of the window. The lattice work is very beautiful, and is filled with stained glass in various patterns; the centre of the window usually consists of larger panes, which themselves are either plain or coloured, and the lattice work makes a frame round them. The glass is fixed in grooves of the wood, and in order to insert it the neighbouring woodwork must be removed. Unfortunately, however, these beautiful windows are not now made, and the Persians are giving them up for what they imagine are French windows, which, being made of wet wood, never shut properly. The only way to buy the old windows is to pick them up second hand, when some khan (or great man) is Europeanizing his house, or at least de-orientalizing it. The windows are more often than not covered with oiled paper or cotton instead of with glass. This is, of course, not transparent; but it is translucent, and keeps the room warm. It is generally removed in summer, during which the windows are almost always open. Glass is now brought from Russia, but it is very expensive as compared with other things; and, as putty is not used, a sudden gust of wind or any small accident often demolishes a large number of panes. Many of the rooms are profusely decorated with looking-glasses; in some cases the whole ceiling is studded with them; but these do not give a faithful reflexion of those that look into them. Generally the rooms have no furniture in them at all except carpets and curtains, and perhaps beds. The Syrians of the Urmi plain are very fond of gaudy pictures of the Russian royal family, and of scriptural or ecclesiastical subjects (especially of the terrors of the Last Judgment), which they bring from Tiflis. These, however, are of late introduction. They never have pictures in the churches, and till lately did not have them in the houses. They will often look at a picture upside down, and it makes no difference to them; just as they read a book upside down, or any way with almost equal facility. This seems to betoken a superior education of the eye. Pictures are not forbidden in the Sunhadus. Their absence may perhaps be accounted for by Mohammedan influence. Some few old ecclesiastical books have them; one book of the Gospels has such effects as a rider (meant to be astride) with both legs on one side of the ass. So also some charms written by priests for special objects have pictures of Saints.

A Syrian's ideas of perspective are hazy in the extreme. In a picture of the Crucifixion, in which a soldier in the foreground is pointing to our Saviour in the distance, the mission scholars thought he was at our Lord's side, and touching him with his hand. Many, too, did not recognize our Saviour on the Cross, reminding one how entirely the understanding of pictures is an acquired art. One has to be a little careful in showing pictures to the Syrian children. Some beautiful pictures of the Nativity published by the S.P.C.K. were sent out for the mission schools, but lost all their teaching value and were greeted with roars of derisive laughter because St. Joseph had on a European hat!

We have left our Syrian eating his breakfast, or more probably (for that does not take many minutes) smoking his cigarette, chubuq or qalyun (waterpipe). He now perhaps goes into Urmi to the bazaar, where he haggles over his purchases and meets his friends. The vendors are generally Mussulmans, though occasionally Syrians. The bazaar consists of streets of stalls and some open squares called caravanserais, which must not be confused with the other caravanserais in the towns and villages where there are stables for horses and camels. The Urmi bazaar is a large one; in the principal caravans-rai are merchants' offices, the post-office, etc., and in the middle a large pool. The open space is usually taken up with great bales deposited by the camels, of which one may see several resting after their long journey, before being taken to their own quarters for the night. From this open space the streets of the retail traders diverge, the shoemakers occupying one, the iron workers another, the drapers a third, and so forth. The best work done is that of the silversmiths, whose filigree work is really beautiful. The better streets of the bazaar are covered in, but all have a road for horses, asses, and camels; and the busy purchasers are hustled aside by riders. In the bazaar also is a *maidan*, an open place covered with gravel, with the two principal mosques; one of them, the "Friday Mosque," being the old Christian Church of St. George, now entirely rebuilt, and containing some fine arabesque work. In this *maidan* corn is sold, and one often sees snake-charmers and conjurers earning their pence from an admiring crowd of *lutis* or loafers. The whole is a busy scene, except on Fridays, when most of the Mussulmans shut up their shops.

It is not quite proper for khans and great people to go to the bazaar in Urmi, far less to buy anything there. If a great man has occasion to go anywhere on the other side of the bazaar, he will make a long détour in order to avoid it. All purchases are made by the servants, who make up their accounts with their masters at intervals; but it is a recognized thing for them to take a percentage, called *modákhel*, on everything they buy, and this is reckoned up quite openly when wages are fixed. If a master were to buy things himself, the only difference would be that the *modákhel* would go into the pocket of the vendor, and probably it would eventually find its way back to the servant.

The Syrian dearly loves his bargain, and does not think hours wasted if he can reduce the price by a few pence. The vendor always asks two or three times what he means to take, and the buyer offers half or a third of what he means to give. The result is usually a fair price, but it takes a long time to arrive at it. It is most amusing to see two friends coming to terms about a piece of property. One recalls Silas Wegg: "Mr. Boffin, I never bargain. . . . I never did 'aggle, and I never will 'aggle. Consequently, I meet you at once, free and fair, with—Done for double the money!" They usually preface all remarks with "We are brethren, we will make no difficulty about the price." "Well, what do you want for the house?"

"Oh, it is your pleasure, you know (*i.e.* what you please), I am content with whatever you say." "Well, but what will you sell for?" "Oh, we are brethren, it is a gift to you, my house is yours." But when a price is suggested, then the real haggling begins; and one cannot but suppose that Ephron's offer of the field as a free gift to Abraham, and Araunah's offer of the threshing-floor to David, were merely polite speeches; they at once accepted the full price. "The land is worth four hundred shekels of silver; what is that betwixt thee and me?" (Gen. xxiii. 15; 2 Sam. xxiv. 22-24). With which we may compare the custom of saying to a guest who admires anything in a house, "It is yours; pray take it." But, of course, it would be very bad manners to accept such a gift.

Having made his purchases, our villager will load his donkey, which is a patient drudge of all work, and return to his own village along the tracks which go by the name of roads, finding perhaps a good bit of road for a mile or so leading up to some agha's house, along which a carriage might be driven, but which begins nowhere. Elsewhere the man and his donkey plod along painfully through the mud, wading through small streams or crossing the river by rickety bridges, which it seems nobody's business to repair, and which generally have large holes in them and threaten continually to fall. Being made of mud plaistered on long poles, they give way after heavy rain or after the winter snows fall. As our friend goes along he meets strings of villagers on their way to or from the town of Urmi. "Strings" is the proper word, because they have to walk in single file, the narrow path seldom allowing two men to walk abreast, at least in muddy weather or in snow. Innumerable donkeys will also be met, carrying every conceivable commodity; they are the regular beasts of burden for short distances, while horses, mules and camels generally are used for long-distance caravans. But the donkeys, though they go slowly, can keep on for an extraordinary number of hours at a stretch, and in the more hilly roads one is sometimes reduced to a donkey caravan when making a journey. The donkeys all have their nostrils split, as this is said to give them a better wind. Many of them are fine animals, and the white ones are affected by the mollahs (the Mussulman ministers of religion) for riding purposes. But the ordinary donkeys have a hard life, and generally end their days by dropping down dead under a heavy load in a snowstorm.

The roads are seldom made, and are merely the result of being constantly trodden down by the passing caravans; hence they are generally lower than the neighbouring fields, and when the latter are irrigated and the streams overflow, the roads are flooded as a matter of course. The result is an incredible amount of mud, which makes locomotion frequently difficult even in summer, and sometimes impossible in winter. There is an utter absence of public spirit in these matters, and but little compulsion; so that matters go from bad to worse. Indeed, the cultivator often looks upon the road as a convenient place to turn his surplus water into. The stream is a far more important thing than the road. It is necessary that the former should be raised in order to turn the water mills; but it is not the least necessary that the road should be raised to keep a dry means of locomotion! A village is supposed to be responsible for its own roads, but no pressure is put on it, unless the visit of a very great man is expected. In Turkey, indeed, the caravan roads along the rivers, which in winter and early spring are yearly ruined by *débris* from the mountains and by snow, are repaired in the late spring by forced labour from the neighbouring villages, and the bridges are renewed in the same way. But in the plain of Urmi, the roads and bridges of the Christian villages are generally worse than those of the Mussulmans. This is because the latter look upon road or bridge making as a work of charity which will secure their entry into Paradise. And, though the short attempts at carriage roads made by some village masters are quite useless, inasmuch as they lead to nowhere, the large bridges over the rivers, of which there are a few in different parts of the country, are a great benefit to the whole community. The bridges over the smaller streams often consist of a single stone or of two poles covered with mud; and yet the Persian horse will go over them without the least hesitation. It must be said, however, that when the roads are dry the riding is excellent, and this is one of the most enjoyable features of Persian life. Horses are cheap, especially in Azerbaijan, and nearly every one keeps one; a very fair one may be obtained for £9 or £10. Indeed, there is hardly any other method of locomotion for human beings. The Persians and Syrians love to go at a jog trot, perhaps varying it occasionally by a furious gallop to show their good riding (during which they often fall!). They cannot understand why Europeans should ride so fast. One day the present writers, accompanied by a bishop, were cantering along the grass, when they met a Persian khan or great man. "Why are those Englishmen riding so fast?" says he to the bishop. "Oh, it is their custom, their pleasure," says the right reverend prelate, with a shrug of the shoulders. "Ah, I understand; no doubt they are drunk!"

The ordinary pursuits of the day in the Urmi plain are mostly agricultural. There are, indeed, a few who follow a trade in the city of Urmi, as shoemakers or carpenters, and a large Christian village just outside the gates, Charbash, consists almost entirely of masons and their apprentices. The daily wages of carpenters and masons are about 1s. to 1s. 6d. a day. In one or two villages, too, are to be found potters making the earthenware jars of all sizes, which are used for carrying water, cooking, eating (they are then glazed), storing, and for all household purposes. But some trades, as working in iron, calico-making, and dyeing, are almost entirely confined to Mussulmans. The greater part of the Christian inhabitants of the Urmi plain are agriculturalists, and in the daytime will be found in the fields or vineyards, or on the threshing-floor, according to the season; if they are labourers they will only get about 5d. a day; but this is more than the Indian labourer gets. Often a man has fields of his own—rather larger than a croft in the Scottish Highlands—or perhaps a vineyard or an orchard; and this is looked to to help out the wages considerably. But if the wages are low, the prices of commodities correspond. Though every one is poor, no one is so poor as many in the great towns of Europe, and starvation, except in the famine years, is hardly known. But the wants of the people are few; the poorer people wear only cotton clothes, which are often made by themselves, and at any rate are very cheap. Cloth clothes cost about the same as in Europe, for though the cloth is dearer owing to its long overland carriage, yet the labour employed is much cheaper. Wheat and barley cost from 7s. 6d. to 16s. per load of 320 lbs., if bought at harvest-time. The barley is almost entirely used as food for the horses, oats not being grown. It is slightly cheaper than wheat. Horses, however, always have to eat their fill of chopped straw before they are given barley (which even then is mixed in the chopped straw), and the poorer people seldom give their horses barley at all. They also give them dried clover in the winter months; in the summer they give them fresh clover, and then they do not give barley.

The buffalo is a greater treasure to the agricultural Syrian even than his horse. He is most carefully tended, kept warm in the stable or even in the house during the winter, and diligently washed in the streams during the summer by the boys, who seem to spend hours on the task, the buffalo standing impassive but contented the while, and when he is not being washed wallowing with infinite enjoyment in the mud or bathing on his own account in the deeper streams, sitting with only his stupid-looking head above the water, and indifferent to all that goes on around him, like a good Mussulman. He is chiefly useful in ploughing and in dragging heavy weights, especially in bringing home the harvest; but oxen and even horses are often used instead, especially in the threshing-floors.

In the autumn some of the fields are ploughed for the early wheat to be sown. The sower takes his bag and scatters the seed, as one sees in the old pictures. But most of the ploughing and sowing is done in the early spring, when the long winter breaks and the snow at last melts. Buffaloes or oxen are generally used; but two men are often seen digging the fields by manual labour. One digs with a spade, and the other helps him by drawing the spade up with a rope, to which a handle is attached. This is perhaps the "two in the field" of St. Matt. xxiv. 40. And now the great thing is to have the country properly irrigated; a complete system of channels spreads over the whole plain, and much ingenuity is shown, especially in the villages on the higher ground and in the mountains. For as the fields are naturally higher than the bed of the rivers, artificial streams have to be carried from some point higher up the river where the level is higher than that of the fields to be irrigated, and when the river makes a narrow channel between hills, this artificial stream has to be cut out of the side of the hill, and often to be carried over a ravine or along the face of a precipice by bridges. For all vegetation irrigation is necessary; the fierce summer sun dries up everything not well watered. There are, indeed, some fields on the sides of the hills surrounding the Urmi plain which trust to the very scanty rainfall and are not irrigated. But their owners never count on getting anything from these fields. If they do, it is so much to the good; if they do not, they are no worse off than they expected to be. Ordinarily, all depends on irrigation. The contrast between an ordinary stretch of ground dried up by a midsummer sun and a little patch watered for a melon field is wonderful. The Syrians well understand the sterility implied in the words, "Ye shall be . . . as a garden that hath no water" (Isa. i. 30). Sometimes water is secured by a series of wells connected by underground tunnels. The tunnels are a few feet from the bottom of each well, and there is a slight fall in each tunnel. The first well is on higher ground, and thus a supply of water is obtained. In other parts of Persia, where there are few or no rivers, this method of obtaining water is extensively used.

Along the streams trees are grown, chiefly pollard willows, which are very useful as fuel, and grow very well. Such is the "tree planted by the waters, and that spreadeth out her roots by the river, and shall not see when heat cometh, but her leaf shall be green; and shall not be careful in the year of drought, neither shall cease from yielding fruit" (Jer. xvii. 8). Without this plentiful supply of wood, which gives to the Urmi plain its name, "the Garden of Persia," its chief attraction would be gone, and the cold of winter would be very hard to bear. In the open Persian fireplaces, and in the newly introduced iron stoves, nothing else can be burnt. It is sold by the weight, and at the present time the better sorts fetch about 7s. a *khulwar* (800 lbs.), but this includes carriage on the backs of donkeys for some distance. The better sorts burnt are apricot, pear, and vine-stocks; willow is cheaper, but burns away quicker. The plane tree and walnut are usually kept for carpenters' work. But the poorer people content themselves with their earth ovens and manure fuel; they seldom use their *rooms* (that is, those which have fireplaces) in winter, but all congregate in the *baita*, or "house."

The irrigation streams are also used to turn the mill wheels. The mills are built of sun-dried bricks over the streams and are of very simple construction, but are valuable pieces of property. The miller receives one-twentieth of whatever he grinds, either in kind or money, as the owner of the corn wishes. The upper and the nether millstone are brought to Urmi from the neighbourhood of the Aras (Araxes), and are rolled along in couples with a beam through their centres, like the wheels of a cart, drawn by buffaloes. When fixed in the mill a wooden lever at the side balances them, and the water then turns them round. When the lever lets them fall slightly their weight prevents their motion. The wheat is brought down from its receptacle into the millstones by two loose pieces of wood, called *chaqchaqs*, or hoppers. These are of some value, and they say of a poor room which yet has one good thing in it, " a deserted mill has still two chaqchaqs." And when a man expects to find something valuable in a house which has been cleaned out by robbers, they say, "The floods have swept away the mill, and he is asking for the chaqchaqs."

The water is brought to the mill on the top of a raised embankment, and falls down a tube formed from a hollowed tree, in order that a sufficient fall may be secured. When the mill is not working, the mill stream is diverted by the raising of a sluice, and makes a circuit to join its proper course lower down. Windmills are not known. The water mills are worked by men only; but in some villages handmills are used, worked by two women, as in St. Matt. xxiv. 41.

A great drawback arising from the irrigation system is the prevalence of malarial fever, which is greatly due to the large amount of stagnant water. The natives of the plain seem to suffer as much from it as Europeans or even more. Quinine and aperient medicines seem to be the only remedy, and these are taken largely. Perhaps the malaria might be very much reduced by a better system of carrying off the surplus water, which at present is allowed to find its way to the sea as best it can, so that all the lower parts of the plain, near the Sea of Urmi, are one great marsh, and quite uninhabitable. But it is curious that some of the mountain villages suffer from malaria no less than the lower-lying villages of the Persian plains.

Among the prominent features of the country we must notice the vineyards and melon fields, which are usually planted close to the villages, for greater security. The vineyards are always walled with mud to the height of from five to ten feet,[1] but the melon fields, vegetable gardens, corn-fields, etc., are more often open. The road to a village often runs through a long series of vineyards, with a high wall on either side, as in the case of Balaam. "The Angel of the Lord stood in a path of the vineyards, a wall being on this side and a wall on that side" (Num. xxii. 24). In the vineyards and orchards are built "towers" (St. Matt. xxi. 33) or rough mud houses, in which all the family live during the grape harvest; but these are permanent, and not like the small temporary erections or slight booths erected in the melon fields and castor oil plantations for the purpose of watching the fruit when nearly ripe lest it should be stolen. It is curious that here we have the reverse of Isa. i. 8,[2] where the prophet mentions the temporary booth (A.V. cottage) in a vineyard, and the rude, but somewhat more permanent "lodge" (cottage, Isa. xxiv. 20) "in the garden of cucumbers," the ὀπωροφυλάκιον of the Septuagint. Such erections are evidently of very ancient date. Jonah erected a booth (Jon. iv. 5), to watch what would become of Nineveh, and Job speaks of the "booth that the keeper maketh" (xxvii. 18).

Both water and musk melons are grown in great profusion. The latter are called "cooked" because while still growing they are buried in the hot soil

---

[1] "I will take away the hedge thereof... and break down the wall thereof," Isa. v. 5; cf. Ps. lxxx. 12; and St. Matt. xxi. 33. By the "hedge" any kind of enclosure seems to be meant.
[2] See the "Speaker's Commentary" here.

in order to ripen. They are sold very cheaply, and even the poorest people make them the great staple of food during the late summer.

The gardens are all arranged below the level of the stream, that they may be properly irrigated; they are dug with parallel ridges, and surrounded by a wall of earth about a foot high. The water is then let in at one corner, and wanders from one part to another, first up and then down, and may be stopped at any point by blocking up the narrow channel between the ridges. This seems to be the method described in Deut. xi. 10, as that of Egypt, "where thou sowedst thy seed, and wateredst it with thy foot, as a garden of herbs." A motion of the foot would turn on or off the water. This was not the common custom in Canaan, which "is a land of hills and valleys, and drinketh water of the rain of heaven" (*id*. ver. 11).[1]

Tobacco also is largely grown in the villages near the hills. But the salt nature of the soil—for the whole plain of Urmi was once covered with the great salt lake which now bounds it, makes the tobacco very strong, and it is very inferior to that grown in the mountains of Kurdistan. It is, however, smoked ("drawn" or "drunk" as they say) by every one, unless some mountaineer comes down with some of his own for sale; but it is only suitable for cigarettes and chubuqs. This tobacco is called *tutun*; that used for the water-pipes is brought from the South of Persia, and is called *tumbaki*; it is not cut up like the *tutun*.

The grapes of the Urmi plain are remarkably fine

[1] See Smith, "Dict. Bible," *s.v.* "Agriculture."

and grow in great abundance; they are so cheap that they are within reach of the poorest. Those intended for use in the late autumn are left in the vineyards, but covered up as a protection against the frost. For winter use, the grapes are strung by the women, tied together by reeds, and then hung from nails in the roof to keep. They then get a new name, *tlu'i*, derived from a word meaning "to hang." These will last, with care, and if the place is sufficiently airy, all the winter, but they gradually dry up like raisins; some people, however, also preserve grapes in sawdust, and these will last till April. Raisins are a great commodity, especially for the fast, and are of many different kinds. They fetch from 1s. 6d. to 2s. per batman of thirty-two pounds. Some attempt has been made to export them to Europe; but the long land journey through Turkey with its many uncertainties, presents many difficulties. It may be hoped, however, that these will gradually be overcome. Treacle, also, is largely made from the grapes. In most vineyards are found a raised bank for drying raisins, a winepress,[1] and a place for making treacle. The wine is not as a rule good; the Syrians have not yet learnt the art of making it. They make it for themselves, and often sell it under the rose to the Mussulmans; but, of course, the latter are not supposed to drink it. This law is more honoured in the breach than in the observance, especially among the well-to-do classes. The red wine is generally used in the

---

[1] Gideon threshed his wheat in the winepress (Judg. vi. 11, R.V.) to hide it from the Midianites. But the modern presses would be much too small for this.

winter, the white wine in the spring, as it keeps better. In the summer wine is seldom drunk, and is very difficult to get. Last year's supply is either finished or turned sour, in which case it will do for vinegar, and does not come amiss, as that is an ingredient in almost every dish. Almost every house has a winepress, and the wine-making is quite simple and primitive. The grape juice, trodden out thoroughly, or pressed out between boards connected together by rough wooden screws, is put into large earthenware jars tapering to a point at the bottom. After the wine has been left to ferment the jars are covered up with a piece of wood, and plaistered over with mud. After about a month it is ready for drinking, but at this stage is rather strong (Isa. xlix. 26, margin ; Acts ii. 13) and sweet. Syrians unfortunately have no idea of drinking wine except a whole cup at a draught, perhaps because there is seldom more than one cup in the company ; and this sometimes leads to intoxication. But drunkenness is not so prevalent as with us. The refuse grapes are used for making arrack, a strong coarse spirit which Europeans seldom learn to appreciate.[1]

Other fruits grow in great abundance, and are stored by the Syrians for winter use, being dried on the roofs by the hot summer sun. Apricots, cherries, quinces, pears, apples, peaches (of which there are several kinds), nectarines, all may be had

[1] It may be interesting to note that near to Jebel Judi, where according to Syrian tradition, the ark rested, is "Noah's vineyard" where grapes still grow. This is close to the village of Hasan in Lower Bohtan, and near the town of Jezireh on the Tigris.

in their season for a song. But the quality is not very good, as compared with the English fruit. The children also delight in the rather sickly fruit of the jujube tree. Strawberries are cultivated by Europeans, but they are never so good as in Western countries; raspberries also and currants will grow in Persia, but they are not a native fruit.

Outside every village is the threshing-floor—a large open place, the most level procurable; generally the only place covered with grass in the neighbourhood. Hither, in July, the hay and clover having been gathered in the month before, they bring the corn to be threshed and winnowed. The whole population has been turned into the fields to reap, and any passer-by makes the pious greeting, "God give you strength." Now the buffaloes bring home the sheaves on heavily laden sledges, or in very rough waggons, the boys singing to them for their encouragement. The sheaves are placed in a great heap, and some are laid round it in a circle, to be threshed by the "ox that treadeth out the corn," walking round in a direction contrary to that of the sun.[1] There are generally two oxen, and they draw behind them a machine arranged with crooked knives which cut up the straw. On this machine the driver sits, and his weight presses it down. The oxen, contrary to the Scripture precept, are frequently muzzled.[2] In Turkey, five or six oxen yoked abreast, without the machine, walk round and round a post

[1] In the Egyptian picture in Smith's "Dict. of Bible," s.v. "Agriculture," the oxen go *with* the sun.
[2] Deut. xxv. 4; 1 Cor. ix. 9; 1 Tim. v. 18. In India also the oxen are muzzled.

in the middle, and so by their feet tread out the corn.

Close by the winnowing goes on. A man takes a shovel (*ruphshta*) and casts the grain in the air that the wind may separate the chaff from the corn. This is probably the "fan" referred to in Holy Scripture, though there two winnowing instruments are mentioned—the "shovel" and the "fan" (Isa. xxx. 24), as they are called in the Authorised Version. It is not very clear what was the difference between them.

There are various other occupations of the men of the Urmi plains. Some go fishing in the rivers —the sea is too salt to allow of fish living in it. Occasionally they throw a preparation containing *cocculus Indicus* mixed with flour, oil, etc., into the stream to intoxicate the fish, and then when the fish rise senseless to the surface, they plunge in and catch them in their hands. But they generally use a circular net; the circumference is weighted, and a cord held in the hand attached to the centre. The net is thrown in flat into the rapid parts of the river, and then drawn in by the cord. The weights in the circumference come together as the net is drawn in, thus making the net a bag, and the fish are enclosed. It is not a high art. The fish themselves are very tasteless and full of bones, and to a European taste scarcely worth the trouble of eating, far less of catching.

The upland villages towards the mountains have more various pursuits, partly like those of the plain, and partly like those of the mountains. Here there are large flocks, *led* by the shepherd, who goes before them and calls their names. They know the voice of the shepherd (St. John x. 1–5). They are said to learn their names in the following way: The shepherd gives them a little salt to eat and calls them by their name over and over again. They do this several days, always giving them salt, so that the sheep learn their name. The salt, be it understood, is to call the attention of the sheep to their names! Such is the account given by an unexceptional authority. In the mountains every shepherd carries salt with him.

It may be as well to explain the nature of the country in which the Persian Syrians live. Between the Turkish frontier and the city of Urmi are, first, a chain of upland plains which run parallel to the frontier (Mérgawar, Térgawar, and Brádust), and then a range of grass-covered hills. Eastward there lie other series of plains, which form the western margin of the Sea of Urmi, and extend for about a hundred miles in length; in breadth they vary considerably, according to the nearness of the mountains to the sea. In the centre lies the great plain of Urmi, which is about twenty miles broad in its widest part, and is watered by the three rivers known as the Nazlu river, the City river, and the Barándus river. These flow into the Sea of Urmi. To the north lies the little plain of Gavilan, which has but little water; its inhabitants have partly the habits of mountaineers, and partly of plain-men. At the north end of the sea is the plain of Salmas, watered by a small river of its own and separated from the other plains by a range of mountains. The Christian inhabitants are chiefly Armenians or Syrian Roman Catholics, (the so-called Chaldeans). The dialect is very different from that of Urmi, and more resembles that of Qudshanis, the patriarch's village. At the south end of the sea is the plain of Solduz, separated from that of Urmi by a range of hills which here come down close to the water. Near this is the somewhat important town of Sa-uchbulak, inhabited chiefly by Kurds, the scene of the late case of abduction by the Kurds of a young lady, a British subject.

All these plains are well watered by the short rivers which rise in the frontier mountains and flow down eastwards to the lake. But, by the time they reach the plains, they are most of them dry in summer, as the water is drawn off into artificial channels for irrigation purposes, and even in winter they are fordable in most places, except after a flood. As a consequence of the abundance of water, these plains are very productive, and might be made much more so under a good government. At present a large area near the mouths of the rivers is a great swamp, which causes malaria and retards locomotion.

The sea or lake of Urmi is one of the saltest pieces of water in the world. It extends for about a hundred miles, more or less north and south, and has no outlet. It is, however, decreasing slowly; for there is no doubt that all the surrounding plains were once under water. It is quite shallow, and at one time there was a talk of carrying a road across it by a causeway to connect Urmi with Tabriz, the capital of this north-western province of Azerbaijan. But, like every project of the sort in Persia, it came to nothing. There are at present a couple of cranky sailing-boats which go across it, and to the islands in the sea, to carry timber and sheep. But as they can only sail with the wind, the unwary passenger who wishes to cross to Tabriz, may find himself detained a week on one of the islands with no food but what he brought with him. These islands are used at some times of the year for pasturing sheep, and they are also the home of the flamingos which flock hither in great numbers in the winter. They come over to the mainland in the spring, and are caught with horsehairs. Several governors have talked (only talked) of putting a steamer on the lake to shorten the journey from Urmi to Tabriz. But the notions of ships held by every one, Christian and Mussulman alike, are hazy in the extreme. Few have even seen a rowing-boat; there are none on the rivers; and their language lacks dozens of words referring to ships and the sea which we use daily.

If any one bathes in the sea, it is as well to take down some fresh water to the shore, for he will emerge perfectly clothed in a white sheet of salt. The water is so buoyant that one can hardly sink in it. But bathing here is not very enjoyable, owing to the shallowness of the water and to the liability of the salt to get into one's eyes and mouth. The Syrians make a pilgrimage to bathe in the sea on St. Thomas's Day (July 3), as there is a tradition that the apostle passed over it on his way to India.

The lake contains no fish or seaweed, and all along the shore is decaying vegetable matter and salt which sends a disagreeable savour over the whole plain and even to the hills behind, when the wind is from the east. There are hardly any villages nearer than two miles from the sea, and the whole borderland is uncultivated. Even the cattle can scarcely find anything to eat on it. It is like the "parched places in the wilderness, in a salt land and not inhabited" (Jer. xvii. 6).

The plains are between four and five thousand feet above the ocean level. Owing to this great elevation, and to the remoteness from the sea, all this part of Persia is very cold in winter. The snow lies deep on the plains for from three to five months. There is usually a heavy fall in November, but this generally melts, and the real snow often does not begin till the middle of December, or even the beginning of January. In the upland and mountain districts it, of course, lasts very much longer. During this time of snow all the cattle are carefully housed, especially the buffaloes, who cannot endure great cold, and the little children, who at other times are busy herding them, are at liberty to attend the village schools. Even in the plains of Urmi, the frosts are very severe, the thermometer often falling below zero (Fahrenheit). Moving about is very difficult at this time; still, the roads from village to village are kept open, and there is a good deal of communication in one way or another. In the mountain districts horse travelling is impossible at this time, and the only means of locomotion is walking very early in the morning on the top of the frozen snow, or *qrushta* ("crust," we should call it). By midday this hard snow has generally melted, and travellers then have to wait till next morning.

In the spring the snow melts very quickly on the

plain. One usually wakes up one morning in March to find oneself in summer. The next two months are the pleasantest in the year. It is not too hot, and everything is green. The wise-looking stork comes and stands on one leg surveying the country which he left the year before for the warmer south. He is called "Hajji (Pilgrim) Lagleg," because he is supposed to have come from Mecca. He is wonderfully tame, and will even stand in the road when a horseman is coming along, and compel him to move out of the path. No one would think of hurting him. He and his mate build their nests with twigs on the trees (where the people often leave baskets for them) and very often on the roofs of the houses, the hen bird clapping her beak with a great noise as a sign of love or of impatience when her mate is away. A little further north, in Armenia, where the churches are more pretentious, the storks greatly affect the spires for their nests, and they look very comical perched on the top of them. But there are no spires in the Syrians' country.

With the spring also the hoopoes return, beautiful birds with their variegated plumage and noble crests. But the Syrians consider them unclean (Lev. xi. 19, R.V.; Deut. xiv. 18). They call them *pupu*, from their note, which resembles that of the cuckoo except that it does not descend. They also call them birds of Solomon, from the old legend that they got their crests from the wise king. A flock of them once sheltered him from a burning sun. In gratitude the king asked them what he should do for them, and they asked for crowns of gold. But finding that they were being killed by greedy

G

men for the sake of their crowns, they begged Solomon to change them for the crest which they retain to this day. They are certainly pretty birds, and welcome harbingers of spring. There are also some cuckoos.

While on the subject of birds, we may notice the red-legged or Asiatic partridge. These are found on the hills, and are caught in traps or shot. But, as they are very shy, the sportsman has to approach behind a great canvas shield which he holds in front of him, and which quite deceives the unwary bird. When caught alive they soon become tame, and the people keep them in their houses, with clipped wings, often for fighting purposes. Quails are also very common, and are very good eating.

The summer in the north Persian plains is certainly hot, but not as compared with southern Persia or India. Europeans rather suffer from the want of freshness in the air than from the actual heat, and it is better for them to move to the hills. As it is too hot for the schools to go on, we have always been in the habit of going into tents on a hill about six miles from Urmi, and the Sisters of Bethany have a house there also, given to the mission by an anonymous benefactress. The Syrians of the city of Urmi usually go to their vineyards if they possess any, or to their relations in the villages, for a summer change. The Persian khans have summer houses in the vineyards, or along the banks of the river.

We may close this chapter with a description of the Persian Syrian's travelling. There are practically only two ways of doing this: (1) by posting, (2) by caravans. In posting one rides post-horses from stage to stage, changing them every time one passes a post-house. These are from fifteen to twenty miles apart. A good rider can, if he is lucky enough always to find horses and the roads are good, get through a hundred miles in a day. But he cannot take any but very light luggage, as he goes at a canter most of the way. In by-roads, like those near the frontier, post-horses are not often used; they are difficult to get, and one may be considerably detained. Also one is obliged when posting to keep to the post-road, which is often not the shortest. At night one can sleep at the post-house, or by preference at some house in the village where one stops, the inhabitants of which will probably be hospitable, even if they be Mussulmans and the traveller a Christian. The usual method is to take a caravan; that is, one hires any number of horses for oneself and one's heavy baggage to go the whole way to one's destination, or from one large town to another. The horses only walk, and this method of travelling is very tedious; it also involves many difficulties with the caravan-drivers, who frequently do not come when they promise, or at the last moment demand a large increase of pay over and above the bargain. The Syrians seldom trouble themselves about much luggage. They stuff a few things into a *khurjin*, or pair of saddle-bags made of carpet, perhaps take a quilt, or trust to hospitality on the way. A European has to be rather more fastidious, and take bedding and plenty of insect powder, or he will get no rest at night. Better than insect powder is a *levinge*, an apparatus consisting of two bags of linen and muslin sewn together. These form a pair of sheets and mosquito curtain in one, and when you are inside and are hermetically sealed up you may defy all the terrors of the night. There are no inns; one has entirely to trust to the hospitality of the villagers upon the road, which they are glad to offer in return for a small present of money. On the less-frequented roads there are large caravanserais standing by themselves, and also in all the larger villages on the caravan road; but these are merely a yard for the camels and horses, with one or two rooms above the entrance for guests, often filthy in the extreme.

CHAPTER V.

EVERYDAY LIFE IN PERSIA—(*continued*).

Women's occupations — Baking — Manure fuel — Maste — Honey —Dowi—Cheese—Storing—Spinning and weaving—Dress—Children little old men—Veiling—Rags—Shaving—Beards—Fair hair and blue eyes—Dying—Women's position—Kissing a woman's hand—Going to the wells at even—Hospitality—A feast—Smoking—Music—The guard and the curfew—Salutations—Presents—Coming of the Vali Ahd—The Peshwaz—" God save the Queen "—Fireworks—Letter-writing—A poem on the three birds from London.

WHILE the men are engaged in their various outdoor pursuits, the women busy themselves with household affairs. At harvest time, and when the grapes are getting ripe, they will also work in the fields and vineyards; but ordinarily their work is at home, and they are usually busy. The Syrian proverb, " The husband is a labourer, the wife a mason," is often true. Even if the husband's earnings are small, the wife by her contrivances and hard work is the better bread-winner of the two. A large portion of her time seems to be taken up in baking; she has to supply the great staff of life to a family which eats more bread than anything else. The usual expression for taking a meal, " to eat bread," expresses the literal truth. Two women are always employed for baking. First they make the dough in a shallow wooden trough, putting in a little leaven from an old baking to leaven the whole lump (1 Cor. v. 6), and cover it over with a cloth. After an interval, one woman takes handfuls of dough and makes them into round balls covered with flour, which the other then rolls out flat, on an oblong sort of cushion stretched out tight on a wickerwork frame, which she holds on her knee; both women sitting on the ground at the edge of the earth-oven or *tanura*. The flat ovals of bread are then placed against the hard clay sides of the oven, and adhere to them by their own moisture; after a minute or two, during which other loaves are being rolled out, they are baked and ready to fall from the sides, and are then hooked out with an iron instrument. Each of these loaves weighs about ten ounces. Bread may also be bought in the bazaars of the towns; but it is seldom so good as that made at home, and is generally adulterated with sand to increase its weight, so that it naturally has a gritty taste. Also bazaar bread is sold according to the market price of wheat, and it is therefore much cheaper to make a store of flour when the price of wheat is low, to bake at home every day, or as often as is necessary.

The bread, when baked, is very nice, even to a European palate, and if made light and well baked, and eaten hot, is most enjoyable. But many cannot accommodate themselves at first to the sour leaven of the East. European bread is easy enough to make if one has an American stove—it of course could not be made in an earth oven—but it is necessary to make one's own yeast, and for that purpose, one must grow one's own hops, unless one can borrow from other European neighbours.

The fire in these ovens is from dried manure fuel, which is so often used in Eastern countries where there is no coal, and where wood is dear; it was common in Palestine (Ezek. iv. 12, 15), and now in many places is the only fuel used. In the plain of Urmi wood is comparatively plentiful, and the cakes of manure fuel are only used for the earth oven. The smell of it is very disagreeable. The only outlet for the smoke of a *baita* is a hole in the roof, and sometimes, if there is a wind, the smoke is intolerable to those who are not accustomed to it. The Syrians do not mix ashes with the manure, as is done in India, to take away the smell. It is the custom for most of the houses in the villages to have a vacant space allotted to them to dry these cakes; but the villagers often use the public roads for this purpose.

It would be impossible to describe all the many ways in which a woman busies herself. After the cows, goats, and ewes are milked, she makes the *masta* (Turkish *ya-urt*) or sour curdled milk, which is probably the "butter" referred to in the Bible, so often associated with honey.[1] In hot countries, where milk will not keep, this curdling is done for purposes of preservation; and the masta, which is more solid than Devonshire cream, is eaten somewhat like butter, and scooped up with pieces of bread.

[1] 2 Sam. xvii. 29; Job xx. 17; Isa. vii. 15, 22. Honey also is constantly eaten, but it is chiefly brought down from Kurdistan.

It would be the natural thing to offer on the spur of the moment to any one, if nothing else were ready, and almost always accompanies every meal. Abraham gave it to the angels (Gen. xviii. 8); Jael to Sisera (Judges v. 25); Barzillai to David, (2 Sam. xvii. 29). The Syrians also make butter (in the European sense) from the masta; that from the buffalo's milk is considered the best. But it is tasteless when compared with butter made from cream. The latter, however, would be too expensive for a poor people; and in summer the milk is likely to turn sour before the cream has formed. From the masta is made a very good drink for the summer called *dowi*. It is simply masta mixed with water and flavoured with herbs. With ice it is very pleasant, though of course its sourness at first deters the unaccustomed palate. Every one makes this for himself, and "no one calls his own dowi sour" as they say; every goose thinks its own goslings swans.

Cheese, also, is extensively used; the best comes from the upland villages towards Turkey. When first made, in the early summer, it is like our milk-cheese, but rather stronger. It is then crumbled up, salted, and flavoured with herbs, and packed very tight in earthenware jars, which are carefully closed and buried in the ground for winter use. This stored cheese is chiefly eaten in the depth of winter, before the fast begins, as it is then forbidden in common with all animal produce.

The good wife takes infinite pains to store up things for the winter. She remembers the proverb her mother has taught her, "The river will not always bring down vine-stocks," and she lays by for the time when the earth is asleep; though she will not have thought of it as "laying by for a rainy day" (that would be a blessed day in her eyes), but for the long spell of snow and frost. It is astonishing how much she stores in her house. In the early spring she lays in wood for next year; she also makes her great conical heap of dried manure fuel, which she coats over with wet manure to protect it from rain and snow, not forgetting to leave a door at the bottom to take the cakes out as they are needed; she buries her jars of cheese, lays in her store of hay, straw, barley, and wheat, the two latter in great wooden chests, which are almost the only furniture in the *baita*, serving also as a convenient screen for the door, and to put anything upon which is not wanted at the moment; then at the proper time she hangs up her *tlu'i* (grapes for the winter), places her water and musk melons round the ledges of her *rooms* (not the *baita*, for there they would be spoilt by the heat), or lays them in the straw; stores in earthenware jars her raisins, salt, split pease,—much approved of for cooking with soup—black beans, red beans, potatoes (but these are not the necessity they are in Europe), rice, treacle, paraffine, clarified butter, which is used for almost all cooking except in the fast, and all other similar commodities; and then, if she has any money over, she lays in her supply of sugar, tea, and coffee from the bazaar in the town of Urmi, though these may be bought from time to time as needed. They come from Europe in great camel caravans, and are now greatly increasing articles of consumption. Lump sugar is the only kind used, and comes mostly from Russia, though sometimes from Marseilles. Composite candles come to Persia from Russia, to Kurdistan from Belgium. Paraffine comes from Baku. Tallow candles are made in Persia. But the old open lamp, fed in Urmi with castor oil, in the mountains with linseed or walnut oil or even with fat, is also extensively used. The wick lies in the spout, and gives a dim light which is not of much use to any one. But as the Syrians go to bed at 9 p.m., and sometimes earlier, and as the light never even in winter quite goes before 5 p.m., they do not need very much artificial light. In Tiari the light of the fire is more used than that of the lamp. The women also spin and weave. In most houses are to be seen spinning wheels; in many, looms; and the simple clothes of blue cotton, such as the children and poorer men wear, are all of Persian manufacture. The better cotton stuffs are imported, and are called "Manchéster" or "América," and "Amerikân." This is the reverse of our practice, when we talk of calico, from Calicut, and muslin, from Mosul. The cloth coats only are not of native material. These, in Persia, are kilted rather fully at the waist and are not, like ours, divided at the back. They are usually bright blue, but also often black. Under this are worn a shirt and under-coat of cotton material, the latter very full and kilted and meeting in front. The shirt and under-coat are confined only by a girdle, either a leathern belt or a long cotton band, wound two or three times round the body. The shirt has no collar attached, but has a nice-looking hem at the top as in a boy's sailor suit. No tie is worn, and the under-coat is fastened (generally with hook and eye) close up under the chin. The trousers are in shape not unlike those of European make, and are sometimes of cloth, but more often of cotton or brown holland. The older men wear

THE SERVANTS OF THE URMI MISSION HOUSE, SHOWING THE DRESS OF THE MOUNTAINS AND OF THE PLAINS.
From the authors' photograph.

shorter and much wider blue cotton trousers. The woollen socks are home made, generally red and white, hardly coming above the ankles, and fastened by a loose thread. The shoes must be easily taken off, and are generally *made* with heels turned down. Great practice is required to keep them on in a muddy road. Very old men and some priests wear a sort of blue cotton cassock in lieu of the undercoat. Most people wear a tall woolly hat of Astrakhan, inside which they usually have a skull cap embroidered with many colours (this also serves as a nightcap); but many of the villagers wear a round hat of brown felt, and the boys usually wear either this or a fez. The Urmi bishops wear turbans in mountain fashion. But the priest's dress is ordinarily the same as that of the laity in the Urmi plain. The boys' clothes are exactly like those of adults, except in size; and, especially if they wear Astrakhan hats, they look ludicrously like little old men. The Mussulman children are the same, and perhaps the most comical sight of all is to see the sons of mollahs, dressed up in long cloaks and white or green turbans like their fathers.

The girls also dress like their mothers, except that they do not wear veils or mufflers till about thirteen or fourteen, in fact usually till they marry. When the mission boys see pictures in the illustrated papers of English little girls in short dresses, they invariably ask, "Are they Mussulmans, Rabbi?"[1] Mussulman women and girls being the only people in their experience who wear short petticoats. If one of the other sex may describe the women's dress without any pretensions to accuracy, it is somewhat as follows. Over a coloured

[1] A pupil calls his master Rabbi (or rather, in modern Syriac, Râbi); literally, "my great one." And a schoolmaster is called a Rabbi. But the title is also given to any priest, and ought not, perhaps, to be given to any one but a priest-schoolmaster. It is a title of honour.

shirt is worn a sort of waistcoat of a different colour; over this an open coat of cloth, if the wearer is rich, unfastened in front, but descending to the knees. The "divided skirt" or loose trousers are so very full as to appear like a dress, and over them an apron is worn, confined by a belt, perhaps of silver. A cap is worn on the head, covered by a muslin veil, one end of which is carried from the back of the neck to cover the mouth in the case of married women, but the rest of the face is exposed. It is considered improper to let the hair be seen. The women generally move this veil aside when they kiss the hand, *e.g.* of a priest; and they are not particular about covering the mouth in their own household; but when a stranger comes in, all hands immediately go up to the mouths, and the veil is drawn. In the case of brides a long veil of any colour falls from the head below the waist, and is used to cover the face entirely. The girls, as has been mentioned, do not wear veils; they wear their hair in plaits, the length of which is often increased by braid. Both the women and the girls often go barefoot, as indeed do the whole population. The pervading colour of the women's clothes is red, which makes a very picturesque contrast with the white veils.

Before leaving the subject of the women's dress, we must notice a most unfortunate and ridiculous addition some of the Urmi women have made to their wardrobe, viz. what they imagine to be a European cotton dress—body and skirt in one. This caricature of a Western lady's apparel is put on anyhow, usually on the top of all the native clothes, and bulges out somewhat like a dress in the old crinoline days; it is the more to be regretted—if one can regret what gives one a hearty laugh—as the native costume is a most happy combination of the useful and the modest; it is extremely becoming, and exactly serves the purposes of everyday life. In the mission boarding schools, both for boys and girls, the native dress is the only one allowed.

The Mussulman women in the streets wear very wide trousers which are in one piece with their slippers; but over the slippers again they wear shoes. They cover themselves completely with a blue mantle, and thus hide their whole faces; only the upper classes wear, in addition, a white veil in front, the *yashmaq*, such as one sees in Constantinople and Cairo. The indoor dress is like a ballet dancer's, but this, of course, they do not show to strangers of the opposite sex. The Mohammedan women in the villages do not wear the blue veil or trousers unless they are leaving home; in the village they merely wear a sort of veil like the Christian women, but their garments are longer than those of the more fashionable ladies, though shorter than those of the Christians.

It will be convenient here to describe the mountain dress, which is quite different from that of the plains, and far more picturesque. Those who are of good family wear elaborately embroidered clothes, the rest are generally in rags. Two pairs of very loose trousers are worn, one of cotton, and one of a thicker material. Inside these the mountaineers, unlike the Urmi men, tuck their shirts, which almost always leave the chest exposed.

An immensely long kerchief wound round and round the waist is the girdle, and holds the khanjar or dagger. Over the shirt is a short jacket reaching only to the waist, even in the case of a patriarch, with perhaps a waistcoat between. Occasionally, however, those who are of good position wear a sort of frock coat. The headdress varies. In Tiari, a simple conical hat of felt is worn over a head shorn of all but one or two pigtails; it is white, black, or brown. In most of the other Ashiret districts the same conical hat is worn, except that it bulges somewhat at the sides, but round it is wrapped the multitudinous folds of the turban, the colour of which varies; priests generally wear black, the colour of the turban, and their beards and hair are their only distinguishing features. Some again, at Qudshanis and elsewhere, wear the Osmanli fez, round which they bind a small turban; and the upper class children there, and also most of the children in Persia, generally wear the simple fez. On their feet the Ashirets wear variegated woollen socks, usually red and white; over them they put on shoes made of wool or felt bound to the ankle by strings. These are much better than leather shoes for the rocks; they are tightly sewn together, and the wool felts when used, so that the soles of the shoes become perfectly hard.

The women either do not wear veils in the mountains, or if they have them they do not habitually cover their mouths. In the Rayat districts, especially when they are at work, their dress does not really differ greatly from that of the men, for whom they are often confused by a stranger when seen at a distance. But they do not have such elaborately embroidered clothes as their husbands and brothers. Perhaps what strikes a stranger most, coming out first to these countries, is that all the Christians and most of the Mussulmans seem to be in rags; or if not in rags to be patched all over, a green square appearing in the middle of a blue coat, or a red square in a green coat. Sometimes the patches are so large or so many that it is impossible to say which is the patch and which the original coat, but the result is often picturesque. No one seems to be ashamed of being in rags; a man probably has a good coat for great days and occasions, but ordinarily a patched or rent coat will do as well as any other. Perhaps this is part of the idea of always trying to seem poorer than one really is, for fear of exciting the cupidity of the government officials.

Before we leave our Syrian, male or female, whose dress we have admired even when ragged, let us look at a most important matter in the man's general appearance—the way he wears his hair. The Mussulman, as is well known, shaves his head and leaves merely two locks behind for Mohammed to pull him up to Paradise by. This is his most distinguishing feature, as in dress he differs very little from the Syrian. The latter, in former days, used to shave his head much more than now. It is usual now to shave the front of the head, leaving the hair behind rather long. It must be allowed that it is not so easy to admire this custom as the dress; but doubtless it is good for cleanliness. The younger generation is taking to not shaving their heads at all. In Turkey most laymen shave the front and middle of their heads, and their cheeks and chins (but never the upper lip), from time to time, especially before a great festival. But priests never shave. In districts, where laymen wear pigtails (as Tiari) or queues, the priests usually or always wear their hair long enough to cover their ears and the back of their necks, but they do not have pigtails. Beards are always worn by bishops and priests, and generally by old men, the usual name for whom is "white beards."[1] No one would think of going without at least a moustache; and though in Persia they trim their beards and moustaches, and even cut them short, yet, to shave clean would be a great disgrace. So that they can well understand what a disgrace it was when "Hanun took David's servants, and shaved off the one half of their beards" (2 Sam. x. 4); and can realize the denunciation of the prophet, that the Lord should shave the children of Israel "with a razor that is hired, namely, by them beyond the river, by the king of Assyria" (Isa. vii. 20). As a severe punishment, the patriarch or bishop will sometimes threaten to have a priest's beard shaved, or perhaps one side only. Women are also punished by half their heads being shaved, or by their plaits being cut off. No doubt David's servants shaved off the other half of their beards themselves, and then waited at Jericho till their beards were grown (2 Sam. x. 5). That would be done now in case such a misfortune happened.

[1] It would be exceedingly unwise for a missionary to go to the East without a beard.

H

Strange to say the Syrians in Persia strongly object to fair hair and blue eyes. This dislike is shared by the Mussulmans. If anybody (especially a boy or man) has fair or even brown hair, he dyes it auburn. Old men constantly dye their beards black or even bright red. The Mussulmans cease to dye when they lose a near relative, and one can tell how long a man has been in mourning by the amount of gray hair between his chin and the dyed part of his beard. There is no pretence about the red dye at any rate. No one ever had hair such a brilliant vermilion. Barbers do a good business. They require hardly any stock in trade, and every one is their customer. No barber's shop is necessary; the men sit down on the ground anywhere in the courtyard, or in the village street, and submit their heads and chins to be scraped without soap. It is not considered necessary to shave more than once a week. Saturday is the favourite day (as also for bathing), as it is the preparation for Sunday.

But the housewife has been left putting away her multitudinous stores. It will be interesting to compare her position with that of her Western sisters. Of course one would expect in a Mussulman country that the women should be entirely in the background; yet one also expects Christianity to teach much. This is undoubtedly the case. The Syrian women are in a much better position than their Mohammedan sisters; they cannot be divorced except through their own misconduct, whereas Mussulmans can divorce their wives at pleasure by paying them their portions; and, we may add (though this does not greatly improve their position, and divorce cannot be considered a desirable thing at all), the Christian women can divorce their husbands if they misconduct themselves.[1] Moreover, their position is safer in that their husbands, however well off, cannot marry any other wives in their lifetime. These things all tend to raise the idea of marriage, and to modify the treatment of women for the better. Yet the estimation in which they are held is far from being what one could wish. There is little of the chivalrous feeling of men towards women which one finds in Europe. The men have not learnt to give "honour unto the wife as unto the weaker vessel, and as being heirs together of the grace of life" (1 Pet. iii. 7). In fact, one does not always realize what chivalry has done for Europe in this respect. It is strange to a European to be invited to dinner at a Syrian's house and to find the hostess serving like Martha, instead of sitting at the head of a table; perhaps only just appearing at the door to kiss the hand of the missionary. But to a Syrian it is far more strange to see the deference paid by Europeans to women. The Mission deacons—most of them married men—were shown a picture in the *Graphic* of the Prince of Wales kissing the hand of the German Empress at Berlin, and with one voice exclaimed, "Nothing should ever induce *me* to kiss a woman's hand." One man, who was really fond of his wife, said once, "If one were forbidden, as in Europe, to beat one's wife when she does wrong, it is better not to be married at all." Too often women are the drudges who are ordered about by the men, do the

[1] See Chap. VII.

hard work, carry heavy loads, whose education matters nothing, and who become prematurely aged through their heavy tasks, and also it seems through their too early marriages. It is impossible to allow this to go on without an effort to make matters better —the men cannot be raised if the women remain as they were; and the Archbishop of Canterbury's mission has therefore made an endeavour to start serious work among the women and girls.[1]

It is perfectly safe, under ordinary circumstances, for a woman to go out by herself; she can go to the bazaar, and from village to village, without her husband's protection. In the evening the path to the well or stream outside the city wall or the village is red with dresses of Syrian women and girls going out like Rebekah with pitchers on their shoulders—"at the time of the evening, even the time that women go out to draw water" (Gen. xxiv. 11, 15; cf. Gen. xxix. 7). Hence the woman of Samaria was all by herself when she happened to go to draw water at midday, the sixth hour. Had it been the evening she would not have had to return to the city before finding "the men" to tell the news to; she would have told her companions who would have been flocking to the well (St. John iv. 6, 28).

One of the noblest characteristics of the Urmi Syrians is their open-hearted hospitality. They are never seen at a better advantage than in their own villages. They never forget to "show love unto strangers," who come to "be guest" to them, as they say (St. Luke xix. 7). Their first care

[1] See Chap. VIII.

on the arrival of a stranger is to tend his horse, prepare their best for the guest, and do all in their power to make him comfortable, before they find out his business. As they will probably not have anything cooked, they proceed to bake bread, kill their chickens, and cook them, just as the angels waited for Sarah's cakes which had to be kneaded and baked upon the hearth, and for the "calf, tender and good," which had to be brought from the herd, killed, and dressed. All this is called by Abraham, just as it would be now by the Syrian on hospitable thoughts intent, a "morsel of bread" (Gen. xviii. 5–9). It is well understood why the friend at midnight was so importunate for the three loaves; "for a friend of mine in his journey is come to me, and I have nothing to set before him" (St. Luke xi. 6). Hospitality is a sacred duty, and in a country where there are no inns it is a matter of course that a traveller goes to the house of a friend, or, indeed, of any one, whether he knows him or not. "Do they turn a dead man away from a graveyard?" they say; and they would as soon think of turning away the weary traveller. They have indeed a proverb, "A guest who comes of his own accord is without honour," but this would never apply to a traveller, and seldom even to a fellow-villager. A man never knows but what his meal may be shared by a stranger; and he is not inconvenienced by having no room at the table, or no plate and knife and fork for him, for these things are not part of his establishment. Living on the floor has this great advantage, that the number of guests can be increased or diminished to almost any extent, without any difference being made in the accommodation. The lady of the house has not to consider the size and symmetry of her table as in the civilized West.

A feast is a very common occurrence. Though the guests will have been invited beforehand, yet, owing to the scarcity of clocks and the uncertainty as to time, a servant is sent "at supper-time to say to them that were bidden, Come, for all things are now ready" (St. Luke xiv. 17). When the guests assemble there is usually a long interval given to pipes and conversation. All sit on the floor, where a gaudy coloured table-cloth is spread, or perhaps a low table six inches high, or a series of trays. All the dishes are placed here at once; in the middle, saucers with pickles, jam, powdery cheese, and preserved fruits; the flat loaves of bread are spread along the edges, and serve as plates as well as for eating purposes, at least one loaf to each person; then all the eatables are brought in, in earthenware or metal bowls; and while they are cooling a long grace is said by the bishop or priest, who signs the food and then himself with the sign of the cross, and ends with the Lord's prayer; then all fall to, the host first saying to his guests, "You have come in peace," to which they all reply, "Thank you." Of course the women do not sit down. They eat afterwards, in a corner, or in another room. The chief guest is placed at the head of the room, and then the others in their due order; the host stays at the bottom, and busies himself with the comfort of his guests, often getting up to give commands to the womenkind who are serving outside. He must go on eating or pretending to eat as long as any of the guests are eating; it would be bad manners for him to have done before all have finished. The sons do not sit down usually in the father's presence, but wait on the guests, and pour out wine for them, one or two cups generally sufficing for the whole company. As all have left their shoes outside the door, it is common for those thus serving to walk over the table-cloth. In the East there is much more formal respect shown by sons than with us, whether among the rich or the poor; a son will wait till his father bids him sit down, and will not smoke in his father's presence, even if he is grown up and married, at any rate when strangers are present.

The guests proceed to tear pieces of bread off their loaves and dip them into the soup, rice, etc., which are in the bowls—they do not take a portion on to a plate for themselves, but dip first into one and then into another bowl. Hence it is natural for two men to dip their hands together in the dish (St. Matt. xxvi. 23). It is a sign of love when one man dips a sop and gives it to another, as our Lord did to Judas (St. John xiii. 26); or he may offer a friend some fruit, or tear off with his fingers part of a chicken (cooked to rags so as to be easily dismembered without a knife) and give it him (cf. Gen. xliii. 34). On no account must the gift be refused; to reject it would be a sign of enmity, and so it is accepted, and if not wanted simply laid down on the bread. It is not bad manners to leave what one has taken.

When a man receives a cup of wine, he turns to his host, to one or all of the company, and says, "Your love,"—that is, "Your good health;" and will receive the reply, "May it be pleasant to you," or "May it descend to your heart." After drinking, the others will point to what he is about to eat, and say again, "May it be pleasant to you." They do not drink wine when they are eating fruit or sweet things, such as jam or honey; these are not thought to go well together. Almost all the cooked dishes are sour with vinegar or *masta*, and very pungent with red pepper. The repast over, and grace said, the guests say "Thank you" to the host, or, "May God increase you," and all set to work to smoke, whether cigarettes, chubuqs, or the qalyun (water-pipe). This differs from the water-pipe of Turkey, the narghile, in having a stiff wooden mouthpiece instead of the coil of the latter. The qalyun is held in one hand, and is not placed at a distance from the smoker. The tops are often very beautiful, and are of chased silver or of china. The *tumbaki* of southern Persia is put in first, and lighted charcoal on the top. A brass pipe communicates with the water in a glass or china bowl, and the smoke is thus drawn through the water to the mouthpiece. The qalyun is passed round like a loving cup, every one taking a few whiffs. Before handing it to his neighbour, the smoker will lift the top with one hand and draw out all the smoke then in the pipe. This is a matter of politeness. The qalyun, in the first instance, is lighted by the servants outside the room, as it requires some trouble and experience to get up a good fire. Similarly a servant offering any one a cigarette or chubuq will light it himself first; and the better trained ones will put their disengaged hand on their breast while offering anything. The pipes are not put into the mouth, but only to the lips. Cigars are not smoked, though they might well be made, if the people knew how.

While all are smoking or playing with their rosaries (which are not used for religious purposes), general conversation goes on; the Syrians talk very little while eating, but wait till they have finished. Perhaps riddles will be asked or "parables" told,[1] or some one will bring in a fiddle or a *zurna*, which is very like the chanter of bagpipes, or a fife, and perhaps a drum, and there will be a song; though for the latter an accompaniment is not the least necessary. Playing is looked upon as a rather professional accomplishment, and it would not be proper at all for a great man to practise it; except, indeed, when he wishes to appear quite European and imports an American organ or even a piano, which he plays with one finger.

The Syriac songs are all sacred, and on Biblical subjects; they are generally in the minor, and sad; a favourite one is on the subject of the expulsion of Adam and Eve from Paradise. Some of them are very beautiful, and a solo is quite enjoyable even to one who is not accustomed to quarter tones. Good singers put in a large number of trills and shakes, and sustain the last note of each line for a long time. But they have little notion of singing together; even if they get the same tune, they seldom get the same key. For secular songs they have to go to the Turkish or Kurdish languages. There are no written tunes, and those mentioned in the

[1] See Chap. XIV.

various service-books are now forgotten. Some traditional airs remain, but there is no musical notation, and the mission scholars were greatly astonished to learn that one could read music like a book. In some of the sung parts of the service-books there are strokes (one, two, or three) in red ink over certain words, but it is not now known how to apply them.

In any case the party breaks up early, as it is the custom to go to bed soon after nine; and in the city of Urmi the guests are obliged to go betimes to their homes, for at a certain hour, varying in winter and summer, the bugle blows and the drums beat and every one must be indoors. The guard perambulates the streets, and any one found in them is treated as a thief, and taken to the lock-up for the night! So the guests leave their host with "Remain in peace," and receive in return the greeting, "God be with you."

The salutations of the Syrians are a very beautiful feature of their life. On meeting a friend a Syrian says, "Peace to you," and receives the reply, "In peace you have come," or simply, "In peace," or "In peace, a hundred times peace," or "In peace and in goodness." In the morning a common greeting is, "Your morning in peace;" in the evening, "Your evening in peace." On a festival, especially at Easter and Christmas, they say, "May your feast be blessed;" and similarly if a man buys a house, or a field, or even a new coat, his friends say, "May it be blessed." After a journey they say, "May your journey be blessed." When a child is born (in Urmi), "May his foot be blessed." In Kurdistan,

"May he be blessed" is said at the birth of a boy, but the birth of a girl is not "blessed;" and they say of a person who arrives just before the birth of a child, "His foot is blessed." On Good Friday and Holy Saturday they do not say "Peace to you," because Judas said "Peace" to our Lord, according to the Syriac version; instead, they say, "Light to your dead." But this custom is dying out among some people in the Urmi plain. When hearing of a death they say, "May God give him rest." When paying a visit of condolence they say, "May your head be pleasant;" and such a visit is called "healing the head" of the bereaved.[1] The name of a dead man is generally preceded by the epithet "the resting," or followed by, "remembered for good." Of a deceased person of distinction, especially in letters and books, they say, "May his memorial be for a blessing," or "May his prayers be on us." The ordinary expression for "Thank you" is "May you be pleasant," *i.e.* pleased. When one wishes to encourage another for doing something well, he says, "May it please yourself," to which a polite reply in the mountains is, "Thank you; may it please you also." An inferior asking another to do something says, "May I be your sacrifice," as in Persian and Turkish. A servant on receiving a command says, "On my eye be it." A host, welcoming a traveller, says, "You have come on my eyes," or, "on the roof of my eyes," *i.e.* "You are very welcome." An instance of politeness is seen when a visitor is asked what his business is; he will

---

[1] One Syriac root expresses, "to be pleased" and "to heal," but in different "moods."

first reply, "I have come for your pleasure," *i.e.* on a friendly visit, and then proceed to relate the business which was the real object of his coming. A child or servant before saying good-bye says, "Forgive me" to his master or parent. A European at first thinks he is going to confess something he has done; but it is merely a formula.

Presents form a very real part of Eastern life; they are chiefly made from inferiors to superiors, and often in the way of bribes; but also merely as a sign of goodwill. Thus on festivals, trays of sweetmeats or fruit are sent. On a recent occasion the Sisters of Bethany made their neighbour, Mar Gauriel, a present of a cake at Christmas; it thus served once as a token of goodwill. Then the good bishop, after an interval, sent it off to Qudshanis to Mar Shimun—a week's journey in winter; thus it served once more. We need not ask if Mar Shimun sent it on to some one else, or what was its condition when finally it was eaten. These presents are very pleasant signs of friendship, especially to welcome a distinguished stranger, to whom large trays of sweets are sent. It is the custom for the recipient to give the bearer of the tray a present in money. When a governor-general comes, as on a late occasion the Vali Ahd or Heir Apparent of the Shah came to Urmi, all the Persian magnates send him presents of trays of sweets with a sum of money, large or small, according to their means, concealed beneath. Woe betide the sender if this is insufficient! The tray is sent back again and the gift refused. The unlucky khan will then have to send double the amount, perhaps a great deal more than he would otherwise have had to contribute. The reason of a visit like this is often simply to raise money, and it is said that on the occasion referred to the khans of Urmi offered the Amir-i-Nizam, the acting governor-general at Tabriz, a large bribe if he would dissuade the Vali Ahd from coming; but it was of no use. If in these cases a present is not received, it is not out of consideration to the poverty of the inferior, but because the superior is displeased. If the latter really feels for the giver, he will accept the present, but make it up to him in another away. Thus if Esau had not accepted Jacob's present, it would have been a sign that he still cherished feelings of revenge against him. Therefore when Jacob "urged him, he took it" (Gen. xxxiii. 11).

The coming of the Vali Ahd to Urmi, in November, 1890, was such a great event, and so well illustrates one phase of Persian life, that the Western reader may like to read an account of it. We had so often heard, untruly, that he was coming, that we put down the report of his intended arrival to popular rumour only. However, he came at last, and the whole place was in a fuss until he went. The soldiers had their uniforms given out—we had never seen them in them before —and vainly tried to make them fit; big men being put into small coats and bursting every button, and small men being buried in large uniforms several sizes too big. Even so there were not enough uniforms, for several men were in ordinary clothes in the rear rank, where they thought they would not be noticed. Such a collection! A regiment of a theatrical strolling company is infinitely better dressed, and more like soldiers. However, their officer, who was a friend of ours, made up for deficiencies by his gorgeous appearance in white cotton gloves and a splendid sword which he seemed afraid to draw.

At last the day came, and according to the etiquette on these occasions all the Europeans, as well as the natives, went out to meet the prince. This would only be the case when a person of this rank or a personal friend was arriving. (But the Syrians would go out to meet any official, as well as their own friends.) We were, of course, dressed in our official costume—a matter of the greatest importance in the East—and sallied forth in caps and gowns, cassocks, hoods, and bands, on horseback, accompanied by all the servants and hangers-on whom we could put into decent coats. All Urmi turned out, and it was a pretty sight to see the avenues and river banks, along which the route lay, a mass of colour; the Christian women in red, the Mussulman in blue—the former looking particularly picturesque. But though everybody was there, one was struck by the smallness of the population for the size of the town. The fact is that an oriental town takes up a large amount of space to a small population.

We rode out to a village called Guktapa, about an hour from the town of Urmi, and dismounted there. Presently a carriage arrived which looked like a hearse, covered over completely with a thick white veil of crochet work. This contained the ladies of the harem. The farashes (officials) applied their wands to the backs of the small boys and common herd and made them turn their faces the other way, while we, as etiquette required, pretended to be walking in a different direction till the carriage had passed. Then all was expectation. At last a voice was heard announcing the coming of the prince, and bidding all "Go ye out to meet him" (St. Matt. xxv. 6); and after an interval the procession appeared, headed by dwarfs, buffoons, and pet greyhounds. Then soldiers, looking magnificent in the distance; though when it was seen that their tunics were of white cotton one ceased to admire. Then came one or two executioners in red, who always attend a royal progress. They had shortly before been deputed to reduce a village to flames, on the other side of the Sea of Urmi, because the inhabitants had not mended the roads to be in readiness for the royal carriage—at least, it was so reported. After them came the Vali Ahd in a carriage and four at a walking pace. It is easier to understand how he must have been jolted during his travels than how he got through all the marshes on the route; a month later it would have been impossible. When he came opposite the various European parties, he stopped and exchanged complimentary speeches and passed on. The Amir-i-Nizam, who is practically the governor-general of the province of Azerbaijan (for the Vali Ahd does not attend to details of business) came with the prince's son-in-law in a second carriage, and after a few minutes' talk with them we all galloped back by a different way to see the procession unofficially on its arrival at Urmi. The whole party stopped at a place just outside the city gate of the Christian quarter of Mart Mariam (St. Mary), and occupied three houses in a large vineyard called Dilgushah or "heartsease," while the soldiers and servants encamped in tents. As the prince passed by, offerings were made him. Sheep were brought to the roadside, and their throats cut there and then. They were then seized by one of the retinue and formed a considerable part of the provision of meat for the whole company during their stay. These wayside offerings are very common; but, for an ordinary traveller, it is usually only a make-believe, the sheep are not really killed, or, if the sheep is accepted, its full price should be given. In harvest time it is especially common to offer sheaves of corn, but these are usually merely an excuse for demanding backsheesh, or peshkash as the Persians call it.

This going out to meet a great personage on his arrival, or "peshwaz," as it is called, is counted as a visit. But it was not expected that the Prince would return it himself. However, it was announced that he wished to inspect all the European schools, and to pay return visits on a certain day. After all, he came a day earlier than he said, perhaps to see how the schools looked on ordinary occasions. All went smoothly, and the Vali Ahd made many pretty speeches, and ordered his steward to make a present to the boys in the school; but this, of course, the steward "ate," as is said in Persia. What seems to have struck the prince most in our school was the sight of the rough and warlike mountaineers. He also went and called on Mar Gauriel, the Bishop of Ardishai and Urmi. This was a great and unprecedented honour, and made the mollahs furious, as he had not called on them individually, but had assembled them all in one of the mosques. One of the mushtehids or chief mollahs would not attend, and was in consequence stripped of his office and exiled to Kerbelai. The whole of the royal visit was marked by attentions paid to the native Christians and to the foreigners, and this was calculated to have an excellent effect on the behaviour of the Mussulmans to the Syrians and Armenians.

The Prince brought his band with him; probably the instruments were those lately given him by Queen Victoria. Every time he came in or went out of his house they played "God save the Queen," which the Persians have adopted, with different words, as their national anthem. But such a parody of Dr. Bull! It was all in the minor and not then in tune. They varied this immortal air with European dance music, and occasionally with Eastern airs.

After a week there was another "peshwaz" to see the royal party off. These processions on leaving are shorter than those at arrival, because in the former case the person in whose honour the procession is got up asks those accompanying him, after a short time, to take no more trouble ("draw trouble" they call it) and to return; and the greater the rank of the person accompanying, the sooner he is asked to return. In this case, the same attention was paid to the foreigners as throughout the visit. The Europeans were asked to ride immediately behind the prince's carriage, and directly they got clear of the city were invited to go up and make their adieux, even before the

governor of Urmi, who had ridden by the side of
the carriage. This is the occasion for a repetition
of the polite speeches, in which "I am very content with you" occurs several times, and the visit
is over. But, to the disgust of the great men
of Urmi, the Vali Ahd announced that he was so
pleased with his visit that he would return in the
spring!

Another characteristic of Syrian and Persian life
at Urmi is their love of fireworks. Just before the
Persian festival of No Ruz ("New Day"), which is
the vernal equinox, there is a great display, a very
pretty sight, although the fireworks are of a primitive nature and very inexpensive. Every house
sends up a large number of rockets, and so the whole
town is one mass of them. They are let off from
the roofs of the houses. There are also Roman
candles and a few other kinds, but the rockets are
the chief thing. The pyrotechnic display goes on
for about six Tuesday nights—Wednesday nights
in the Eastern reckoning—before No Ruz, but
the last day is the great one. This custom of fixed
days for fireworks is said to be peculiar to Urmi,
and to be really a relic of the old fire-worshipping
religion of Persia—Parseeism.

Zoroaster was a native of the old city of
Baqchiqal'a, in the plain of Urmi, where according
to Syrian tradition St. George was martyred.[1]
There are now no Parsees in Urmi, or indeed in
any part of Persia, except the Great Salt Lake
Desert, but they have left a relic in the great ash
heaps which are to be found in several places,

[1] See below, Chap. XV.

notably at the village of Degalah, close to Urmi. The name Urmi may, perhaps, be a corruption of Hurmizd, the Good Principle of the old Persian religion, as Ahriman was the Evil Principle. The connecting link may be seen in the form Urmis found in some of the books (though Urmin is also found), and in the present adjective used by the mountaineers "Urmizhnayi" for men of Urmi; or sometimes "Urmijnayi."

A very real part of the Syrian's life is his letter-writing. Almost the whole epistle is taken up with compliments, and the gist of the letter comes in a sentence at the end. At the top of the sheet is written *Jah* with three dots above and one beneath, to denote the Trinity in Unity. The following is a short note written to two of the missionaries from the father of two pupils:—

"In the year of Christ ——, December, 30 in it. To you Apostles from the Western regions to the Eastern regions, and a shining light of Jesus, and governors and shepherds of a little flock in the East, the Moses and Aaron of our land, who brought the people of Israel from the darkness of Egypt, the Peter and Paul of our time, who are by name ——, reverend and beloved, Love and Peace. Having wished you peace, these :— I entrust Yonan and Ishu [Jonah and Joshua] to you, who are to them spiritual fathers, that you may lead them in all love and fear of God. And I know you care for them well. I rejoice greatly that they are under your rule, and this great love that you have showed me and my sons will never be forgotten by my heart all my days.

"I cannot with pen and ink show you my love for you. These few words are enough for your wisdom. Remain strong and pleasant; from your loving servant ——. Amen."

Or a schoolmaster will fill a whole page with

titles and phrases, and add in a corner, "If you ask, I am well; and please send six slate-pencils by the bearer. From your loving and deficient servant." The letters are written in Old Syriac, except sometimes in the plain of Urmi, where people have now begun to write in the vernacular. In the mountains, however, it is still quite common for people, who can read the classical Syriac perfectly, not to be able to read or write the language of everyday life.

It is not proper for a great man to write his own letters. He employs a scribe, to whom, when all is written, he gives his seal, which he keeps in a little bag in his pocket. The scribe smears a little of the glutinous ink on the seal, wets the edge of the paper where the impression is to be made, and then with a hard pressure affixes his master's signature; he wipes the seal and returns it to its owner. He then, perhaps, adds a line on his own account, as "The humble writer —— sends you peace," or "asks your prayers;" just as Tertius saluted the Romans (Rom. xvi. 22).

The composition of the Syrians is usually confined to letters. Occasionally, however, they break out into poetry, as in the following poem of welcome to the present writers and Mr. Athelstan Riley, when they first came to the country. It is translated from the vernacular Syriac.

"May the Lord bless the Archbishop of Canterbury
  He has sent to us three birds;
One is Mr. Riley by name—
  Welcome are to us these brethren.

"This one is energetic—well done to him ;
　　Like John the Baptist, he wears a belt.
　He has published the Creed—
　　Welcome are to us these brethren.

"In Urmi there is much said of him ;
　　We hope his schools will be established.
　Like Simon, he always wears a sword—
　　Welcome are to us these brethren.

"One of them, his beard is dark ;
　　His figure resembles that of Saint Thomas,
　In Urmi he will work every day—
　　Welcome are to us these brethren.

"Canon Maclean is his name,
　　He has left his home, his father, and his mother.
　Christ became his mouth's taste—
　　Welcome are to us these brethren.

"One of them, his beard is yellow,
　　His smell is sweet like that of a rose ;
　In Urmi he has laid a net—
　　Welcome are to us these brethren.

"His name is Browne—he is exceedingly gentle,
　　Through his work many will come to penitence ;
　His mustard grain will grow very much—
　　Welcome are to us these brethren.

"Ye are welcome, all of you!
　　But ye have not eaten my bread,
　Only tea of mine ye have taken ;
　　I —— who am with you.

"May the Lord bless that kingdom
　　Which abounds with his blessings,
　Which has sent abroad so many gospellers,
　　For ever shall she be praised.　Amen."

CHAPTER VI.

CONDITIONS OF LIFE UNDER THE PERSIAN GOVERNMENT.

Autocracy impotent to govern—Relation of master and servant—The two Jews—The landlord system—Aghas—Village tenure—Taxes—Tenure of vineyards, fields, and orchards—The kokha and malik—Oriental justice—Disabilities of Christians—Apostasy—Petty oppression—The plaintiff—Bringing up old cases—Danger of going bail—A crafty governor—A governor's account of his duties—A word worse than a blow—Testimony to a claim—One way of earning a reputation—Bribes—Intrigues—Public security—Punishing criminals—The bastinado—Frontier raids—Need of trades—Going to Russia—Usury—Earnest money—Inheritance of property—Wills.

AN autocracy is often, or generally, impotent; and when the resources of the country are small and corruption reigns supreme, the result is an almost utter absence of stable government. It is supposed, in theory, that whatever the sovereign wishes is done; but as a matter of fact his commands are not carried out, especially in the more remote provinces, unless pressure can be put on the subordinate governors in each case to do so. Persia is a good example of this. It is governed, not for the good of the people but of the governors. Each official has autocratic power over those under him, which is only limited by the autocratic power of his superior. Theoretically, when a superior governor makes an order, all who are beneath him carry it out to the letter, but as a matter of fact an underling, unless hard pressed, will not execute a command until bribed to do so. And when orders are merely given, as is so often the case, to secure a bribe from the one side who wish to have it carried out, or from the other who wish to have it rescinded, it may be imagined that the government is impotent. There is no certainty; a merchant is never sure of getting in his debts, and a villager is never secure against the oppressions of the tax-gatherer or the judge, and all live in a chronic state of doubt as to what the morrow will being forth.

The system of government in Persia depends entirely on the general relation of master and servants. The servants are the children of the master and altogether in his power. Just as the law with us will not interfere in ordinary cases between father and son, so in Persia the superior officials are loth to interfere in a case of master and servant. On the other hand, the master protects the servant against all outsiders, whether the latter are right or wrong. He may oppress him himself, but will not allow any one else to do so if he can help it; and if a servant does wrong, he naturally expects the master to defend him. Owing to this relation between them, there is a certain freedom in the attitude of the one to the other. Although the servant is respectful, and always uses a polite and almost abject formula in addressing his master, yet there is an absence of servility about him. A butler, for instance, will join in conversation with the master at table quite freely, and even contradict him when he is wrong. Similarly, in schools, there is an absence of that restraint which marks the attitude of an English schoolboy to his master. The pupils, while respectful, are yet familiar with their teacher. They show a readiness at coming back to school, often before the time, and a sorrow at leaving their schoolmaster which would surprise a European boy. The same thing again accounts for the accessibility of a Persian governor to all and sundry. The peasant can get access to the judge to lay his petition before him almost as readily as the rich man; though, indeed, inasmuch as he does not bring the same bribe, he will not so easily get his wishes carried out, and he may be hindered by the judge's servants, who expect to make something out of every case.

An indication of the absence of servility is perhaps the free use of the imperative mood by the Syrians. A servant will use the imperative to his master or a child to its parents without any disrespectful intention. At first a stranger might be offended; on reflection he sees a beautiful characteristic of the people—the affection between a man and his dependants.

The Syrians tell a story which amusingly illustrates the relation of masters and servants, and shows how the former can sometimes get round their obligations. Two Kurdish chieftains had each a Jew under his protection, doubtless in consideration of some substantial subsidy. The Jews got rich, and the two Kurds laid their heads together to see how they could fleece them. The first said to the second, "It would not be respectable for me to take money from the Jew who is under my protection; but you fleece my man, and I will then fleece yours." So the second Kurd fleeced the first Kurd's Jew, who complained to his patron. "Oh, he has robbed you, has he? Well, never mind. You shall be revenged. *See how I will fleece his Jew!*" Neither Jew got much out of that arrangement.

The landlord system also arises out of the relation of master and servant. Almost all the Syrians live in villages, each of which is governed in feudal style by one or more aghas or landlords, who have very considerable power, whether for good or evil, over their "subjects." Sometimes the village, with its adjoining field, is in the hand of one agha; sometimes it is divided among many. Almost always these aghas are Mussulmans, but in a few cases they are Christians who have made some money, and have bought small villages or parts of them. The position of agha is much sought after, and is often sold at a very high price.

Though the aghas have in many ways much power, and often oppress and punish their "subjects" (for the governors seldom interfere between them unless in very grave matters), yet in other ways they have less power than an English landlord. Thus, for example, houses are held on a much securer tenure than in England. Except in the town of Urmi, the ground always belongs to the agha, and rent is paid for it; but the house is built by the tenant, in any style he likes, and it cannot be taken away from him as long as he pays the ground-rent.

Moreover, he can sell it if he pleases, but on the understanding that the purchaser becomes a "subject" of the master of the village. In fact, the feuing system of Scotland is in force, except that there are no feu charters. If a man sells his house, he gives a deed to the purchaser, and this is the latter's sole title. In the first instance a man who wishes to become a tenant will apply to the agha for a site, bringing with him a present of a few shillings or of three or four loaves of sugar, or something of the sort. The agha will be glad to get an extra subject, for the sake of the ground-rent and taxes which will be paid by him. Indeed, some aghas themselves build houses in order to attract tenants. In that case the houses are given rent free (except for the ground-rent), but on the other hand the tenants cannot sell them, and are liable to be evicted at any time.

The taxes paid by the Christians are as follows:— Every male above sixteen pays a poll tax of 3s. in lieu of military service. At one time the Persian government tried the experiment of enlisting the Syrians, but this has not been continued. The Mussulmans, on the other hand, can be forced to serve. If a soldier is enlisted, he is given a piece of land for the support of his family, and a very small salary, with uniform and gun. If Mussulmans do not serve they have to pay a tax. For every house (of seven or eight souls, perhaps of two or three families, for the married sons do not as a rule at once separate from their parents) the Syrians pay a tax or ground-rent of 4s. 9d. Beyond this no house rent is paid, as explained above.

LIFE UNDER THE PERSIAN GOVERNMENT. 123

Every man gives his labour for two days to the agha, or the price of it; each house also gives the agha two fowls, a load of manure fuel, some eggs, and a fee on the occasion of a marriage; for every she-buffalo, 2s. a year; for every cow, 1s.; for every ewe or she-goat, 6d.; but all these are free until they bear. For the Serperast, the Mussulman governor of the Christians, the tax from each house is 8d., with a small present of firewood. It will thus be seen that, if the law were strictly kept, the taxes would not be excessive, especially as there are some exemptions, as in the case of priests. It must, however, be remembered, that, owing to the lowness of wages and of the price of their produce, the taxes of the Syrians are equivalent to taxes of three or four times their amount in Europe.

This method of taxing is called "Gyur-al," or "see and take." It is a Turkish word, for this language is the vernacular of the Mussulmans of Azerbaijan, not Persian. There is another method in a few villages, called "makhta," by which each house is valued at so much. In either case the agha pays from a third to a half of the total taxes to the Shah. It should be added that, owing to the depreciation of the Persian monetary unit, the qran, which is now about $7\frac{1}{2}d.$, the English value of the taxes is much lower than what it was a few years ago.

Vineyards are held on the same tenure as the houses. Either they are bought from another tenant, or else they are prepared *ab initio* by the cultivator, a plot of ground having been granted by the agha, as for houses. For every sixteen.

Persian yards square, the Persian vineyard *tanap*, an annual rent of 6*d.* is paid to the agha, or about 7*s.* 6*d.* an English acre. As long as this is paid, and the vine-stocks remain in the ground, the tenant cannot be evicted. Vineyards are very frequently sub-let for a year: a good rent is 10*s.* to 12*s.* a tanap. There are generally an immense number of these vineyards found in every village. A field *tanap* is 256 vineyard *tanaps*.

Grassfields and orchards are reckoned as vineyards; they are held on the same tenure, and the same rent is paid for them. In the case of ploughed fields, however, the tenant can be changed by the agha every year. If the latter gives the seed, the tenant returns, as rent, two-thirds of the produce to the agha; if the tenant provides everything, he gives one-third of the produce.

Similarly, if the landlord has planted the vineyard, and it is only cultivated by the villagers, he receives a definite proportion of the produce, as in the parable of the wicked husbandmen (St. Matt. xxi. 34; St. Mark xii. 2; St. Luke xx. 10), where St. Mark's and St. Luke's account show us that the lord of the vineyard only received a portion of the fruit.

Sometimes a tenant buys a property from the agha at £7 to £15 a tanap. He then pays 5*s.* yearly as taxes for the land.

In every village one of the Christians is appointed kokha or kokhaya. He is responsible for collecting the taxes, and is generally the spokesman of the village. He receives no salary, but he does not pay poll tax. Next to the qasha, or parish priest, he receives a great deal of honour from his fellow-villagers, and he generally has something to say in every village matter. In a very few villages of the Urmi plain there is a superior sort of kokha, called malik, as in the mountains. He sometimes has a small salary, and receives a fee on the occasion of weddings. The maliks or kokhas are the general supervisors of the temporal affairs of the village.

The general condition of the people in Persia has certainly improved in the last fifty years, since there have been Europeans and Americans amongst them. The Mussulman does not now look upon the Christian as a certain and easy prey. The Christian does not now have to dismount when he passes a Mussulman of any consequence, as he was obliged to do but a few years ago, a practice which recalls to us Rebekah alighting off her camel when she saw Isaak (Gen. xxiv. 64). And this is but a sign of the times. The Persians are now forced to be more considerate to their dependants, and have begun to learn the meaning of the Syrian proverb, "If a man does not walk on his head, he will not know the measure of his footsteps;" that is, Great men ought to consider their inferiors. Generally, it may be said that the hardships of the life of the Christians in Persia do not come from the ordinary peasant Mussulman population, which is often as poor and nearly as much oppressed as themselves, but from the officials and landlords. And it is not now often, thanks to the efforts of consuls and missionaries, that the inhabitants of the Urmi plain have very great instances of oppression to complain of; it is rather the constant round of petty acts of injustice, inseparable, as it would seem, from the wretched system of government, which make the difficulties of their life.

It is from the administration of what is called justice, that most of the hardships of the Eastern Syrians in Persia arise. It must be confessed that this is, to a great extent, their own fault. A more litigious people probably never lived; although they know that in the majority of cases they themselves, whether plaintiffs or defendants, will get no advantage, but that they will only fill the pockets of their Mussulman governors. Yet they go to law over the veriest trifle, and utterly forget the precept of St. Paul, which forbids a Christian to drag his brother before the tribunal of the infidel. The earnest efforts of missionaries have to be directed to the eradication of this unfortunate and suicidal characteristic of the Syrian people.

There are two laws in Persia directed against the Christians, which, if they were often carried out, would be a crying injustice. As it is, it is a matter of astonishment that they are allowed by the nations of Europe to remain on the Persian statute-book. One is, that if any member of a Christian family become a Mussulman, he or she can claim the whole property of her "house," which may consist of several families. Now, although a Christian man seldom apostatizes, it is by no means uncommon for a Christian woman to fall in love with, and marry, or be carried off by a young Mussulman. The Syrians, whose notion of necessity is a weak one, then say that she has apostatized "without any remedy," that is, she could not help it; or "from the root of the ear," which means the same thing.

Necessity with them means but a strong temptation, because they have not the moral backbone to resist great pressure.

In cases of abduction, the Persian authorities are generally very careful to examine the woman, to see if she has voluntarily become a Mussulman, and send for her own people to reason with her; and even if she persists in her apostasy, a good governor will only give her her share of the family goods. But under a bad governor, the law may at any time be carried out, or used as a means of extorting bribes, and it is a disgrace that it should be allowed to remain. A Christian who has apostatized cannot return to his or her own faith without great danger. It should be added that, as a woman cannot be produced in court, except veiled, cases of impersonation sometimes occur.

Another injustice in the Persian law is that the evidence of Christians is not received against that of Mussulmans, and this is often the cause of great hardship. In these two cases the Christians ought to be righted by the intervention of the European governments; and this was strongly recommended, in 1880, by Mr. Abbott, British consul-general at Tabriz, in a report on the Nestorian Christians;[1] but nothing has been done.

Injustice is continually being done in a small way. The governor of the town of Urmi has, for dealing with the Christians, a deputy called the Serperast. This official depends for his livelihood to a great extent, and for keeping up a staff of servants entirely, on what he can get in the way of fines out

[1] Blue-book on the Kurdish invasion of Persia in 1880, p. 35.

of the Christians. Hence it is his interest to stir up quarrels and magnify trifles, and above all, when a case is brought before him, to secure a conviction. People are encouraged to make complaints (and indeed the Syrians need no encouragement), and the defendant is almost always mulcted in costs, if in nothing else. If two men fight, and both are equally to blame, they each hurry off to the Serperast, and whoever arrives first is the plaintiff, and generally gets off scot free, while his unfortunate opponent (who perhaps was the assaulted party) is put into prison for a day or two, and a heavy fine is extorted from him. The Syrians say in such a case, "Instead of the buffaloes crying out, it is the cart which complains." Persian justice says, "We must punish somebody," but does not care whom, as long as its pockets are filled by the transaction.

Justice can never be depended on in Persia. It by no means follows that if a man has the right on his side he wins his case or even escapes a fine Bribes are freely administered on both sides; without this no one can expect judgment to be given in his favour. Often, when the bribes are equal, or for some reason the judge do not wish to decide it, the case will be sent to some neutral third party for arbitration. Under a bad governor an old case, settled long before, may be brought up again for the purpose of extorting money. In one such case an affair five years old, and settled at the time, was brought up against two men, the sole connexion of one of whom with the matter was that he had gone bail for the other!

The case was as follows. Two Christians were coming into the city, probably half drunk, and were, according to the account of the survivor, attacked by a Mussulman, who shot one dead. He in his turn was stabbed by the companion of the murdered man. Thereupon both parties were had up before the governor. The Mussulman got off on plea of self-defence, and the Christian was heavily fined. No "blood money" was given to the relations of the murdered man. Five years after, the widow was ill advised enough to petition for the blood money, and this was ordered to be paid—about 30 tomans, or less than £10. It is about 300 tomans if a Mussulman is killed. But the money was ordered to be paid in equal shares by the Mussulman, the companion of the murdered man, and another Christian who happened to have bailed him five years before. At the same time each was ordered to pay 25 tomans to the governor as a fee. Hereupon the Mussulman, out of revenge, got up a story that at the time of the murder, five years before, the companion of the murdered man robbed him of 70 tomans, and this was ordered to be paid. Thus a man, especially a Christian, if he once gets into the clutches of the officials of the law, does not know whether he will ever be free from it. His case may be brought up against him at any time. That described above was fortunately settled by the governor being removed, and by his successor knowing the rights of the matter from having investigated it originally.

The same governor made a good thing for himself out of a difficult case in a rather amusing manner.

A murder was committed near Urmi, and the dead man's body was found at an equal distance from several villages, partly Mussulman and partly Christian. As no one knew, or would tell, who did the deed, the governor took the fine he would have exacted of the perpetrator from *each* of the villages. Of course the fine went into his own pocket.

In the villages small but continual oppressions are carried on by the aghas, with whom in ordinary matters the governors do not interfere; this can only be prevented by a stringent oversight of the villages by the government. It must be remembered, however, that it is so weak that it cannot prevent local injustice. Much has been done by the residence of Europeans among the people to check these, and the people are the first to acknowledge that they are much better off now than they were fifty years ago, and that the missionaries have been the cause of the improvement in their temporal prospects. For instance, a case happened not long ago in which an agha had grossly oppressed his "subjects," taking extra taxes from them, compelling them to work for him for nothing, carrying off Christian women for his harem, and so on. The missionaries joined in making a strong representation to the governor, with the result that the agha had to make restitution and to give a promise in writing, called an *iltizân*, that he would be of good behaviour for the future. But he afterwards returned to his old practices. What is wanted in these cases of oppression is that the European consuls should claim *as a right* to interfere, and that they should interfere much more frequently.

The following is the account by a governor of Urmi of his own functions, in a letter to the English missionaries who had represented to him a flagrant case.

"My Soul!

"I have received your highness' letter, containing an accusation against a servant who had been sent to —— to collect rents, and who had troubled there a priest, one of your students. It was necessary to make an examination of the case; and the servant was kept in prison for three days, and yesterday punished in a military manner.

"I have a special petition to make to your greatness; that you will tell your students that from sunrise till four hours past sunset, I am sitting in the hall to see and attend to all the petitions of Mussulmans and Christians, of all men of whatever nation or language they may be. They can see me without any hindrance, so that they do not need any one to intercede for them, and need not be the means of troubling your nobility. And if the Serperast does not judge their case rightly, they can send their petitions by post or telegraph to the blessed dust of his holiest and blessed presence, the Lord Vali Ahd (may my spirit be his sacrifice); or to the presence of the most happy, high, and blessed Amir-i-Nizam."

(Date).

No one, of course, will take this letter literally. The Christians have little or no chance against a Mussulman unless backed up by the Europeans.

An extraordinary number of the cases which come before the Mussulman judges arise simply from one man having called the other names, "reviling" him, as they call it. We say that words break no bones; but the Syrians, on the other hand, think that an opprobrious epithet is far worse than a blow. "A blow can be wiped out, a word never," they say; and they can well understand how deeply Shimei's curses cut David. His words were far worse than the stones he threw, and were remembered till David's dying day (2 Sam. xvi. 5; 1 Kings ii. 8). So now, matters which we should dismiss with a laugh, are brought up seriously to the judgment hall. A mission scholar who was severely rebuked for stabbing another with a knife, exclaimed in tones of indignant self-excuse, "Why, Rabbi, he called me a dervish!"

Litigants have a curious way in Persia. If, for example, they claim something, they get several people, preferably Mussulman mollahs, to write them a letter, saying that the claim is well founded. It makes no difference if, as is nearly always the case, the witnesses have, and can have, no earthly knowledge of the matter. Of course they are paid for their signatures, or rather seals. This letter is then taken to the governor with a bribe, and if the governor is corruptible, he writes them a letter allowing the claim. The other side then goes through the same process, and the governor gives them also a letter, this time disallowing the claim. The result is generally that everything is left undecided, and this means further litigation, and more fees to the officials.

An amusing story is told of the proceedings of some of the early European settlers in Persia. It was important to establish their reputation; and to call a man an opprobrious name with impunity would do it in the firmest way possible. So they called on the governor, called him by some name particularly insulting to a Mussulman ear, and at the same time slipped a gold watch into his hand.

The governor's avarice got the better of his indignation, and he said nothing to the speech while he received the gift. The Europeans' reputation was securely established.

Every official in Persia, from the Shah downwards, has his price. "Give money, and bring the mollah out of the mosque," the people say. Money can do anything, and no one can expect an office of any kind unless he pays for it. In the same way a *khal'at* or robe of honour given by the Shah or a great official to an inferior, as a token of approval, is nearly always paid for. It is received with great honour, and there is a *peshwaz* or procession to go and meet the bearer as he conveys it to the city. All the friends of the recipient go and "bless" the present, although they know that it has been duly bought and paid for. And so ranks in the army are bought by people who have never served, but who like to have a handle to their name. Sometimes a man gives a bribe to get an office and fails, and the superior authorities thus find out that he is a man of substance, and squeeze him more than if he had obtained the post. In that case they say, "We went to get something out of our beards, but we had to add our moustaches to them."

The general effect of oppressions is greatly to diminish the sense of justice and truth in the people. A nation that is habitually oppressed becomes naturally untruthful. This applies fully as much to the ordinary Mussulman population of Persia as to the Christians. They are quite as untruthful as the Syrians and Armenians. Indeed, the Mussulman will consider it a good action to deceive one of another religion, but the Christian will always acknowledge that his lie is a sin; only he lies, he says, from necessity, to prevent oppression. So with the sense of justice. If a Christian commits a crime, every one in the community does his best to get him off punishment. The shame is not that he should commit the offence, but that he, a Christian, should be punished for it. For instance, a Syrian lately was put to death for committing several murders—an almost, if not quite unique case fortunately. The whole Syrian population tried to get him off, and applied to the European missionaries to interfere. It was quite unintelligible to them when they were told that it was God's law that he should die, and that he would certainly be put to death in England. Because he was a Syrian, the missionaries were expected to try and procure his pardon. And the prosecutor in the case, another Syrian, was utterly sent to Coventry, and no one would give him the usual "Peace."

Too often the injustice of Persian judges is helped on by intrigues among the Syrians themselves. Moved by pique, or jealousy, or enmity, one man will set on the officials to squeeze his neighbours, forgetful, in the impulse of the moment, that his own turn will come next. One cannot read the books of Ezra or Nehemiah, or the sixth chapter of Daniel, without remarking that intrigues like those of the Samaritans and others against the Jews are going on over and over again in our own day. They will rather be subject to the Egyptians than be delivered by a Moses (Ex. v. 20). And it is this very want of union which makes it so easy for a Mohammedan government to keep the Christians in subjection. The Syrians have not yet learnt that union is strength, or as they themselves put it, that if two chestnuts were to become one they would crack a walnut.

It must be said, in justice to the Persian government, that public security, if not all that could be desired, is yet much better than might be expected. One cannot go for a walk a mile from Constantinople or Smyrna for fear of brigands; but one can go alone anywhere in the plain of Urmi, as in the greater part of Persia, without the least danger. Nor is it necessary to take soldiers (unless as a guard of honour for great persons) on all the ordinary roads. Perhaps this is due to the great severity with which highway robbery is punished. When caught, a robber is generally put to death; either his throat is cut in the market-place, for hanging is of course forbidden by a religion which does not allow men even to wring a fowl's neck; or if a terrible example is to be made, he is blown from a cannon outside one of the gates of the city.[1] If, however, the governor is merciful, or the offence is not a great one, he is let off with having a hand or his ears cut off, or the sinews of his hand severed, or even, if he has great influence, with a heavy fine. The executioner, like our judges, is robed in red, to inspire awe into the offender. In other parts of Persia, under very cruel governors, robbers and murderers have been built up alive into pillars

[1] This reminds us of another death "without the gate" (Heb. xiii. 12). Cf. the story of Naboth (1 Kings xxi. 13) and the parable of the wicked husbandman (St. Matt. xxi. 39).

136 LIFE UNDER THE PERSIAN GOVERNMENT.

to die slowly, and left by the wayside as a standing menace to evil-doers.

The ordinary punishment for lighter offences is the bastinado. This takes the place of long imprisonments, which are not often inflicted except in the case of political offenders. It is no great disgrace to "eat sticks" as it is called; even high officials are thus beaten. The culprit lies down on the ground and his bare feet are placed in a loop attached to a long pole with handles which are held by the attendants. This is called a *felek*. The executioners "lay on" and thrash the offender till their sticks break; fresh sticks are then substituted till a sufficient number are used up. Bribing generally has a good deal to do with the ease with which the sticks break. It is of course not such a terrible punishment as it would be to those whose feet are not hardened by constantly walking barefoot; but a man who has "eaten sticks" is often lame for weeks or even months.

The frontier districts between Persia and Turkey, which are inhabited partly by Kurds and partly by Syrians, are far from safe for any but European travellers, whose reputation gives them protection. It is not at all uncommon for travellers from Urmi to the patriarchal village to be pillaged by Kurds and stripped of everything they have with them, even of the clothes they are standing in. Even if travellers escape robbers, they are probably squeezed by the customs officials of both Turkey and Persia, who are merely placed on the frontier for the sake of the money they can get out of passers-by. Even the Turkish and Persian consuls on either side have

LIFE UNDER THE PERSIAN GOVERNMENT. 137

to live almost entirely on the fees they can get out of the poor travellers, and it is a common thing for a traveller to be seized by the servants of his consul in order to get money for passports and other documents out of him.

If only the Syrians could have more trade, a great step would have been taken to promote their welfare. The Armenians have become the principal traders of the East. They are the chief merchants in almost every city. It would be a great thing if the Syrians could follow their example, at however great a distance. They cannot all be priests or schoolmasters, however well educated, and there is little else open to them except labourers' work. Hence a very large number of them go to Europe, either to work or to beg. Most of the workers go to Tiflis and to other Russian towns, where they engage in various trades and generally save considerable sums, for they are a thrifty people. The beggars go to all European countries,—the bolder sort to the West, with some excuse, such as a school or orphanage, to extract money from the charitable, and the less enterprising to Russia, which is close by. They think there is no business so honourable or profitable as this; in the latter respect at least they are right. But even if they go to work and not to beg, there are many evils connected with the system. The men go off to Russia, and often leave their families in want. If they remain away long (so lax are the rules for divorce), they may find their wives married again in their absence. Moreover, they seem to learn European vices easily, without being able to assimilate European virtues. If they emigrated with their families and settled permanently in foreign countries, there would not be the same objection to their leaving home; and a few have done this. There are some Syrian villages near Erivan in Trans-Caucasia. They have conformed to the Russian Church.

But what the Syrians want is the establishment of trades in their midst. There are, indeed, some considerable difficulties, which arise from the character of the people themselves as well as from their surroundings. The Syrians are not at all a commercial people, and they have no business habits. They have to learn the value of time and punctuality, and the advantage of credit. At present there is no credit; no one believes any one else, and one of the first essentials of commerce is wanting. No doubt the unbusinesslike character of the Syrians arises from their long captivity, as one may call it. They are only just beginning to shake themselves free from the servitude of a domineering Mohammedanism; and there is no reason why in time they should not become, like the Armenians and Jews, a commercial people. They may perhaps one day be, with the Armenians, the merchants of Persia; for it is not likely that the Persians themselves will ever become commercial. Another difficulty in the way of trades is the refusal of the Mussulmans to buy from the Christians. They profess to consider things made by the infidel unclean. Already, however, this feeling is passing away. Already the best carpenters in Urmi are Christians. Already the

Persians come to the Christians to be doctored, or to have their photograph taken, or to have their clothes made. And no doubt, when the communications between Persia and the West improve, and intercourse becomes more frequent, the Mussulmans will buy from the Christians without the least scruple. In this connection we may mention the curious fact that Mussulmans will allow a Christian to drink out of his glasses, but not out of his earthenware bowls. Once when we were travelling we borrowed a samovar (urn) from a Mussulman. On our returning it he was just about to put it away as it was, when a mollah turned the corner. The Mussulman thereupon scrupulously cleaned every portion of the vessel that had been defiled by the infidel.

A drawback to trade, however, besides (or perhaps because of) the uncertainty due to an unstable government is the extraordinarily high rate of interest charged for borrowed money. Twenty per cent. is a not uncommon rate, and it is never less than ten per cent. As a very large number of the people are in debt, it is no wonder that so many go to Russia and other European countries to get a little money by hook or by crook to pay their liabilities. This usury would have horrified their forefathers, who only allowed (and that grudgingly) one per cent. interest, and reduced even that small rate by a later canon (Sunhadus iv. § 8). It is not uncommon for a borrower to give something in pledge, as security, or in lieu of interest. A mare, or a cow, or a field is given, and the produce goes to the creditor. This custom is allowed and regulated in the Sunhadus (iv. §§ 8, 9).

In buying, selling, or hiring, it is usual to give earnest money, as this fixes the bargain. A caravan driver will often give the hirer something—money, or a knife, or an article of dress—as security that he will not play him false; or if the hirer has a hold on him otherwise, the caravan man receives some money, and this legally prevents his breaking his word. The same applies to all bargains; and it is especially necessary to pay some earnest money in buying hay, corn, and other commodities, which go up and down in price, lest the seller should take advantage of the state of the market, to go back from his word.

Property descends to the children, or goes to the widow or widower in fixed proportions under Persian law. The Old Syrian law, still in force among the independent tribes in Turkey, gave from one-fifth to two-thirds to a widower (according to whether there are children or not), and from one-tenth to one-third to a widow.[1] The rest goes to the children, by any wife or husband, a son taking double a daughter's portion. Failing children, the parents of the deceased inherit; or failing them, brothers and sisters and their descendants; failing them, the grandparents; failing them, uncles and aunts and their descendants; failing them, the great-grandparents; failing them, the great-uncles and aunts and their descendants. But a man's share is double a woman's. Relations not by blood do not inherit (Sunhadus iii. §§ 1-10).

Wills are not very commonly made; indeed in the mountains never. And even if they are made

[1] But usually, in practice, a widow and a daughter get nothing in the mountains.

they are often disregarded. The authorities differ on the subject. One says that all wills, oral or written, even those made by boys of twelve, are to be confirmed; others, that wills made to defraud heirs are not to be confirmed, and may only be regarded if there are no heirs (Sunhadus iii. § 13).

CHAPTER VII.

MARRIAGE CUSTOMS.

Betrothals—The parents' consent—Rebekah and Isaak—Table of affinity—A Syrian's account of the customs of his people—The wedding procession — The religious ceremony — The knitting of the bridechamber—Contributions to the marriage—Lamps—A Mussulman's wedding festivities—The dowry—Several families under one roof—A man and his daughter-in-law—Eloping—Remarriage—Divorce.

WITH the Syrians, as with us, the betrothal precedes the "blessing" or marriage; though with them the two rites are not united as now with us, but are separated by an interval, often of some months or even years. Hence there is no such thing as an "engagement," but when the contracting parties or their parents have arranged the matter, the betrothal takes place. The bride and bridegroom are nearly always very young, as is usual in the East; he is sometimes but fourteen years old, and she often not more than twelve; but the Sunhadus rules that this is to be the absolute minimum. "The woman must be fourteen years old, or twelve at least, and give her free consent" (book ii. § 4). Although this custom of early marriage has its disadvantages, yet

MARRIAGE CUSTOMS. 143

without doubt it has the good result of greatly tending to morality. The following is an abridged account from the Sunhadus of the method of betrothal, and in the main accords with modern custom. Betrothal must be performed in a church [but now generally in a house] by priests and deacons and laity, with prayer and blessing, cross, ring, and *khnana*.[1] In the morning the priests send the ring to the woman by four nuns or discreet laywomen, who, if she consents, put it on her hand. If she does not consent, nothing more is done. If she does consent, the betrothal is carried out. Both bride and bridegroom drink of the blessed cup, and the sponsors, or groomsman and bridesmaid, who are also the sponsors at baptism as explained in Chapter XII., are signed with it. There must be at least five witnesses besides the families of the parties. Two documents are prepared; and the assent of the parties and the amount of the man's settlement and the woman's dowry is written down. After being sealed and witnessed, one document is given to the man, one to the woman. Betrothals not thus performed, or with non-Christian witnesses, are invalid, and all who take part in them are excommunicated and censured. In a place where there is no priest they assemble witnesses as before; take cross, ring, and *khnana;* say Our Father, and Holy God, Holy Mighty, Holy Immortal have mercy upon us. Glory be to the Father, and to the Son, and to the Holy Ghost. Holy God, etc. From everlasting to everlasting, for ever and ever. Holy

---

[1] Sacred earth taken from the tombs of the martyrs. It is now used at weddings, but not as a rule at betrothals.

God, etc. The betrothal is thus completed. If before the marriage a priest is available, he completes what is lacking; but if not, the marriage is similarly performed (Sunhadus ii. §§ 2, 3).

The bridegroom always makes his suit through his father, if alive, or, if not, through an elder brother or near relation, or through some great man or a malik; and as a matter of custom a man is not betrothed except with his parents' consent and with that of all his elder unmarried brothers; though the canons only say that a man's betrothal cannot stand against his parents' consent if he is dependant on them, but if not it does stand; and they do not mention the elder brothers at all (ii. § 9). A woman's hand is always asked through her father, if he is alive. Thus, in the case of Dinah, "Shechem spake unto his father Hamor, saying, Get me this damsel to wife... And Hamor the father of Shechem went out unto Jacob to commune with him" (Gen. xxxiv. 4, 6). If the father is not alive, the woman is given away by her brothers, or, if she has none, by her paternal uncles, who may marry her to their own sons, or to others. The marriage of first cousins is thus permitted by canon, although in practice it is unknown, and public opinion would be too strong to allow it. It is supposed to be uncanonical. If a woman has no brothers or paternal uncles, she is given away by her mother; but, if she have no near relations, by the parish priest (Sunhadus ii. §§ 5, 6). The bride and bridegroom have often not seen each other before they are betrothed, especially if they are not of the same village; and marriages are often arranged by parents for family considerations, and the young people's wishes scarcely considered. There often is a sort of understanding between lad and lass, but courtship, as understood in the West, is scarcely known; and it is a natural result of the system that the idea of conjugal love is not a high one. The Syrians frequently express the greatest astonishment at the devotion Westerns so often display to their wives, and the sacrifices made for their sakes; they too often chose a wife for her capacity as a good servant or as an economical housewife. At the same time there are conspicuous exceptions; but the love more often comes after marriage than before it. Betrothal is a binding contract, and, ordinarily, betrothed persons cannot be separated either before or after marriage, except for reasons for which divorce is allowed (Sunhadus ii. § 7). But exceptions are made in the case of the woman being deserted for a number of years by a man who has gone to a distant country—three, if he does not maintain her in the mean time, seven if he does maintain her; and some authorities hold betrothal to be voidable if they do not marry for ten years, and there is an incompatibility of temper (ii. §§ 7, 8). The practice is somewhat more lax; and betrothals are occasionally, though rarely, voided. In any case betrothals made irregularly, that is, without the intervention of the priest, and not in accordance with the canons, are not binding.

It is curious to notice the strict parallelism between the betrothals of the Eastern Syrians and that of Rebekah and Isaak as narrated in Gen. xxiv. The whole chapter reminds us of everyday customs—the women going out at evening to draw water from the well with their earthenware jars on their shoulders, the camels kneeling down outside the city to drink, the chopped straw eaten by the camels, a peculiarity of the East (*teven*, the word still used, and probably meaning building material, because always mixed with the mud or mortar), the presentation of the nose-ring (A.V., earring) and bracelets, and the apparent knowledge of Rebekah that the acceptance of these gifts meant assent to proposals of marriage, with regard to which we may compare the provision of the Sunhadus, mentioned above, that the acceptance of the ring by the woman is the acknowledged token of her assent. And above all the management of the betrothal contract by the relations, neither the bridegroom nor bride appearing on the scene (for Rebekah seems only to have been consulted as to whether she would go *at once*), the long address of the servant, the presentation of raiment by the bridegroom besides other gifts (for the bridegroom provides the trousseau, not the bride [1]), and the close veiling of the bride when she comes in sight of Isaak (as later when Leah was substituted for Rachel) all agree with the customs of to-day. This is only a sample of the conservatism of the East; oriental customs throw light on almost every chapter of the Bible narrative.

The Syrian Table of affinity is a very long one, and contains sixty-two forbidden relationships for the man, and the same number for the woman.

---

[1] But in Qudshanis, at any rate in the Patriarch's tribe, the bride's parents provide the trousseau.

MARRIAGE CUSTOMS.

The only relationships which we do, and the Syrians do not reckon are between a man and his brother's (or sister's) daughter-in-law, and between a woman and her brother's (or sister's) son-in-law. The reason for the long list is perhaps to be found in the custom prevalent of having several related families living under one roof. The married sons, at least at first, nearly always live under the same roof as the parents, and all are one "house;" hence many people often live in the same dwelling-place who are only distantly connected; and it is usually felt to be undesirable that a bridegroom and a bride should have been of the same household.[1] For instance, two brothers may not marry two sisters. Also a man may not marry his baptismal sponsor or her daughter, or his father's or mother's sponsors or their daughters; and similarly for women (Canons of George, Metropolitan of Assyria, in the Ashitha Sunhadus). Also a man may not marry a woman betrothed to his brother who has died between the betrothal and marriage. The rule with regard to non-Christian marriages is curious. A Christian man may marry a heathen woman with a view to converting her or the children of the marriage, but a Christian woman may not marry one who is not a Christian. In practice, however, the only case which ever arises is that of a marriage with Mussulmans; and of course the Mohammedan law strictly forbids any marriage with a Christian unless the latter apostatizes.

This place may be chosen for giving an account

[1] But sometimes in Tiari, at any rate, a man and woman of the same "house" marry, so as to keep the bride in her father's house.

of the customs of the people written by one of the mission scholars, although it is not altogether about marriage customs. It was an essay written for an examination, and is given here as it was composed, being literally translated.

On the Country and Customs of the Syrians.

"The first thing I wish to tell is where the Syrians live. They have not a special country to themselves, or a king of their own to govern them, but they are scattered as sheep which have no shepherd in different countries; but most of them live in the Eastern part of the world, under the shadow of Nasir-id-din Shah,[1] one of the noblest kings, and one who loves his subjects. The country where the Syrians live is very agreeable and pleasant, and full of fruits of many kinds, but has not much money or expensive commodities. Thus this portion of the flock of the Syrians lives in more comfort than the other subjects around them [the mountain Syrians, in Turkey]; but even they give too high taxes for the king. Now, however, some of the tricks of the aghas [masters of the villages] have been broken by the European apostles [missionaries], and there is a certain amount of security and peace. We hope God will raise up the church anew, that the Syrians may be worthy of the glory of God.

"Now I wish to explain somewhat about the customs of the Syrians. If we turn back to a time considerably before now and look at some of the customs of the Syrians, we shall see many curious things in them. For example, the dress of the Syrians at that time was as follows: They put on a long coat of native stuff, but now we see that the coats are made like soldiers' coats, and short like the lutis [disreputable characters, men without any profession]. The old custom is changed. Also the trousers were of blue holland, somewhat broad as we see some wear them now, below blue, and above red or white. And then,

[1] In reality the Persian Syrians are only one-fourth of the whole number. Our author is a Persian subject.

too, the hat was of felt, blackened with age; but now the hats are of Bokhara,[1] and with them is worn an undercoat like those of soldiers, of various kinds;[2] and also European shirts. The shoes were sandals, but we have changed them for many different kinds; sometimes they are like English or Russian shoes with stiff heels, or saghrii.[3]

"One of the best of the customs of the Syrians is when a stranger comes into our house. We put before him everything that we have to eat, though we may not have invited him to our table. Also we wash his feet.[4] Secondly, the Syrians sleep on the floor, not on bedsteads. A little before now we had no plaistered rooms, but *bati*[5] black with the smoke of the oven; and when it is winter or cold we put low tables over the ovens and sit under them.[6]

"The food of the Syrians is as follows: Meat cooked in soup; pounded meat; vegetables stuffed with meat or rice; and now there are many other dishes, such as pillau (two kinds), omelette, treacle-flour, butter-flour, *hasida*,[7] rice milk; and there are others not so nice as these.

"Weddings are performed in the following manner. First, one day they go to the father of the girl with trumpets and drums; they put a ring on her, eat and drink and go away.[8] After this, they take presents of sweets, etc. After this, one day they kill an ox for the great day of the wedding; and then they take trumpets and drums and a jar of wine in their hands and invite the villagers, as far as the master of the wedding orders; and thus also they send to other villages and invite their relations and friends. Then they begin to play airs of various kinds, and go to the house of the bride with *khena*[9] and bless it. Next

---

[1] The Russo-Persian woolly hats, made of the material known in Europe as Astrakhan.
[2] Like the waistcoats of the last century.
[3] An open shoe of superior make, much worn by mollahs.
[4] This must usually be taken in a figurative sense.
[5] This is the plural of baita. See page 51.
[6] For the ovens see above, page 51.
[7] An indescribably nasty and oily compound of wheat, butter, etc.
[8] This is the betrothal.
[9] A yellow dye much used for the hands and hair. Mussulman women like Jezebel (2 Kings ix. 30, margin) also paint their eyes, but the Syrian women do not do this (cf. Jer. iv. 30; Ezek. xxiii. 40).

day the groomsmen bring the bride in the morning. They eat bread in the house of the bridegroom, and then they go and bring the bride. After they have eaten and drunk, they adorn the bride in a different kind of dress from that of everyday, and put a tinsel ornament on her head; and place her on a horse. Then they give three cheers (but in former times with us they used to take the bride seven times round the oven); and she asks forgiveness from her father and mother;[1] and so they bring her.[2] They adorn the bridegroom and take him up to the roof with his best man. They make a framework filled with apples, pears, pomegranates, raisins, and the fruit of the jujube tree, in the form of a cross. Then the bridegroom takes one of the apples and signs himself with the sign of the cross in the name of the three Persons, and throws it at the bride; this he does as often as he pleases. Then they are joyful on the great day of the bridechamber. This they keep up for nearly seven days and seven nights.

"The churches of the Syrians are quite like in old times in form; but their doors were smaller than now. The Syrians have taken their religion from Mar Nestoris.[3] They were very zealous at first, and a great church; and the Syrians who lived in it were husbandmen. But now they have somewhat increased."[4]

In the wedding procession referred to in the above account, the bride is closely veiled, so that her face is completely hidden, both when she is on horseback, and also throughout the marriage ceremonies. This is clearly a custom dating from time immemorial, and is not due to the influence of Mohammedanism merely, as it is mentioned in the case of Rebekah, and the fact that the veil is worn during the whole

---

[1] An Eastern phrase for saying good-bye.

[2] This often or generally takes several days. They take the bride first to one friend's house, then to another, and so on; and lastly to the bridegroom's. They must never retrace their steps in this process, but always go forward, however wide the circuit be.

[3] This is a strange statement even for a Syrian.

[4] The exact opposite is really the case. The Syrians are now a mere fraction of what they once were.

of the wedding, and reaches to the knees so as to conceal almost the whole of the bride's figure, accounts for the facility with which Jacob was deceived in the case of Leah (Gen. xxix. 23). The veil is also worn by brides for a considerable time after marriage—in some places for seven days, in some more—and they do not show their faces to strangers.

Our author does not mention the religious ceremony or "blessing" as it is called. And indeed, it is overshadowed by the social festivities even more than with us. It ought to take place in the church, but frequently or usually is in the house of the bridegroom. It consists of many prayers and anthems, which refer at length to the examples of the Old Testament fathers. The *khnana* or sacred earth [1] is thrown into a cup of wine and water, and also the ring, and both bride and bridegroom drink of it; the groomsman and bridesmaid stand on either side, and are signed by the priest with the cup, but they do not drink of it. The bride and bridegroom are then crowned with threads of three colours intertwined. They are of red, blue, and white, and signify respectively that killing, death, and life, are in the hands of God. This ceremony is called the "Order of Crowning." Crowns are also used at baptism. Dr. Badger erroneously says this practice is confined to the Roman Catholic Uniats of Mosul ("Nestorians and their Rituals," vol. ii. p. 212).

The prayers and anthems are lengthened or shortened according to the discretion of the priest; and great as are the differences in all Syrian liturgical

[1] See above, page 143.

manuscripts, no books have so many discrepancies as the marriage services. At the end of the prayers, the priest first, and then the people, kiss the bridegroom and touch the head of the bride. But the bridegroom does not publicly kiss the bride as in old times, and as often happens with us. In Kurdistan only the near relations and sponsors attend the ceremony in church. In Tiari, when they have returned to the house, the groom and bride sit close together, as in Urmi, and visitors kiss his cheek, and the top of her head through the veil. In Qudshanis the bride sits apart, and visitors only kiss the bridegroom. All who kiss him, kiss also the groomsman. This is not the case in Urmi.

There is another religious service of some interest, known as the "knitting of the bride-chamber," and performed in the evening. The name refers to an old custom of making a wickerwork screen, in the large *baita*, or family room, to fence off the bride-chamber. The marriage service-book is placed under the bridal pillow.

The festivities go on for several days, often for a week, as in the case of Leah (Gen. xxix. 27) and Samson (Judges xiv. 12). Also, as in the latter case, they are in the house of the bridegroom. Everything is done according to the command of the "friend of the bridegroom" (St. John iii. 29), who is also the "governor of the feast," as at the marriage in Cana of Galilee (St. John ii. 8–11), where also we notice that the bridegroom gives the feast.

At a wedding, it is the custom to pay a fee to the *agha*, or master of the village, to the *malik*, or head man of the village, if there is one,[1] and to the parish priest. On the other hand, it is often the custom to go round the village to ask for subscriptions towards the expenses of the wedding. If you take a hair from every beard, they say, you will make a beard. If a man is asked for a contribution which he wishes indefinitely to postpone, he says, "Do not be sorry, my donkey; the summer is coming, and I will reap some clover."

As we have noticed the likeness of Syrian customs to those mentioned in the Bible, we must not omit to contrast some points. In the parable of the Ten Virgins, the bridegroom goes by night himself to fetch the bride, and lamps are naturally used by the virgins, and are the conspicuous feature of the parable; lamps fed with oil were used by the Jews, as torches were used by the Greeks and Romans.[2] But now the procession to fetch the bride is always in the daytime, and the bridegroom himself never goes to the bride's house, but his friends fetch her for him; whence the usual expression for "to marry a son," is "to bring a bride" for him. Yet, perhaps, a relic of an older custom is to be found in the practice of carrying a couple of unlighted candles in front of a bride as she is being taken from her father's to her future husband's house.

The festivities at a Mussulman wedding do not differ greatly from those of their Christian neighbours. A description of one such marriage at Urmi may suffice. It was in the house of a general

---

[1] If there is only a kokha or kokhaya he does not receive a fee. See above, page 124.

[2] Trench on the Parables; St. Matt. xxv. 1-14.

of division, and on a large scale. He was the father of the bridegroom, who was doubtless a mere boy, though neither he nor the bride appeared on the scene; it being etiquette, on these occasions, for both parties to be absent from their own wedding festivities. There is also a feast in the house of the bride, but the principal one is in that of the bridegroom. In this case the festivities were kept up for several days. On the first day, the lowest classes were invited, then their superiors, while the last few days were for the "upper ten." All the Europeans were invited on the ninth day, and even after that, the festivities went on for three or four days. Open house was kept, and the host must have gone to a very great expense, for Persia, in providing entertainment of all kinds for so many guests. The chief amusement was dancing on the tight-rope by a Syrian, who really did some remarkably clever things; he rowed himself across on a tray, and ended by putting his feet in large saucepans, and so walking across the rope. The guests were also regaled with the strains of the Urmi military band, which prides itself on playing European airs; but as each instrument was out of tune with the others, the Westerns, at least, were not much wiser, until this was explained to them. Afterwards, there was an entertainment by some gipsy boys, who are, in Persia, all professional dancers; they are not nomads as in Europe, although they keep to themselves and remain a distinct people. Owing, no doubt, to the presence of Europeans, everything was quite *comme il faut*, though it is understood that this is not always the case. Then came dinner on the floor, after which the European guests all went to pay their respects, and to give their congratulations to the host, who had been entertaining in another part of the house some Mussulman grandees, — amongst others, a Kurdish highwayman, whom the Persian authorities long tried to catch (in which case he would have had his throat cut, or would have been blown from a gun); but whom, as they were unsuccessful, they came to terms with, and appointed as a sort of protector of his own district, like Rob Roy, and now treat with the greatest honour. The host received his Western guests with the greatest respect and effusive compliments, and insisted on giving them a private exhibition of some dancing on stilts, by the Syrian rope-dancer; after which, leave was taken with another effusion of pretty speeches, those to whom this was new being agreeably surprised at having been amused instead of bored.

Among the Syrians, both the parents of the bride and of the bridegroom give a portion to the young couple, and there is often much haggling as to the amount. No doubt this formed a serious part of Hamor's "communing" with Jacob. "Ask me never so much dowry and gift, and I will give according as ye shall say unto me, but give me the damsel to wife" (Gen. xxxiv. 12). The Sunhadus lays down that the portion provided by the bridegroom's parents should be the same as that provided by the bride's family; or, according to some authorities, the latter should be half as much again as the former (ii. § 13).

The young couple live, as a rule, in the house of the bridegroom's father after marriage, and do not set up an establishment of their own. As they are at first mere children, this is a natural arrangement, and many families live in the same house. Later, the sons often (but by no means invariably) separate from their father, and there is then a general division of goods, which often causes much quarrelling. This practice of having several families under one roof leads to a curious prohibition: a man may not speak to his daughter-in-law. There is a Syriac proverb, "My daughter, I am talking to you; my daughter-in-law, listen." This is said when a man speaks to another, not for his own sake, but for the benefit of a third party. The father-in-law may not scold his daughter-in-law when she does wrong, and so the daughter has to fulfil the function of a "whipping boy."

If the parents do not consent, the young people sometimes take matters into their own hands and elope. They are then generally forgiven and married in the usual manner. The Sunhadus, however, is more strict. It lays down that if a woman is carried off by force against her own will, she may marry the man if she wills and if the parents consent. But if there is collusion, she may not marry the man who carried her off, but should be given to some one else, and the man must be punished and pay a fine to the woman. If a woman carried off by force had been previously betrothed, the previous betrothal remains binding; but if she had consented to the elopement, the man who had been betrothed to her may receive her or not, as he pleases (Sunhadus ii. § 12).

Generally, it may be said that the early marriages

have a very good effect on the morality of the younger people; and women very seldom fall before marriage. But in some districts in the mountains adultery is lamentably common, and is readily condoned. It is usually supposed, however, that the husband is ignorant of the matter. Occasionally he kills the wife and her paramour; sometimes he is deterred from fear of their families, at any rate unless he has positive proof. There are no restrictions on digamy, even among priests. The Sunhadus, indeed, quotes a Western canon of St. Ambrose and "the Greek Kings"—Constantine, Theodosius the Younger, and Leo—to the effect that if widows and widowers remarry within ten months, they are not to be received with honour; but adds that in the East there is no canon on this subject (book ii. § 16). Generally a widower, at least, marries very soon after his wife's death. It is very uncommon for a man to remain unmarried, even if he has been a widower more than once. Almost every one, man or woman, marries at least once; though there are a few exceptions in the case of men or women who remain unmarried for the sake of religion, and abstain from meat, and who are then called monks[1] or nuns. Some, like Solti, Mar Shimun's sister, remain unmarried for domestic reasons. This lady presides over the household arrangements of the patriarch's house. Bishops also, and their successors, remain unmarried.[2]

The laws and practice of the East Syrians allow divorce *a vinculo* in several cases. "Judicial separa-

---

[1] A monk is called Raban, lit. "our great one."
[2] See page 186.

tions" are not recognized by the Sunhadus or in practice; the innocent party is, though the guilty party is not, allowed to marry again (book ii. §1). Divorce is, with this proviso, allowed: (1) if the parties wish to enter the religious life, but only by mutual consent, and not then if there are little children (ii. § 17, and vii. § 2, canon 5); in this case they may not return to one another afterwards; (2) for adultery; (3) for apostasy; (4) for murder; (5) in case of an incurable bodily defect existing at the time of the marriage and unknown to one of the parties; (6) if the parties quarrel much, and reproof has no effect on them, after ten years, but not if there are any children; (7) if one of them is carried away captive, after three years, but it is recommended that they abide a long time if they can; (8) to a wife, if her husband goes to a far country, after seven years, if he does not maintain her, or after ten years if he does maintain her, though "she ought always to remain true to him." Also the Sunhadus quotes "the Greek Kings" as saying, "If a woman sleep in a strange house against her husband's will, or go to the theatre, or go to a strange village without father, brother, husband, or son, divorce is allowed" (ii. §§ 17-26).

Generally, "those guilty of unlawful intercourse, in any way, are excommunicated till they amend, as also all who have any dealings with them. If they die without repentance, let them be buried with the burial of an ass, and let no one attend the funeral. Any Ordinary transgressing this canon is condemned to the same punishment" (ii. § 27, canon of Mar Awa).

MARRIAGE CUSTOMS.

Laxity in the matter of divorce is a natural consequence of living in a Mussulman country, where any man may obtain a divorce by paying his wife her proper portion, with or without reason. The only wonder is that, in practice, the Syrians are not more lax than they are. The judge in divorce cases, as in many others, is the bishop, who is thoroughly recognized by the Mussulman authorities for this purpose, even in Persia and in those parts of the Syrian country where the Turkish government has a thorough hold on the people, and the Sunhadus is the statute-book by which divorce is regulated; the canon law in this respect thus receiving civil sanction. Divorce is granted not only on the petition of the husband, but also of the wife.

CHAPTER VIII.

THE SYRIAN AT SCHOOL.

Intelligence of the children—Their affection for their teachers—System of schools in the Archbishop of Canterbury's mission—The village schools—High schools—Learning by heart—"Is England in London?"—The upper school for deacons and older students—Early marriage—Trying to bribe a missionary—Mountain and plain boys—Punishments—"Pouring into prison"—Marks—Games—Writing and illumination—A "beautiful pen"—Printing Syriac—Order and method—"Fleeing"—Inquisitiveness—Inability to swallow too much—Breaking up—The girls at school—Rivalry with the boys—Learning to be good housewives—Outcome of education—Providing school-books—Bookbinding.

THERE can be no doubt that the children show quite the best part of the Syrian character. Not old enough to have contracted the faults due to poverty and oppression, they show all the affectionate disposition and warm-heartedness of their parents, with a docility, anxiety to receive instruction, and aptitude to learn which would surprise a European visitor. They have certainly the advantage of most Western children of the same class of life in intelligence. The absence of servility in the Syrian character has already been referred to. This is especially seen in the relations of teacher and pupil. Many an English schoolboy considers it not only the proper, but the almost inevitable thing to hate his master. The Syrian children know nothing of this. Though eager enough to get home for the holidays, they are only too glad to come back to school, and often come considerably before the proper time. They set off with their bedding and boxes on a donkey to Urmi, if they are from the plain, the first thing in the morning, and come to kiss the "apostle's" hand with a smile long before they are expected. They clearly do not know what Black Monday means. The mountain boys are not quite so regular. They have the frontier to pass, with its exactions, and a long journey to travel to school. Moreover, they are not accustomed to discipline like the children of the plain, and do not see the necessity of being tied down to any particular day.

The girls and very little boys are generally brought by their fathers or their mothers; but most of the boys are well able to take care of themselves. They are not likely to be taken in by the Mussulman sweetmeat vendor who hangs about the school premises like his prototype in the West. They can haggle with him as well as their parents, and indeed may safely be trusted to buy things for home in the bazaar without loss. Their very dress proclaims them little old men. There is no such thing as children's clothes; a boy wears the same garments as his father, except that they are smaller.

The children are certainly most anxious to learn, and are very docile. It is easy to keep order, and punishments are not often necessary. The chief

M

trouble is through the quarrels that arise. One boy calls another names, and a fight ensues. Whoever gets the worst of it will fly in tears to the nearest "apostle." Tale-telling is unfortunately not put down by public opinion. We have found in cases like this that the best way is to tell the disputants to come back again and relate their tale next day. By then they will have forgotten all about it.

BOYS IN THE MISSION SCHOOL, URMI, WITH THEIR TEACHER.
From the authors' photograph.

The best way of explaining the Syrian child's life at school is perhaps to describe the system of schools of the Archbishop of Canterbury's mission. These are of three grades, and during the year 1890–91 numbered seventy-eight elementary or village schools; four high schools for boys under seventeen, and one for girls till they marry; and an upper school for young men over seventeen, who are most of them already deacons.

The village schools are all open for nearly four months in the winter, from the end of November to the middle or end of March. This is the time when the children are free from herding the cattle and can be spared to go to school. In the more important villages a few schools go on reading till the beginning of summer. In most of these elementary schools the boys and girls read together. Some begin with the spelling-book, which has been printed on purpose for them at the mission press; others have advanced as far as reading the New Testament in the vernacular.[1] A few have begun classical Syriac. Some of the girls learn to sew, if there is a female teacher. All, both boys and girls, learn Bible history and the village catechism issued by the press at Urmi, and some advance as far as the larger catechism intended for the high schools. The children may safely be said to know far more about the elements of the Christian faith than an average Etonian or Harrovian. All also learn mental arithmetic, at any rate in the plains. Some also do arithmetic on slates, and write copies, one or two perhaps learn Persian or Turkish, as the case may be. The boys in the mountain schools learn more Old Syriac, and less (or no) arithmetic—this is sadly deficient, even in Urmi—and less reading in the vernacular. The reason of this is that almost the only books hitherto printed in the modern

[1] We may, perhaps, here express our sense of the good work done by the American Bible Society in connexion with the American Presbyterian Mission at Urmi, in issuing the sacred Scriptures in classical Syriac, and also in the Urmi dialect. The translation into the vernacular was first made by the venerable Dr. Perkins, at Urmi, about 1835.

language are in the Urmi dialect, and cannot readily be understood in the mountains.

The teachers are either deacons and other senior scholars from the Urmi schools or, especially in the mountains, parish priests. The schools within reach of the missionaries are examined every few weeks by them, and at the end of the session there is a more complete examination, on which to some extent depends the amount of salary paid to the teacher. But "payment by results" is only adopted in a modified sense; a teacher who has only a handful of backward scholars may receive the highest salary if he has made good progress with the material available. The cost of each school is usually only about £4 or £5 a year, and many or most of them are supported by individual subscribers, who receive reports of their own schools at the end of the session. The numbers in some schools rise to sixty or seventy; there will then be two teachers; perhaps one a deacon and one a girl from the school of the Sisters of Bethany. In the smaller villages, on the other hand, or where the Old Church is weak, and in many of the mountain villages where the people have not the same zeal for education as in the plains, there will only be perhaps ten or fifteen pupils or even less. A pleasing feature is the occasional presence of young men of twenty or more, who are not ashamed of coming and sitting among their young brothers and sisters to make up for time wasted in their boyhood.

The high schools are established at different centres: in the town of Urmi, where there is one for boys, and one for girls; in the village of Superghan near the Sea of Urmi; in the village of Ardishai south of Urmi, where the high school and village school are incorporated in one; and one in Turkey. These are all boarding schools. Except in the last, and in the girls' school at Urmi, the children, if they live within a reasonable distance, go home from Saturday to Monday; and for this reason no work is done on Saturday afternoons and Monday mornings, which are the two half-holidays of the week. The curriculum of the boys at Urmi and Superghan includes Holy Scripture, the larger catechism, classical Syriac, arithmetic, grammar of both classical and vernacular Syriac, history, geography, Persian or Turkish, the former of which is compulsory for all subjects of Persia, the latter for those of Turkey; writing copies, or "a beautiful pen," as the Syrians call it—and indeed good Syriac writing is beautiful to behold—dictation and composition; and, as a voluntary subject, English.

The children are wonderfully quick at picking up things, and especially in learning by heart. They will learn long passages with a most astonishing ease. But often, though they can rattle off a long passage from the catechism or from a geography or history, they will not take in the meaning; and the teachers have to be most carefully supervised to see that they do not get the children into a habit of learning by rote only. As an instance of this, they have learnt in geography the names of the different countries with the name of the capital after each, and they will bring out England—London, France—Paris, as if they were one word, without having the least notion, like the man in Hajji Baba, whether

London is in England or England in London. Indeed, they commonly speak about people living in "London" when they mean England. So they will talk about Norway—Sweden as if they were one word. They will even say, in reply to the question, "Who was the first man?" "Adameve." So, too, they will read their own vernacular without the least regard for stops, and without a notion of the sense. Perhaps the absence of capitals in Syriac has something to do with this; it is not so easy to see at a glance where a new sentence begins.

The boys in the village schools often read off certain psalms or passages from the Gospels with fluency, but can hardly spell the words of a new passage. One sometimes finds a boy "reading" what is over the page before he turns over! He has it by heart.

The students of the upper school are not quite so quick at learning as the younger boys. Their curriculum is much the same as that of the high school, but they have more advanced lessons in classical Syriac and theology, and they also learn to understand the service-books, which are in the classical language, and are taught preaching. One of the deacons preaches in the mission chapel once a week; two write sermons on a selected subject, which are criticised at the preaching lesson, and one is then chosen to be delivered before the assembled schools. This mission chapel is meant primarily for the missionaries and sisters, but on week days the scholars attend in the nave (which is then curtained off from the chancel, somewhat in Syrian fashion) for their daily prayers. On Sundays those who have not gone home go to Mart Mariam, in the town of

Urmi, for the prayers and Liturgy (if it is celebrated), and also for the special preaching and catechising which are held there in the afternoon.

Most of the students in the upper school are already ordained deacons; many or most are already married. They are, however, somewhat ashamed of acknowledging the fact, and it was somewhat startling to find, after some six months, that many of our young deacons whom we looked on as mere lads, were fathers of families! They had not told us. Lately, when one of the boys (he was no more) was offered some copying work to do, as he was poor, he did not send the outspoken excuse, "I have married a wife and therefore I cannot come," but merely wrote, "Please forgive me, for I have business." It was the same thing. The days before the fast are the great time for marriage, for during the fast custom, though not the Sunhadus, forbids them to marry; and at that time of merry-making it is common for the deacons to come and ask a few days' holiday. "Well, what do you want it for?" will be the inquiry. Nothing but blushes and suppressed laughter from outside listeners results, until the "apostle" comes to the rescue with, "I suppose you want to get married?" "Yes, Rabbi," is the meek reply, and the applicant goes off rejoicing. One day the father of a boy, certainly not more than fifteen, came into the "judgment hall," as the reception room is called in Persia, and after much humming and hawing, during which he sedulously kept his hand behind his back, announced that he had come to ask the missionaries' leave for his son to be married. "To be married?" ejaculates the astonished European. "And how old is the bride?" "Well, I dare say she will be twelve," is the hesitating reply. Being told that as the bridegroom elect's father he ought to know best, he departs with many thanks, and after he has gone, it is discovered that he has been holding behind his back all the time a loaf of sugar, or "blue jacket," as it is euphemistically called on such an occasion, which he has left as a *douceur* to reconcile the missionary to the precocious matrimony of his son![1]

The better students of the upper school read only in spring and autumn; in the winter they are teaching village schools. In this way the influence of the central schools is felt all over the country. When they are absent, their place is taken by a more backward set of students of the same age. The boys of the high schools read for some eight months and a half, from September 1st, old style, to June 1st, new style. At Urmi, both the upper and high boys' schools are in the same courtyard under the immediate eye of the missionaries, who live among the scholars. Here mountaineers and boys of the plain are educated together, and though jealousies and even fights sometimes occur, as when an Urmi boy speaks of a Shapatnaya[2] in a tone of contempt, which the mountaineer returns in full, calling him an Urmijnaya, these soon pass off, and the school life has an excellent effect in soothing natural animosities between mountain and plain.

---

[1] For the sake of European honesty, it must be added that the bribe was not accepted!

[2] Shapat is the old name of the country on the Turkish side of the frontier.

As a whole, the scholars of both schools get on exceedingly well together, in spite of the great clannishness which exists. But mountaineers do not like to have "Urmijnayi" in their dormitories, and *vice versa*. Even among the Urmi boys themselves the same thing exists. The boys of each district stick together. On one occasion, when almost all the boys had gone home for a holiday, one little mite came and said, " Please, Rabbi, may I go and sit in the deacons' school? because there are none of the boys of my river left in our school, and I cannot talk to the boys of other rivers (dioceses)!"

The punishments consist of impositions and sometimes the stick, administered, however, only by the missionaries. For some time it seemed difficult to know how to punish the students in the upper school if they offended. One could not beat an ordained clergyman! At last the happy thought occurred to some one—perhaps to one of the boys— of shutting up refractory deacons in a dark wood room for a number of hours, longer or shorter, according to the nature of the offence. So now, to the great glee of the small boys, and no small discomfiture of the offender, he is "poured into prison." This acts as a capital deterrent, and is taken very well. The offender is sometimes a little sulky at first, but generally forgives his rabbi in a most friendly manner after a little time. Sometimes the best way of punishing a wrongdoer is to hold him up to ridicule before the class. But the small boys do not approve of having the stick confined to them, and came and petitioned that at any rate all in the upper school who were not ordained, the unordained deacons, as they called them, might be beaten.[1]

There is a great rivalry over the marks, and the scholars are spurred on by them to great exertions. "Marks are sweeter than the stick," they truly say. Every week they change places, according to the marks they have earned the week before. And the total marks, with those of the examination, determine what boys shall be promoted to the upper school, and which senior students shall have schools.

All are most anxious to learn English. We were very much averse to teaching it, fearing that it would lead to begging in Europe, and at best that it would do no good, and merely take up time which should be devoted to oriental languages or other studies. But we were obliged to give in to the popular clamour. So now boys are allowed to learn English, if they are sufficiently proficient in other things; but Persian or Turkish is compulsory for all. These as being the "languages of the kingdom" (as they would say) are necessary for all. It is especially necessary for them to learn to read Persian or Turkish handwriting, which is far more difficult than the printed character, in order to decipher official documents.

Throughout, however, the greatest care is taken in the mission schools not to Westernize. The children live in a thoroughly oriental manner, and are taught to take a pride in their own national customs. They are not allowed in school to ape

[1] We may refer to an interesting paper on schools by Rev. A. H. Lang, in the mission quarterly paper, No 3.

European dress and manners; and their food and habits are kept studiously Eastern. No good can come from producing a hybrid imitation of western ways.

The boys are not good at outdoor games. They have a few, such as leapfrog, marbles (or rather "pebbles"), and a kind of draughts, played with stones on a board drawn with chalk on the pavement. Also, when they are given an entertainment, they play "sacks on the mill," and ingenious games of that sort, and various sorts of rounders; on the links near the sea they play hockey, which they call *hul-hul*. But they do not take to athletics at school of their own accord, until they are taught. They are much fonder of sitting in their class-rooms —which are also their dormitories, for Syrians sleep and live in the same rooms, rolling up their beds in the daytime—and writing out in a "beautiful pen" a copy of the Catechism, or a history, or a *shamashutha*, which is the deacon's part in the Liturgy. Writing is really with them a fine art; it takes a long time, but is often a beautiful sight when finished. The title-pages are often adorned with designs, for which they use different-coloured inks made by themselves. The black ink is a very sticky preparation made from gall-nuts, native sulphate of iron, etc., and most of the boys, especially those from the mountains, are very efficient at preparing it. European ink is not suitable for the thick writing, being too liquid. Reeds are used; for a "beautiful pen" cannot be produced by even the thickest of steel nibs. The boys sit on the floor with one knee up, against which they lean their paper. They do not want tables or chairs. They look upon their productions, when done, with justifiable pride. The Eastern Syriac character is quite different from the Syriac used in England and Europe generally, which is Western or Jacobite. It more closely resembles the old character, the Estrangêla, or Estrángelo as it is called in England, which is now only used for title-pages of books, etc. It does not correspond with our capitals, but rather with our black letter. All the three Syriac characters, "Estrangêla," "Nestorian," and "Jacobite," are cursive; the letters are all capable of being joined on to those which precede, though not all to those which follow. And this makes a difficulty in printing. In the Roman printed alphabet, no letter joins on to the preceding; but the Syriac printed character exactly resembles the written, and there have to be at least two types of each letter, one to join on, and one to stand alone. But besides this, the vowels are formed by dots below and above the letters, and this immensely multiplies the types which are necessary. A Syrian compositor has to have some five hundred types for his twenty-two letters. This adds very greatly to the labour of setting up type.

The first thing the Syrian boy has to be taught is order and method. This seems to be a thing an oriental cannot teach, and a constant supervision is necessary to see that the school routine works properly. The want of method is seen in Syriac books. For instance, they have no paragraphs. The use of red ink to a certain extent modifies this difficulty, the beginning of a new subject being usually marked in this way. But often subjects are mixed up in the books in a most distracting way. The daily services are a good example of this. There is no "Order of Morning and Evening Prayer." One takes a collect from the book called the *Takhsa*, some anthems from one part of the "Before and After," others from another part, the litanies and psalms from the psalter, and so forth; the order of the service is purely traditional, and is not written down.

It has been said that the Syrian boy is very docile. But he sometimes "flees" without a word to anybody. Perhaps he has a quarrel with one of his schoolfellows, and in a hot-headed way he runs off on the spur of the moment to his own village, or perhaps he has been punished for some fault and resents it. The first the missionaries hear of it is when his name is called over next morning and no answer is returned. "Where is So-and-so?" "Oh, he has fled, Rabbi!" More often than not he comes back again and asks for readmittance. Sometimes his father wishes him to leave school to go to work, or for some other reason; and then he will often simply "flee," not coming to say good-bye, or "ask forgiveness," as they call it, lest the missionary should disapprove. Another difficulty is that the scholars will flee to one of the schools of the other missions for some small reason such as the above; not because he wishes to change his religion, but in a fit of pique, or because he would have a better chance of getting a school to teach elsewhere, or for some such reason. The Syrians have a great idea of both eating their cake and having it. An Old Syrian, for instance, thinks he can go to a Roman Catholic or Presbyterian school, and get the advantages that are to be gained out of them, without himself becoming a Roman Catholic or Presbyterian. The only way of checking this going from one high school to another, is by having an understanding between the missionaries that such runaways will not be received. This readiness of the Syrian to turn his coat for a trifling advantage is, in our opinion, a decisive argument against the proselytizing method.

Sometimes when a quarrel has arisen the school is divided into two factions, each supporting one side. The boys, like their elders, are hot-headed partisans. One day a mild rebellion broke out in the Urmi upper school on account of a quarrel which was brought to the missionaries to judge. They gave their award, but this did not satisfy one of the disputants, who thereupon persuaded all his partisans, who were the majority, to "flee." One morning only a handful answered their names. "Where are the rest?" was the inquiry, which elicited no response until some one ventured the remark, "There is a rebellion, and they are not going to read any more!" However, as no notice whatever was taken of their absence, to their surprise—for they expected that a deputation would be sent to beg them to return—the runaways all came back before the day was over, rather shamefast. They were let off with a severe reprimand, and only the ringleader was punished.

In their lessons the deacons and boys are of a very inquiring turn of mind, and will sometimes take up the whole lesson, if they are allowed, in asking questions. Occasionally they lay traps for the missionaries, to see if their answers agree with one another, and after receiving a reply to some query they have propounded will say, "Yes, we receive that; Rabbi Mr. —— said the same thing the other day." They are rather fond of saying, "We cannot receive that;" but they do not mean any impertinence by it; they merely imply that they have not sufficiently grasped it. They will not take things on trust. It is a strange comment on the life they are accustomed to that they do not *expect* their teachers to tell them the truth; it is natural for them to think that a schoolmaster would use "economies." A class of boys was being taught by one of the missionaries a few elementary facts in astronomy, as that the earth is round, and the like; and all replied glibly enough, "Yes, Rabbi," till at last one small mountaineer allowed his incredulity to get the better of his respect, and said, "Are we really to believe all *that?*" It need not be said that one of the first things to teach is truth; they have also to learn to be honourable, not to look over their neighbour's slate and so on, but to cultivate a public opinion which will look down on, and not up to, a boy who successfully lies and cheats.

The scholars do not have many holidays during the session—a few days at Christmas and Easter, and at the Carnival, which they call "Across the fast," and on the principal holy days, and a day at mid-lent; but, on the other hand, they have a "long vacation" of three months and a half in the summer, when it is too hot to read or teach. Before the long vacation, at the end of May, there is a breaking-up day both for boys and girls, when the scholars are allowed to invite any of their own friends to an entertainment and *tamasha* or "spectacle" as they call it when they try to speak English. A conjurer or an acrobat is provided, who provokes roars of laughter from an appreciative audience in whose lives there is not much fun. Afterwards all sit down to dinner in relays.

The mission girls' school at Urmi is conducted

GIRLS IN THE SCHOOL OF THE SISTERS OF BETHANY.
From the authors' photograph.

by the Sisters of Bethany. Naturally, the scholars cannot go home weekly, like the boys, and they live almost all their time in the school. A priest teaches them classical Syriac and some of the other lessons, and the Sisters and others the rest. The girls learn Holy Scripture, catechism, geography, classical Syriac, dictation, writing, arithmetic, and a few a little English. But they are especially taught to be good housewives—to knit and sew, keep house, be clean and neat, mend clothes, and wash. Saturday is given up entirely to teaching these things, though they are not confined to that day. The girls themselves are very anxious to learn all that the boys learn—Persian, Turkish, and so on; but it is far more useful to train them to be good wives. They, of course, know all that goes on in the boys' school, and are very jealous if they do not have the same holidays; and they even complained one day that the boys were having an examination and they were not! It must be said that when they are examined they show remarkable quickness. They are more backward than the boys, because a girl's education is considered much less important than that of her brothers; but, on the other hand, they are more intelligent and quicker at picking up things. They are very docile and give but little trouble. As the Sisters' courtyard adjoins the churchyard of Mart Mariam, the girls all go daily to morning and evening prayers at the old church. It is thus not necessary to have a large chapel in which they can have their daily offices. On Sunday afternoons they also go to Mart Mariam for catechising and sermon.

It is curious that they naturally, and until taught otherwise, sew in the opposite way to ourselves. They usually use the right hand, but by no means always, and they turn their work away from them, beginning at what we should call the wrong end; sewing seems to depend on reading and writing in this respect. M. Huc mentions that the Chinese impel the needle perpendicularly down and up, the

Tartars up and down, while Europeans impel it from right to left ("Travels in Tartary, etc.," vol. i. chap. iii.). So the Syrians impel it from left to right. In arithmetic also, in adding up columns of figures, they will often begin at the wrong side; and a priest who professed to teach this science was found making his scholars add up the lefthand column first!

A few of the upper girls return to their villages in the winter to teach the little girls. They then return to school in the spring. But this is only in the larger villages, where funds will allow of the schools being held.

The mountains are not nearly so well provided for in the way of education as the Persian plains. This is chiefly due to the hostility of the Turkish authorities, who will always close a school if they can get hold of it. A deacon's school, which was held at Qudshanis one winter, had to be stopped because of the continual annoyances given by the officials to Mar Shimun in consequence of it. But there are a good number of village schools, especially in the Ashiret country, and there is also a small high school, where picked boys are boarded and educated, those being selected who are likely to be ordained; and it is hoped that more may be accomplished before long.

It is not difficult to educate the Syrians; the question is, What is to be done with them when they are educated? Some can become priests, some schoolmasters; a few can be employed by the missionaries, as printers, binders, etc. But, in the absence of trades, it is not easy to know what to do with the rest. There are three ways out of this difficulty: (1) Some say, Do not educate them, but let them go on in their ignorance, tilling the ground and getting what they can out of it. But one cannot allow them to continue in their dead-alive oppressed condition, either from a spiritual or from a temporal point of view. There is, however, thus much truth in this opinion: the Syrians should not be so much over-educated as to be ashamed of their own country and life, and ape Europeans. (2) Others say, Let them emigrate. This means, let them go to Tiflis or to Europe to work or beg. The evils of this course have already been pointed out. (3) A third remedy is to promote trades in their own country. This seems to be the best course, and that which the Syrians most wish. But it is not an easy thing to do, and must be accomplished gradually.[1]

In order to equip the schools, it is necessary to provide school books. These have to be specially printed, in the East Syriac type; and indeed specially written. Syriac has such a poor vocabulary that it is almost impossible to take a book in a European language and translate it directly. School books have to be written specially with a view to the Syriac language, and to Syriac methods of thought. For this reason the printing press is necessary in an educational establishment. The Syrian youths show great quickness at picking up the printer's work, difficult as it is as compared with that of printers of European languages. Even to them, English, though a foreign language, is

[1] See above, page 137.

decidedly easier to set up than their own Syriac. Yet, in a few months, with the help of the missionaries (who knew nothing about the art), and of an English book on practical printing, they managed to learn their trade sufficiently to print passably in red and black. Binding also has to form part of the educational establishment, for all the books printed have to be strongly bound to stand somewhat rough usage. In this the mountaineers could give good lessons, for they bind excellently in wooden boards all the manuscripts they write. But this method of binding is too expensive for schoolbooks. The wooden boards, which are often half an inch to an inch thick, are sometimes, but not always, covered with leather.[1]

[1] Besides the educational system described in this chapter, the French Roman Catholic and American Presbyterian Missions have both boys' and girls' schools, on a large scale, together with hospitals, printing presses, etc. The writers wish especially here to call attention to the beautifully printed books lately brought out by the Lazarist Mission, such as the Chronicle of Bar Hebraeus (published at the Lazarist house in Paris, and printed at Leipsig).

CHAPTER IX.

THE EAST SYRIAN CLERGY.

The three orders and nine divisions—Comparison with the ranks of the angels—All the offices filled by our Lord—The present head of the Church of the East—His style—The succession to the Patriarchate and to the bishoprics—The old method—Mar Shimun's authority—The other Patriarchates—Independence of Seleucia—The metropolitan—The old provinces and missions of the Syrians—The bishops—Old method of election—A bishop's functions—Swearing a kind of ordeal—Fees and first-fruits—Ordinations—The parish priest—His functions and position—Dress of the clergy—The old tonsure—Election of a parish priest—Begging in Europe—The five-legged ass—Deacons—Their duties—Minor offices—Monasteries.

THE Syrians divide their hierarchical system according to the ranks of the angels; they reckon three orders, the episcopate, presbyterate, and diaconate; but each order has three divisions. Thus the diaconate consists of readers, whose duty it is to read the lections from the Old Testament and the Acts of the Apostles; sub-deacons, called by the Syriacized Greek name *hiupatiáqni*, who keep the church and watch the doors and light the candles; and deacons, *shamashi* or *mshamsháni*, who say the Litany or Bidding Prayer (the Syriac *karuzútha* is a combination of the two), and certain exhortations in the Liturgy and other services. But the first two of these subdivisions are now obsolete. Similarly the presbyterate consists of simple presbyters, "whose duty," says the Sunhadus (book vi. § 1), "is to make the Offering" (Eucharist); of chorepiscopi or *periadúti* (both so called in Syriac), who visited the villages and monasteries in old times as representatives of the bishop of the diocese; and of archdeacons, *arkidiagóni*, whose name, as understood by the Syrians, means "head of the service," and who are therefore placed as overseers of the bishop's church—as it were deans of cathedrals. The office of chorepiscopus remains no longer; and even when the Sunhadus was put in its present form, probably in the thirteenth century, it no longer existed, though its functions were performed by periaduti, who had formerly been deputies of the chorepiscopi. The episcopate also is divided (in this case both by the books and in practice), into three subdivisions; of simple or diocesan bishops, who "ordain all readers, subdeacons, deacons and presbyters, give a blessing to a periaduta, and say a prayer over archdeacons;" metropolitans, "who ordain their suffragans"—though in practice all bishops are "ordained" by the patriarch; and patriarchs "who ordain metropolitans and confirm bishops" (Sunhadus, book vi. § 1). These distinctions are important, as showing which of these divisions were and which were not ordained. There were no ordinations for the archidiaconate, which is little more than a title of honour given to an influential parish priest, and for the office of chorepiscopi. These offices always were held by priests among the Eastern Syrians.[1] The holders are mere priests who have certain functions superadded. But all the three kinds of bishops are ordained or consecrated (there is only one word for these two expressions in Syriac), and there is a separate form of ordination for each in the Ordinal. For, translation being in all ordinary cases forbidden, any one appointed patriarch, metropolitan, or simple bishop has no higher rank than that of a priest, and needs consecration. The canons refer to St. Gregory of Nazianzum's refusal to become Bishop of Constantinople because he had already been raised to the episcopate, and to some other cases, in refusing to allow translation; but they add that if he has been violently expelled against his own will from a see, he may be translated to another, even to a metropolitanate (viii. § 14). It is doubtful what would be done as to ordination in that case. Probably only the prayers of the Ordinal proper to a metropolitan would be said. The canons give no clue.

There is a slightly different reckoning in the "Book of Heavenly Intelligences and of the Church in Heaven and on Earth," erroneously attributed to Mar Shimun Barseba'i, and included in the Ashitha Sunhadus.[2] In this the chorepiscopi rank above the archdeacons, and the latter are included among the visitors, *sa'uri*. The chorepiscopus has a blessing

---

[1] Smith, Dictionary Chr. Ant. s.v. "Chorepiscopus."

[2] The reputed author lived at the time of Nicæa (Assemanni Bibl. Or., vol. iii. part i.); the book refers to the council of Chalcedon and to the Jacobites, and has many similar anachronisms.

said over him "not like an ordination," but the archdeacon and visitor are said to have been ordained in old times, though not at the time the book was written. The scheme of the hierarchy is given as follows:—

    I. *a.* Catholici or Patriarchs = Cherubim.
       b. Metropolitans = Seraphim.
       c. Bishops = Thrones.
   II. *a.* Chorepiscopi = Dominions.
       b. Visitors = Virtues.
       c. Priests = Powers.
  III. *a.* Deacons = Principalities.
       b. Subdeacons = Archangels.
       c. Readers = Angels.

It is interesting to notice that the Syrians claim that our Lord himself served these nine divisions of the three orders; he was a reader when he read in the synagogue at Nazareth (St. Luke iv. 17); subdeacon, when he "cast out all them that sold and bought in the temple" (St. Matt. xxi. 12); deacon, when preaching[1] "Repent: for the kingdom of heaven is at hand" (St. Matt. iv. 17), and in washing the feet of the disciples (St. John xiii. 5); priest, when baptizing in Enon near to Salim (St. John iii. 23, *sic*), and when celebrating the Eucharist; periaduta in visiting the villages and towns, healing the sick and casting out devils, and also in sending out the Twelve and the Seventy; archdeacon, in arranging the manner of their service (St. Luke ix. 2, x. 1); bishop, when ordaining the

---

[1] The Syriac word for preaching is the same as that for saying the Litany—Bidding Prayer, which is the deacon's special function.

apostles (St. John xx. 22); metropolitan at the same time, and when giving them the commission to baptize (St. Matt. xxviii. 19), also when bidding St. Peter to strengthen his brethren (St. Luke xxii. 32); and patriarch when giving the promise to St. Peter (St. Matt. xvi. 18, 19), and when bidding him "Feed My sheep" (St. John xxi. 15-18). The Sunhadus adds that no bishop may officiate, even though ordained, until confirmed by the patriarch, for the apostles did not go forth until confirmed by the Holy Ghost at Pentecost (Sunhadus, book vi. § 1, and "Heavenly Intelligences," *passim*).

All these divisions of the three orders are included in the one term "priesthood," *kahnutha;* and thus a deacon, though not a *kahna*, is a member of the *kahnutha*. St. Ephrem, the Syrian, was only a deacon, yet he speaks of himself as belonging to the "priesthood." This has misled the translator of St. Ephrem in the "Library of the Fathers."

At the present day the head of the "Church of the East" bears the dynastic name of Mar Shimun (literally, my Lord Simon). His baptismal name is Ruil (Reuben), and he heads his letters with "Ruil Shimun." His successor, when he comes to the patriarchal throne, will also be called Mar Shimun, the full title being, "The Reverend and Honoured Father of Fathers and Great Shepherd, Mar Shimun, Patriarch Catholicos of the East." But a prescribed form of letter in the Ashitha Sunhadus gives a far longer form of address: "The Father of Fathers, Chief Shepherd, Head of Overseers, Absolved and Absolver of the absolved, Holy, who anointest high priests and priests for consecrating, Earthly Angel, and Bodily Seraph, the Peter of our times, the Paul of our age, the Timothy of our days, chosen among apostles, and sought out among fathers, bestower of benefactions, overflowing with absolutions, our Lord and our Father, Mar N. Catholicos, Patriarch of the East," etc. All of which is religiously copied down by those who write him a letter, and the gist of what they want to say has in consequence to be relegated to a postscript.

The succession is, in practice, managed thus. There are always in the family several youths who have never eaten meat or married, and whose mothers did not eat meat during their pregnancy. One of these *nziri*, as they are called (Nazarites), is chosen, either during the lifetime or at the death of the patriarch, to be his successor. The disappointed candidates then sometimes eat meat and marry, and so are disabled from holding the episcopal office. A similar arrangement holds for a bishop's successors. No bishop or his successor may eat meat or marry; that is to say, they are *monks* in Syrian language. This was not always the case. In the thirteenth century the bishops were "generally chosen from the monks" (Sunhadus, vii., Preface); but the canons say that the people "are not to look among the rich men for a bishop, but are to choose any fit person, whether a stranger or not. If a monk is elected, great care must be taken to see that he is orthodox" (viii. §§ 2, 4).

This approach to an hereditary episcopate seems to be an arrangement of the last three or four hundred years; and it will probably be considered an abuse. It is certainly in opposition to the canons, which provide that "no bishop may nominate his successor" (viii. § 4). But it may perhaps be doubted whether a better arrangement could be found in the present condition of the people. Anything like a popular election, in an oppressed nation who have never learnt to exercise any sort of franchise, would lead to many scandals. And the present system has the advantage of raising up an aristocracy in its best sense, which would otherwise be entirely lacking. In any case such is the present arrangement, and the people are much attached to it, nor would they readily brook a change. It was the custom of their fathers for each bishop to have one or more nephews or cousins as his Nazarites or Natar kursii (holders of the seat),[1] and to bring them up as his successors, and it is a very good custom too.

In the case of the patriarchate it seems that formerly, when it was necessary to choose a successor, the two great independent tribes of Tiari and Tkhuma agreed together and selected one of the Nazarites of the patriarchal family, and this has constantly led to disputes. The far East has been no exception to the rule that popular election to the episcopate is ever the cause of strife.

When the successor is elected or chosen, he is consecrated by the metropolitan. This is a relic of the old procedure, which is the only one known to the canons. When the patriarchs lived at Seleucia-Ctesiphon on the Southern Tigris, it was the custom

---

[1] This is the barbarous modern plural of *natar kursi*. It should be *natrai kursi* (or, as in classical Syriac, *kursia*).

for the Bishop of Kashkar, one of the bishops of the patriarchal province, or if he was dead the Bishop of Zabi, to write and summon the four metropolitans who came first in precedence; though, according to some, two others were associated with them. These then attended, each accompanied by three bishops, and with the consent of the people of the patriarchal cities, Seleucia and Ctesiphon, elected, ordained, and enthroned a fit person in the great church of Kukhi. At least three metropolitans were obliged to attend, but in time of persecution two sufficed, with the bishops of the patriarchal province; the metropolitan of Elam, or Elymais, in South-West Persia, presided (Sunhadus ix. §§ 2-4; "Heavenly Intelligences," s.v. "Patriarchs"). All these rules and names are now but a memory. There is only one metropolitan, and it is never, alas! anything but a "time of persecution."

Mar Shimun exercises temporal as well as spiritual jurisdiction, especially over the tribal or independent Syrians of Tiari, Tkhuma, Jilu, Bas, Diz, and the other valleys of Central Kurdistan. His temporal jurisdiction is to a great extent recognized by the Turkish authority, who are sufficiently politic to make him an annual subsidy. They have often no means of getting at his people except through him, and at his pleasure.

He is looked upon as the source of all gifts to the church; he holds all orders and offices, and dispenses them as seems good to him. His name, Catholicos, is interpreted to mean "holder of all," because he has all the divisions of the priesthood and all jurisdiction. Metropolitans and bishops may not undo what he has decided; "he has authority over all, as the brain and skull over the limbs, to bind and loose in heaven and earth, and he holds the keys of the height and the depth" ("Book of Heavenly Intelligences," s.v. "Patriarchs"). The same authority says that no one may judge him—Christ is his judge; and so also the Sunhadus says in one place (ix. § 5). In the same section it enacts that "his brother patriarchs are to judge him;" but this refers to a united Christendom; and in another place the penalty of degradation is assigned to a patriarch for certain offences (ix. § 5; viii. § 20); so that there seems to be some confusion on the subject.

The Syrians reckon five patriarchates: those of Rome (the first); Alexandria; Ephesus, afterwards moved to Constantinople; Antioch; Seleucia (their own). They do not reckon Jerusalem, but say it is to have special honour, and is not subject to Cæsarea. Perhaps the reference is to the seventh Nicene Canon. They recognize that Seleucia was once dependent on Antioch, and that its metropolitans went there to be consecrated; but a change was made for the reasons given in the following summary of a letter purporting to have been sent by the four "Western Patriarchs" to the "Church of the East":—"Formerly Seleucia was the first metropolitanate, and its metropolitan ordained bishops in all the East—Assyria, Media, Persia—and was their ruler. But now, in consequence of recent troubles, when two patriarchs (*sic*) from the East were crucified on the doors of the church of Antioch by the Jews and Manicheans, we grant it independence;

its holder is to be a patriarch, and may make metropolitans as he wills, with the consent of two bishops present with him; the number three must not be diminished.... On the death of the patriarch, let the metropolitans and bishops assemble, as many as possible, and ordain the patriarch, and they are our ministers, we acting by them. All ecclesiastical jurisdiction is given him, and all bishops ordained by metropolitans must be confirmed by him, and receive a letter from him before they ordain or do any episcopal act. If there is an accusation against him, the matter must be examined by the other patriarchs, and not by his disciples ; and if it is a time of peace, Persia will execute our decrees." This letter purports to have been brought by Aghbata, Bishop of Bith Lapat or Elam (S.W. Persia); and he therefore was made first metropolitan, and had precedence in the patriarchal election, and ordained the patriarch. The date given is, "forty years after the martyrdom of St. Peter and St. Paul, 280 years before Nicæa" (Sunhadus, ix. § 5). Chronology is not the strong point of the Sunhadus. On this letter Dr. Neale remarks that it is a "palpable forgery" (Notes in Badger's "Nestorians and their Rituals," vol. i.). The lateness of its composition is seen from the fact that the canons assigning deposition to a patriarch who does wrong could not have been made in the face of it, and some of them date from the ninth century; whereas this letter might have been forged after that date in the interest of a patriarch who wished to avoid trial.

The patriarch is the judge both of metropolitans and bishops; metropolitans seem never to have had any coercive power over their suffragans. "If the metropolitan can settle a dispute or accusation against a bishop amicably, well; if not, it is the duty of the Catholicos to decide it. A metropolitan may not govern his brother bishops by force, only by persuasion" (Sunhadus, viii. § 17). But, apparently, even the Catholicos can only act in synod. "A patriarch may not suspend any bishop or metropolitan without the consent of the three metropolitans of Elam, Nisibis, and Prath Maishan (Busra); if one of these is dead, then of the metropolitan of Assyria ("Book of Heavenly Intelligences," *s.v.* "Bishop"). For this reason metropolitans met at the patriarchal city, first yearly, but later, once every four years, to hear all complaints; but the very distant metropolitans merely sent letters of assent once every six years (Sunhadus, viii. § 19). And anathemas might only be pronounced by councils (§ 22). A *provincial* synod could not depose a bishop except by leave of the patriarch (§ 22); these met twice yearly at the metropolitan's, and were only for minor matters (§ 11, and "Heavenly Intelligences," *s.v.* "Metropolitans"). And a metropolitan might not ordain in the diocese of one of his suffragans (Sunhadus, viii. § 17). The patriarch only is the judge of all, and may ordain where he pleases, for he is the "universal father" (*id.* and vi. § 6 Canon 8).

Excommunication by the patriarch is still a very serious punishment; and, especially in the mountains, no one will speak to those who are under Mar Shimun's ban. It can, however, always be revoked " inasmuch as it is a command to the offender to repent." Deposition, on the other hand, " makes a man as dead, and is only given to the clergy. If a clerk deposed repents, he does not get his degree back" (viii. § 22).

Among those who obey the rule of Mar Shimun there is only one metropolitan, usually called *Matran* for short, whose dynastic name is Mar

THE METROPOLITAN, MAR KHNANISHU, AND PRIESTS.
From a photograph by the Rev. Y. M. Neesan.

Khnanishu, that is, My Lord Mercy-of-Jesus. His baptismal name is Isaak, and he signs himself, Isaak Khnanishu. He is the second in rank in the church. There are now no provinces, as there were in ancient times, and Mar Khnanishu does not exercise even the somewhat limited metropolitical authority recognized by the canons. He has two bishops in his neighbourhood who are, more or less, dependent on him, and who may perhaps be called his suffragans; but his known integrity procures for him a respect and influence far beyond his immediate neighbourhood. It is his office to ordain the patriarch, and he may also ordain bishops; but in practice this is generally done by the patriarch himself.

Metropolitans were, according to the Syrians, appointed by St. Paul in the "mother cities," bishops in the small cities (Sunhadus, viii. § 19, canon 2). At first Seleucia was only a metropolitanate; but when it became a patriarchate the following provinces were made, and were given precedence in order of creation: (1) Elam or Elymais, (S.W. Persia); (2) Nisibis; (3) Prath of Maishan or the lower Euphrates (Busra); (4) Assyria, or the district of Mosul and Arbela. These four were said to have been made before the Council of Nicæa. (5) Bith Garmai or the Gramqayi, of which Bith Sluk or Shahrgard was the see town (said to be "Inner Assyria"); (6) Pâris (Fars, Southern Persia); (7) Merv; (8) Khulwan (or Khalakh?); (9) Hariu (Herat?); (10) Hindustan; (11) China; (12) Samarcand; (13) Armenia; (14) Sham or Damascus. There were also four others which came to nothing (Sunhadus, viii. § 15; "Heavenly Intelligences," *s.v.* "Patriarchs." The latter omits Hindustan, China, Armenia). The number and remoteness of the metropolitan sees testifies to the missionary zeal of the forefathers of the Eastern Syrians at a time when "their numbers, with those of the Jacobites, were computed to surpass the Greek and Latin communions" (Gibbon, ch.

xlvii). Indeed, there were at one time twenty-five metropolitans, and it is now scarcely doubted that the early missions of this faith spread to China, where the famous monument of Siganfu "describes the fortunes of the Nestorian Church from the first mission A.D. 636 to the current year 781." The latter year was in the time of the Catholicos Khnanishu ("Anan-jesu"), and the monument was raised by Yezdbuzd, priest and chorepiscopus of Chumdan, the capital of the Chinese Empire.[1] Of these metropolitans, the bishop of Paris or Fars had special ritual privileges, and might wear his *biruna* (mitre or episcopal headdress), and carry his staff till the end of the Liturgy, like the patriarch, both on the bema and in the sanctuary ("Heavenly Intelligences," s.v. "Metropolitans").

There are now, besides the patriarch and metropolitan, three bishops in Persia, seven in Turkey; but several of these have only nominal dioceses. The patriarchal diocese, on the other hand, is enormous, far too large to be properly supervised by one man, considering the mountainous nature of the country. It includes most of the tribal Syrians. The non-tribal dioceses appear to be divided very unscientifically, and to be subject to frequent change. In the plain of Urmi there have been at various times several bishops, but either at their death there was no *natar kursi*, or some other reason prevented the succession being kept up, and the different dioceses have been consolidated into two. On such an occasion the vacant see falls to the patriarch to do as he pleases with. The hierarchy now is as follows:—

---

[1] See Dean Milman's note to Gibbon, ch. xlvii.

1. Mar Shimun (Simon. Baptismal name Ruil or Reuben), Patriarch and Catholicos of the East, who resides at Qudshanis (Kochanis). Diocese: Qudshanis (itself in the non-tribal country, but reckoned Ashiret or Independent), Tiari, Tkhuma, Diz, Walto, Tal, Mar Bishu, etc., and the non-tribal districts of Albeg, Sŭra, and others.

2. Mar Khnanishu (= Mercy of Jesus. Baptismal name Iskhaq or Isaak), Metropolitan or Matran. Diocese: Shamsdin, in Turkey; Tergawar, and Mergawar, two upland plains in Persia, near the Turkish frontier.

3. Mar Auraham (Abraham). Patriarch designate, first cousin to Mar Shimun. Diocese: Upper Berwer, near Qudshanis (non-tribal).

4. Mar Sergis (Sergius). Diocese: Jilu and Bas, two tribal districts in Turkey.

5. Mar Ishuyaw (= Jesus gave) of Duri. Diocese: Lower Berwer, south of Tiari (Turkey: non-tribal).

6. Mar Yonan (Jonah). Diocese: Village of Ukri on the Zab, in Lower Berwer.

7. Mar Sliwa (= Cross. Baptismal name Shlimun or Solomon). Diocese: Part of the plain of Gawar, in Turkey, near the Persian frontier (non-tribal).

8. Mar Saurishu (= Hope of Jesus). Diocese: A few upland villages in Persia, near Urmi, and in the plain of Gawar, in Turkey.

9. Mar Dinkha (= Sun-rising). Diocese: The village of Tis in Shamsdin (Turkey), taken from the Matran's diocese.

10. Mar Yukhanan (John). Diocese: Village of Tulaki, district of Tergawar, Persia (taken from the Matran's diocese).

11. Mar Gauriel (Gabriel. Baptismal name Yaqu or James). Diocese: The country watered by the Barandus and Urmi city rivers, in the plain of Urmi (Persia), and district of Solduz, south of the Sea of Urmi. See village, Ardishai; residence, city of Urmi.

12. Mar Yonan (Jonah). Diocese: The district

MAR GAURIEL, BISHOP OF ARDISHAI AND URMI, AND TWO NAZARITES.
From the authors' photograph.

watered by the Nazlu river (north part of the Urmi plain), the plains of Gavilan and Salmas. But there are very few old Syrians in the last. Residence: Superghan (or Sipúrghan), on the Sea of Urmi.

There are one or two other bishops still alive who have been consecrated by Mar Shimun, but they do not now hold dioceses under his jurisdiction. The dioceses in the plain of Urmi, follow the rivers which run down from the mountains of Kurdistan to the Sea of Urmi, and a man will describe himself as belonging to "such and such a river."

The present method of filling up bishoprics has been explained. The old method was very different. On the death of a bishop, the metropolitan collected the bishops of the province, and went to the city and called together the congregation; the whole assembly then elected any proper person, though the choice generally fell on a monk. The metropolitan and bishops then ordained the elect, all laying their right hand upon him,[1] and the metropolitan saying the service of ordination. They then sent the new bishop with a letter to the patriarch for confirmation. Several bishops were to be summoned, at least three; and if there were no bishops in the province, the metropolitan might summon those of other provinces. Special provisions were made against the election of an unwilling person, or of any one who had been condemned for any offence, against the nomination by a bishop of his successor, and for the deposition of any bishop who obtained his office through simony. When the bishop was ordained, the metropolitan sent his chorepiscopus to enthrone him in his see; no one in the bishop's jurisdiction might do this. According to some authorities, the see town must consent to whomsoever the metropolitan wishes; according to others, the metropolitan must ordain whomsoever the see town elects (Sunhadus, viii. §§ 1-9; "Heavenly Intelligences," *s.v.* "Bishops.") The precedence of

---

[1] See below, page 200.

the bishops was not according to the date of their ordination, but according to the foundation of their sees; and the precedence of provinces was similar. All the bishops of an older province took precedence of those of a newer province ("Heavenly Intelligences," *ubi supra*).

A bishop is called in the books, and in letters, *Episqópa;* but popularly *abúna, i.e.* our father. In the plain of Mosul, this latter name is also given to superior priests. In Urmî a bishop is addressed as *Mámu, i.e.* little uncle; in the mountains either as "my father" or "my beloved," (this is rather more familiar), or "my revered one."

The functions of an East Syrian bishop differ considerably from those of the Western episcopate. As he has not to administer confirmation, he has a great part of the work of our bishops taken off his hands. Confirmation is administered by the priest, directly after baptism. But, on the other hand, the oriental bishop has many peculiar functions of his own. A great part of his time is taken up in settling disputes, reconciling enemies, hearing divorce and often, especially in the mountains, other legal cases. One curious function they occasionally have to perform is that of swearing a man. Oaths never seem to have been exacted from all witnesses, but to have been looked on as a sort of ordeal; they are of rare occurrence, and are looked upon as a great solemnity. They are not administered by a lawyer as a matter of form, but by the bishop with much admonition and exhortation. Sometimes, when a Mussulman governor in Urmi is in doubt about a case, or is indifferent (having been equally bribed by both sides), he will send one of the disputants to the bishop to be sworn. The bishop takes him to the church, and after some prayers swears the man on the Gospels, and gives a certificate to that effect. An oath thus taken is considered most sacred by both Christians and Mussulmans. Generally, when there are two disputants, and the burden of proof lies with one, the other has the choice, according to the Sunhadus, whether he himself will go through the ordeal of an oath, or whether he will make his adversary swear (book iv. § 17).

Each bishop used to be obliged to summon his diocesan council twice a year, through his chorepiscopus; the inhabitants of all the villages came to do him reverence, and join with him in the Sacrament. Monks ordinarily came once a year (Sunhadus, viii. § 10). The only remnant of this custom is in the habit of the villagers of coming at Christmas and Easter to "bless the bishop's feast."

It is hardly to be expected that a poor people like the Syrians would give any large amount for the support of their clergy; and even the bishops are often very poor. Most of them have a few fields or vineyards, which their brothers and nephews, or even in some cases they themselves, cultivate. Most of the income of the bishops comes, however, from the *rishitha* or first-fruits, which the villagers voluntarily pay every year. Once in three years all villages are supposed to give offerings to the patriarch, and one of his family makes a tour in the various districts for this purpose. In this way the whole of the patriarchal household is maintained. The sums given to the parish priests by the villagers are miserably small; often the priest gets nothing at all but the fee he receives in connexion with marriages and baptisms.[1] For this reason ordination is considered no bar to secular work, and most of the village clergy substantially make their living by a trade, or in some other way.

The bishop's chief function is to ordain priests and deacons; the minor orders of subdeacons and readers having become obsolete, they ordain youths to the diaconate at once. Formerly, says the book ascribed to Mar Shimun Barseba'i, chorepiscopi might ordain readers and subdeacons, but not priests or deacons; this, however, was stopped by the "Synod of the Chalcedonians." We may note the anachronism in a book purporting to be of the fourth century! There is no canon of Chalcedon to this effect. In all ordinations, whether of bishops, priests, and deacons, only the right hand is laid on the head of the ordained; this is expressly laid down in the Ordinal, and is several times referred to in old Syrian books (*e.g.* Sunhadus, viii. § 1). Perhaps this is to be explained by the fact that they understand the "right hands of fellowship" (Gal. ii. 9) to refer to ordination. The ordination takes place at the sanctuary door, the bishop first cutting off locks of the ordinand's hair in the form of a cross. No ordination may take place in an unconsecrated place; but in the days when there were deaconesses, they were ordained in the baptistery or "house of the deacon," which is on the south side of the sanctuary and is connected with it by a door (Sunhadus,

---

[1] The Sunhadus forbids compulsory baptismal fees, vi. § 6, Canon 7.

vi. § 4). Priests and deacons are gradually led up before the altar by the bishop, who says a prayer at each step. They prostrate themselves a great many times before the altar, and are kissed on the cheek by the bishop, they meanwhile kissing his hand. The priests do not join with the bishop in the laying on of hands. This is a Western custom. After the service, all the friends of the ordained persons kiss them and say, "May your ordination be blessed." This is a very ancient, and once universal practice.[1] In the plain of Urmi a feast generally follows the ordination.

The present canonical age for ordination is very much lower than with us. The Sunhadus says: "Readers may not be ordained till past boyhood, however learned; subdeacons when nearly grown up, deacons a little later, priests about eighteen. But, according to the ancient rule, not before thirty" (vi. § 4, Canon 2). With this last rule the "Book of Heavenly Intelligences" (*s.v.* "Priests") agrees. In practice priests are seldom ordained quite so young as eighteen, but the usual age for deacons is seventeen. Sometimes, also, bishops are ordained quite as youths or even children, when their predecessors die and there is no other *natar kursi;* and it is not at all unknown for deacons to be ordained when only ten years old.

Although the parish priest receives but a small stipend, he is a person of great position in the village; indeed, he is generally the chief man, and receives considerable honour; his parishioners kiss

---

[1] It is mentioned in the "Apostolic Constitutions" (viii. 5). Smith and Cheetham, D.C.A., *s.v.* "Kiss."

his hand, he is called respectfully "Rabbi" or "Rabbi Qasha,"[1] and he is placed in the chief seat at feasts. His duties are many. He "consecrates baptism and offers the Offering [Eucharist], reads the Gospel on the bema [a raised platform outside the sanctuary wall], betroths a woman, buries the dead, absolves transgressors, and performs all the necessary parts of the priest's office except consecrating an altar with oil, reconciles transgressors, absolves sinners with penitence, and binds and looses because he has received the priesthood. He lays his hand on the sick that they may recover" ("Heavenly Intelligences," *s.v.* "Priests"). He has to settle minor disputes, in concert with his "white beards" who, it may be remarked, exercise a considerable influence over the priest's actions, for they are not at all "priest-ridden." But all graver cases have to be referred to the bishop, both in practice and by law. The priest may not excommunicate when the bishop is near ("Heavenly Intelligences," *s.v.* "Priests").

The priest is almost always ordained in the village where he has been brought up, and indeed he remains all his life in the same village. Strictly speaking, when a man has once been ordained to a cure he may not leave it to go elsewhere, nor on the other hand may the bishop substitute any one else for him, except for some offence after trial. In that case the displaced priest may not seek a place elsewhere. But if it is not for gain that a priest wishes

---

[1] Qasha = Priest. It is a corruption of the older name Qashisha (= elder, or presbyter). In the books the name *kahna* (sacerdos) is also used.

to leave his parish and to go elsewhere, a bishop or visitor may give him leave (Sunhadus, vi. § 5; "Heavenly Intelligences," *s.v.* "Priests"). The priest thus has fixity of tenure, and as a matter of fact a bishop finds it very difficult to displace him; but he may not seek promotion to get a larger stipend. Parish priests are very often sons of priests; the priesthood of the village thus frequently going in the same family from generation to generation. There is no restriction on their marriage. The celibacy of the clergy was abolished A.D. 499 by a synod at Seleucia, under the Catholicos Babæus, when even Catholici were permitted to marry.[1] The Sunhadus implicitly allows clerical marriage by saying that monks may not marry like the rest of the clerks and laymen (vii. § 2, Canon 5). Dr. Badger (vol. ii. p. 180) quotes two canons which explicitly allow the marriage of a bishop; but these passages do not occur in the copies seen by the present writers. In practice there is hardly such a thing as an unmarried priest; they could probably be counted on the fingers of one hand. And the clergy are allowed to marry after ordination. In the marriage service there are special anthems to be sung when the bridegroom is a priest. Nor is there any prohibition against re-marriage.

Priests do not now wear a special dress in everyday life, though in the mountains a black turban is often or generally affected. It looks rather surprising to a Western to see a venerable ecclesiastic with a flowing white beard, vested in a short schoolboy's jacket, as one does in all parts of the moun-

[1] Smith and Wace, D.C.B., *s.v.* "Nestorianism."

tains. In the plain of Urmi, the priests dress in the coloured garments and Astrakhan hats of laymen, but the bishops wear turbans and flowing robes, and look quite ecclesiastical. The canons say that all clerks are to differ from laymen in dress and in tonsure, and in girding the loins; they are not to wear rings or carry knives in their belts (vi. § 6, Canon 1). One priest (Qasha Daniel), in the village of Zawitha in Tiari, has the hereditary privilege of wearing a hanjar because his is one of the families of watchers (probably against the Kurds of Berwer, a neighbouring district). Perhaps this dates from the days of the rule of the Kurdish Miras, before the great massacre by Bedr Khan Beg of the tribal Christians, in 1843.

The tonsure referred to in the canon quoted above is not that known as St. Paul's, which was the Greek form, and was total;[1] but only the middle of the head was shaved by the Eastern Syrians. The author of the "Heavenly Intelligences" says that they adopted this form to distinguish themselves from the Jacobites. "Some say that when the Apostles preached, the Jews caught them and shaved the middle of their heads [as a disgrace]. We are like Simon, who shaved the middle of his head, and the Jacobites are like Paul who shaved the whole of his head" (*s.v.* "Tonsure"). Here, the tonsure is only ascribed to monks, together with "black dress," but the Sunhadus orders it for all clerks; nothing, however, is said of black dress for them. These rules are now a dead letter.[2]

[1] Smith and Cheetham, "Dict. Chr. Ant.," *s.v.* "Tonsure."
[2] See above, page 97.

The old law of Constantine that the clergy were to be free from taxes, which caused so many to seek minor orders unworthily, still survives in the arrangement by the Persian government that no parish priest need pay the poll-tax which is exacted from Christians in lieu of compulsory military service. Although this only involves the saving of some 3s. a year, it is a much-cherished privilege, and is often the cause of complaints to the government, when a village master or his servant exacts the tax in spite of the law.

The procedure laid down for the election of a parish priest is carried out now almost exactly, except that the bishop acts as his own chorepiscopus. When a priest dies, the chorepiscopus is ordered to go to the village and to gather together the villagers and cause them to elect a parish priest. This done, the bishop ordains him. No one may be ordained except by his own bishop, not even by the metropolitan, but the patriarch may ordain whom he will. And every village with from thirty to sixty houses of Christians should have a priest (vi. §§ 5–7.) But in practice, while many villages, especially in the plain of Urmi and Rayat districts in Turkey, have no priest, and have to be served from a distance, many other villages have a large number of supernumerary priests, who perhaps go through their whole lives without learning how to celebrate the Holy Eucharist. In the village of Ashitha, in Tiari, there are no fewer than sixteen priests, and more than seventy deacons to one church. This is abnormal, but still there are often too many priests and deacons in a village, who have in many cases been ordained without proper qualifications, and without any "title." A bishop sometimes only makes up his mind to ordain a man on Saturday night, and ordains him on Sunday morning. He knows the capabilities of a man by personal knowledge or by report—for the ordained will have lived in the same village all his life; and if he can read classical Syriac, and therefore go through the service, the bishop ordains him without further examination. This, however, is not such an evil as it would be with us, as every one knows the qualifications of the candidate much better than would be possible in the West, where people move about from place to place so much more; and the bishop is greatly guided by public opinion. He would scarcely ordain a priest, and probably not a deacon, unless the villagers wished it. A worse evil is the tendency of so many priests in the plain of Urmi to go off begging to Russia, and often to other European countries. The Russian authorities have made praiseworthy efforts to stop this; but it is easy for a man to cross the frontier as a layman, and then to use his priestly office as an excuse for getting alms from the Russian peasant, who is as generous as he is superstitious. Many of these beggars pass as pilgrims, *muqdusi*; and it is said that some once got into trouble in a rather amusing way. They found a dead donkey, and taking one of its legs, they threw earth on it to make it look as if it had been buried, and palmed it off on an unsuspecting village as a leg of the ass on which our Lord rode into Jerusalem, saying they had brought it from the Holy City. Having made a good sum by its sale, they proceeded to sell the other three legs to different villages, and to make a large fortune. They ought then to have returned home, but their greed led them to their fate, for they took another donkey and sold another leg. But by this time the arrival of these wonderful relics was made known far and wide; and, as even the most ignorant villager knows that no ass has five legs, the would-be pilgrims were caught and all their gains taken from them, and they themselves, to use their own phrase, were " poured into prison." This story is probably as old as the hills, but it serves to illustrate the tales the people tell of one another.

It is sad that priests should nearly always be the heroes of these tales, and sadder still that many should be ordained on purpose to go and beg; but as the author of the "Heavenly Intelligences" says almost in the words of our own Article, although there are evil priests in the Church, yet the way of God laid on their heads is true, and the offering which they offer is a pure one because it is the Holy Ghost which sanctifies it; and so their baptism is also a true one, for the mercies of God are not destroyed, and the people do not suffer for the wickedness of the priest, and only the priest suffers himself (*s.v.* "Priests").

Deacons are much more necessary with the East Syrians than with us, as neither the Eucharist nor baptism can be administered without them (Cautelae Missae, No. 21); and, moreover, they have a definite part in every service. Hence their large number, and the early age of ordination, by which almost every village is supplied with at least one deacon.

Those which have no deacon have to procure one from a neighbouring village. A priest can no more celebrate the Eucharist without a deacon, than a deacon can without a priest; although, if there are two priests, one may take the deacon's part. The deacon is little more than an acolyte; he is never, in practice,[1] allowed to baptize, and it is only of late years, in the plain of Urmi, that the bishops have allowed the more learned deacons to preach. Thus there seems no reason why the deacons should not be ordained young. Their ordination is no bar to their secular occupations or to marriage. For instance, the late mission steward at Urmi was a deacon, and also one of the servants; and indeed, there is hardly any deacon who does not work in the fields or at some trade. They point to the example of St. Paul in justifying this; and it may be admitted that our rigid Western system would never work with them. The diaconate is not regarded as a mere step to the priesthood as with us; a deacon is not looked on as "a clergyman who is not exactly in full orders." With the Syrians the ordination to the priesthood is the great step. A man frequently remains a deacon all his life, and often is not promoted to, or does not seek, the higher grade. The good old Raban Yonan, who died a deacon, used to say he was unworthy to be ordained priest.

The duties of a deacon are to assist the priest at the Liturgy, to say the litanies or bidding-prayers (which form a part of the Liturgy as well as of the daily and other offices), also to say the shorter exhortations and exclamations which are a great

[1] See below, chapter xii.

feature of all the services, and to which we may compare our own exhortations. These are not a peculiarity of our modern Anglican formularies. And it may not be superfluous to point out that the Scottish Liturgy has two such exhortations, which would (in the East) be especially the deacon's part, though only one is ascribed to the deacon, viz. that before the offertory. The Syrian deacon also lights and swings the censer, clangs the cymbals, draws the veil, gives the "peace" from the priest to the people; he may also make the holy loaves for consecration and for the *Antidoron*, and may mix the chalice ("Heavenly Intelligences," *s. v.* "Deacons"), though these things are properly done by the priest; he prepares the sanctuary, and "adorns the altar"; he reads the "Apostle" in the very rare cases in which it is now read at all, pours water on the priest's hands at the lavabo; and one deacon, wrapping round himself the sanctuary veil, holds in both hands the large paten for the priest to communicate the people, while another administers the cup. But a deacon may not "say any collects, offer the offering, or consecrate the water and oil of baptism, or do any priestly acts." The author of the "Heavenly Intelligences" says that subdeacons may also read the litanies. But that subdivision of the third order is now obsolete.

The canons say that a youth must not be ordained even subdeacon until he knows the psalms by heart. Prodigious as the powers of the Syrians are in this respect, I doubt if any could now repeat the whole Psalter without book, even among the priests. Deacons must have the consent of the parish priest

P

and laity of their village before they are ordained. This is the Syrian form of the *Si Quis*. The canons also say that there must be no more than seven deacons in any village or city. But this is a dead letter, and was so when the "Heavenly Intelligences" was written (*s.v.* "Deacons;" Sunhadus, vi. §§ 4, 5).

There are now no deaconesses. They are, however, recognized both in the Sunhadus and "Heavenly Intelligences." They must be sixty years old, and their duty is to officiate at the baptism of adult women.

The books also recognize, besides subdeacons and readers: (1) exorcists, who were to be monks; these were not ordained, but received a commission from the bishop. There are none now. (2) Sacristans, who are to be deacons or priests. They care for the Sanctuary, prepare the elements, administer the cup, and with the priest consume what remains of the Holy Sacrament. (3) Stewards, who have charge of the church furniture. (4) Doorkeepers, who keep the nave of the yard, call people to prayer by beating the semantron (*naqusha*) or oblong board which in old-fashioned churches takes the place of a bell; and they also announce to the faithful, when any one dies, that they may attend the funeral ("Heavenly Intelligences," *ad fin.*). The last three offices in some places exist at the present day.

There are now no monasteries. The old monks did not eat meat, and only made one full meal in the day. They followed the rule laid down in the Sunhadus. The monasteries were diocesan, and supervised by periaduti, who were the representatives of the bishop and responsible to him. But a few monasteries were independent, and under the direct rule of the patriarch. No bishop or metropolitan might enter these except occasionally and as a guest, and they were strictly non-diocesan (Sunhadus, book vii.).

CHAPTER X.

THE DAILY SERVICES.

The semantron calls people to prayer—Hours of prayer—The evening service—Taking off shoes—The kiss of peace—"Farcing" the Lord's prayer—Congregational singing—The two choirs—The psalms and anthems—Specimen anthems—Specimen collects—The blessing—Night service—Morning service—Service on Sundays and holy days—"Gloria in Excelsis" and "Benedicite"—The multiplicity of books—Parts of the service special to priests, and to deacons—Compline—Lights—Summer chapels—Praying towards the East—Absence of pictures—The cross—Standing and kneeling—Praying for oppressors—Devotion to the martyrs and the Blessed Virgin—Variety of the intercessions for the living and the dead—Invocations of the saints—Method of dividing the Psalter.

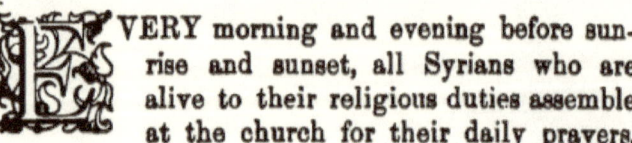EVERY morning and evening before sunrise and sunset, all Syrians who are alive to their religious duties assemble at the church for their daily prayers. They certainly put our apathetic and respectable Western to shame in this respect. They do not consider they have done enough if they attend a midday and perhaps an evening service on Sundays; even on ordinary week days many a village church is filled with a devout congregation of people dressed in their everyday clothes. Even

THE DAILY SERVICES. 213

if they are in rags, it is no shame for them to be seen standing in the church and offering their daily prayers and praises to their Creator. The women, indeed, usually are occupied on week days in their homes with domestic duties; but the men before and after their day's work assemble, often as a matter of course, when summoned to prayer by the beating of the semantron. "As Noah," says the author of the "Heavenly Intelligences" (*s.v.* "Semantron"), "beat wood on wood to warn people to enter the ark, so we beat the semantron. It is a type of the trumpets of the day of judgment." It is rather a matter of regret that this old-fashioned instrument should now be gradually giving way to the modern bell, introduced from Russia.

As watches and clocks do not form part of the ordinary furniture of such an old-world people, the prayers have to vary with the sun. In a mountain village, for instance, the evening prayers will be begun when the sun has reached a certain point on the hills. Great was the indignation one day when, owing to some accident, the mission boys were not summoned to prayer till the sun had set and the muezzin on the neighbouring mosque had called his people to prayers. "Oh, Rabbi," they exclaimed, "why have you kept us so long from our prayers? It is a *sin* for us to begin after the Mussulmans have begun theirs!" Perhaps it is the most natural arrangement with a people who have so little artificial light, and whose churches are so dark.

We proceed to describe the evening service. The first thing done on entering the church, as also on-entering any room, is to take off the shoes and leave them at the door. At the end of service, every one picks out his own just as we pick out our own hats under similar circumstances. How each of us can find his hat is as much a mystery to them, as how each of them can pick out his own shoes from a number of seemingly identical pairs is to us. With them the removal of the hat is a small matter. They do, indeed, unlike the Mussulmans, take off their hats or turbans during the actual time of prayer, but they do not consider it irreverent to wear them in the church when prayers are not going on. But it would be grossly irreverent, in their eyes, to keep on the shoes. They quite understand why Moses was commanded to put off his shoes from off his feet: "for the place whereon thou standest is holy ground;" and why "the captain of the Lord's host said unto Joshua, Loose thy shoe from off thy foot; for the place whereon thou standest is holy" (Ex. iii. 5; Josh. v. 15). A mission scholar once remarked, on seeing the European missionaries' celebration: "What astonishes me most in your service is that you wear shoes." It struck him as a priest wearing a tall hat at the altar would strike us. This, however, cannot always have been the case, as the Sunhadus forbids priests to enter a church or any public assembly without shoes or stockings, or to celebrate divine service without priest's clothing, or in sandals; but it recommends special shoes if they may be had (vi. § 6, Canon 2).

The custom in Tiari, and some other mountain districts, differs somewhat from what has been

THE DAILY SERVICES. 215

described above. There shoes are not worn, but sandals of skin or felt are bound upon the feet; these sandals are not removed on entering either a house or a church. But they are exchanged for special slippers in the baptistery by any clergyman who wishes to enter the sanctuary. He will also cover his worldly clothes with an albe and cotton breeches, and wear a stole before going in.

Hanjars (daggers) and other weapons, and pipes and walking-sticks, are not taken into church.

On entering the church, the people often kiss the cross on the door post; and then proceed to the *quasi*-altar in the nave, or in the summer chapel, as the case may be, where the cross is lying, and devoutly kiss it, crossing themselves and bowing. The bishop, or the senior priest present, first advances, crosses himself, and kisses the cross, saying, "Glory be to God in the highest (thrice), and on earth peace and a good hope to men, at all times and for ever." He then stands on the north side of the nave near the cross, and all the people advance in order, kiss the cross and then the priest's hand, and pass down in line, touching the hands of those who have already kissed the cross, and raising their own hands to their lips. But if there are other priests present, the deacons and laymen kiss their hands also. Meanwhile they say the Lord's prayer, "farced" in a peculiar manner, thus—

Our Father which art in heaven, Hallowed be thy Name. Thy kingdom come. * Holy, holy, holy art thou. * Our Father which art in heaven. * Heaven and earth are full of the greatness of thy glory. Angels (*lit.* the watchful ones) and men cry to thee, Holy, holy, holy art thou. * Our Father which art in heaven, Hallowed be thy Name. Thy kingdom come. Thy will be done in earth, As it is in heaven. Give us this day our daily bread (*lit.* the bread of our need). And forgive us our trespasses (*or* debts). As we forgive them that trespass against us (*or* our debtors). And lead us not into temptation. But deliver us from the Evil one.[1] For thine is the Kingdom, and the Power, and the Glory, for ever and ever, Amen. * Glory be to the Father and to the Son and to the Holy Ghost. From everlasting to everlasting, Amen. * Our Father which art in heaven, Hallowed be thy Name. Thy Kingdom come. * Holy, holy, holy art thou. * Our Father which art in heaven. * Heaven and earth are full of the greatness of thy glory. Angels and men cry to thee. Holy, holy, holy art thou.

The Lord's Prayer is always said with the doxology; sometimes simply, sometimes farced as above. When it is finished the deacon says, "Let us pray, peace be with us," and the priest says a collect.

The collects, which may only be said by priests, are very short, and nearly always end in the same way. The following are specimens—

Thee, O my Lord, heaven and earth and all that is in them are bound to confess and worship and glorify, for all thy helps and graces towards us, the greatness of which cannot be repaid; Lord of all, Father, Son, and Holy Ghost for ever. *Amen.* (*Prayer of the Lakhumara, at Morning Prayer on Ferias.*)

May thy grace, O my Lord, shine forth upon us when thy justice judges us; and may thy mercy come to our aid in the day when thy Greatness shines forth, Lord of all, Father, Son, and Holy Ghost for ever. *Amen.* (*One of the concluding prayers at Evensong.*)

As the services are all in the classical Syriac,

---

[1] This is the East Syrian interpretation. It is paraphrased, "The Evil one and his hosts."

THE DAILY SERVICES. 217

they cannot be generally followed, except at well-known points, by the laity, especially by the old men and the women. But all who can read the old books now press forward to the books, of which there are seldom more than two, and often only one, and stand round them. It is a matter of indifference whether the letters are upside down or sideways on, or what we should call right side up; they can read with almost equal facility in any case. Thus ten or a dozen men may read from one book of large type, some peeping over the shoulders of others. This facility in reading upside down is not merely because the language is familiar, for it is found that those who are learning any European language can read it almost as easily with the book turned one way as another.

The singers divide themselves into two choirs, called respectively, "before" and "after." The weeks are divided into those "before" and those "after," according as whether the first choir on the north side, or the second choir on the south, begins the service. If the first choir begins one anthem, the second choir begins the next, and so on alternately. The practise of singing in two choirs is ascribed to the precept of St. Ignatius, who saw in a vision the angels singing antiphonally, and taught the church of Antioch, and through it the whole of the East, to do the same. As the churches are nearly always dark, rude tapers of beeswax are held in the hand over the books. As these grow dim every few minutes, they are snuffed by the hand, and the greasy condition of the manuscripts testifies to the zeal of the holder to sing rather than to his care to prevent the wax falling. Certainly the Syrians have a thorough notion of congregational worship. All their services are sung; but all who can read join in at the top of their voice, whether they are musical or not; often not to the same tune, and generally not in the same key as their neighbours. One of the mission boys, whose voice was of the loudest, had a knack of singing a fifth below the leading voice, and the discord may be imagined! But all is very hearty and earnest, and one would not exchange the Syrian evensong for a most beautiful musical rendering in many of our cathedrals. The Syrians would consider a read service as unworthy of the time and place.

They begin a selection of the Psalms. There are seven such, one for each day of the week. The arrangement of verses does not follow the "division of the Hebrews"; each clause is usually much shorter than in our version, and there is no division into verses. Hence the Psalters printed by the Bible societies are useless for liturgical purposes, and one has been specially issued from the mission press (1891).[1] About seven psalms are said at each evensong in this place. On ordinary days it is usual for one member of the one choir to recite them antiphonally in a sort of recitative with one member of the other choir; on holy days and Sundays they are generally sung by the whole choir, and take much longer.

---

[1] The Lazarist mission has also included the Psalter in their beautiful Book of Daily Offices, printed at Leipsig. This has some alterations from the old Syrian books, and is therefore not favourably received by the Old Church.

THE DAILY SERVICES. 219

After the psalms comes a collect, and then a feature common to all East Syrian services, called from its first words *Lakhumara* (Thee, O Lord). All join in repeating—

Thee, O Lord of all, we confess; and thee, Jesus Christ, we glorify, for thou art the Quickener of our bodies, and thou art the Saviour of our souls. * I was glad when they said unto me, we will go into the house of the Lord. * Thee, O Lord, etc., * Glory be, etc. From everlasting to everlasting, Amen. * Thee, O Lord, etc.

The verse of the psalm varies on different occasions. If prayers are said in a private house, they say, "In every place art thou, O God." At the Liturgy they say, "I will wash my hands in innocency, O Lord, and so will I go to thine altar." At Baptism they say, "The voice of the Lord is upon the waters; the God of glory thundereth."

After another collect, said by the priest, they recite the *Shuraya*, or short psalm, and the first anthem, called "Before." These both vary, not only according to the day of the week, but according as to whether the week itself is "before" or "after." All anthems are divided into paragraphs; each choir sings one to its proper tune, and the other choir takes up the next to the same tune, and so on to the end. They are sung rather slowly, and take up much more time than a corresponding amount of the psalms. Each paragraph is prefaced by a clause from the Psalter which gives it its keynote. These anthems are a special feature of all East Syrian services, and give an opportunity to all who can read of joining heartily in the worship. The first anthem for Monday evening (*i.e.* what we should call Sunday evening) in the week "before" is given here as a specimen. In all these anthems the stars denote the places where the choirs change. The full stops denote the metrical divisions, like lines in our poetry. The anthems are in metre, not infrequently very irregular; and rarely they rhyme.

Help me, Lord, for there is not one godly man left. Lo, there is not one godly man left, and the faithful is minished, and the just is destroyed, and there is no good man among men. With a double heart every man speaks, and with dissembling lips. Each man with his neighbour. Of envy and guile and slander is our inner humanity (*lit.* son of man) full. Love is rooted out from our thoughts, which is the chief of the commandments. There is great fear lest we all be destroyed in Thy anger. For thy faithfulness is silent with us. And hath given place to thy grace.[1] O our Lord, have pity on us.

The Lord is faithful in his words. Our Saviour gave the promise of life to those who desire his love, and made them rich in his knowledge. And filled them with the wisdom of strength, and taught them to pray at all times. Our Father which art in heaven, hallowed be thy name, thy kingdom come to us. Thy will be done on earth as it is in heaven. Give us the bread of our need. And lead us not into temptation. But deliver us from the Evil one, for thine is the kingdom. The power and the glory.

Glory be to the Father, and to the Son, and to the Holy Ghost. O Mary, who didst bear the medicine of life to the children of Adam, in thy petition we will take refuge. And in the confident hope of the prayers of St. John we will conquer the Evil one and his host. And by the prayer of the prophets, apostles, martyrs, fathers, and teachers. And by the prayer of our holy Awa, confessor, and of St. George. And the great power of the Cross. And the hallowing of the holy Church. We will beseech Christ to have mercy and pity. Upon our souls.

After the first anthem comes another collect, and

---

[1] *i.e.* all we have is of grace.

THE DAILY SERVICES.

Psalms cxli., cxlii. follow daily; then an invariable portion of the "Letter psalm" (cxix. 105-113), and Ps. cxvii., all under one Gloria. Another collect precedes the second *Shuraya* (short psalm) and anthem which vary both according to the day of the week and to the week itself, and closely resemble the first. The deacon then advances to the cross, kisses it, puts on a girdle over his ordinary dress, and a stole over the left shoulder ("Heavenly Intelligences," s.v. "Deacons"), kisses the priest's hand, and repeats two litanies[1] which are said daily. The priest says a collect, and the deacon says, "Lift up your voices and worship the living God, all ye people;" then kisses the priest's hand, lays aside his stole, and returns to his place. All then join in the "Holy God."

Holy God, Holy Mighty, Holy Immortal, have mercy upon us. * Glory be to the Father, etc. * Holy God, etc. * From everlasting to everlasting, Amen. * Holy God, etc.

The priest says two collects, between which the deacon proclaims, "Bless, O my Lord. Lower your heads for the laying on of hands and receive a blessing;" and the "Evening Anthem" follows. This varies according to the season, and is taken from the "Kashkul" on ordinary ferias. In practice, however, as few churches possess a "Kashkul," another anthem known by heart to every one is usually substituted, followed by a collect, by a variable portion of Psalm cxix., "Hallelujah" (thrice), "Our Father" (said simply), and two more

[1] These correspond to the Greek "ectene," and are partly litanies and partly bidding-prayers.

collects. In this place comes one of the anthems of the martyrs, of which there are fourteen, one for each morning and evening of the week (though those for Sunday are usually omitted). It is natural that a people who have hardly ever known what it is to be free from oppression, and who have had so many martyrs of their own, should have a special reverence for those who have laid down their lives for Christ; and they have a particular love for these anthems. That for Monday evening is given here as a specimen.

Glorify the Lord, O ye righteous. Holy martyrs, pray for peace. That we may celebrate your festivals with joy.

For it becometh well the just to be thankful. The martyrs who longed to see Christ. Obtained wings through the sword, and flew to heaven.

Sing praises lustily unto Him. The martyrs in their love say to Christ. For thee we die daily.

Seek the Lord and His strength. O ye martyrs, ask mercy for the world which taketh. True refuge in the strength of your bones.

These called upon the Lord, and He heard them. Let us call on the martyrs and take refuge in them. That they may pray for us.

As a city surrounded with a wall. Ye fence in the breaches. Before the persecutors in the times of affliction.

From this time forth for evermore. May the prayers of the martyrs be a wall to us. And drive away from us the attacks of the crafty.

Offer unto Him the sacrifice of thanksgiving. O ye martyrs who were sacrifices to the high priests. May your prayer be a wall to our souls.

I will always give thanks unto the Lord. Blessed is your fight, O holy martyrs. For by the blood of your necks ye gained the kingdom.

His praise shall ever be in my mouth. Blessed is Christ who strengthened his saints. Here on earth, and above in heaven.

They that love the Lord hate the thing which is evil. Ye martyrs of the Son, that love the Only Begotten. Pray that there may be peace in creation.

Look on Him and trust in him. The martyrs saw the Son crucified on the tree. And lowered their necks to the sword, and were crowned.

Bow down thine ear, O Lord, and hear me. The cross of our Lord was stained with blood. The martyrs saw it and lowered their necks.

He divided the sea, and let them go through. The cross of Christ was a bridge to the martyrs. And the just crossed by it to the country where there is no fear.

More to be desired are they than gold and than precious stones. The martyrs are like pearls. For their images are fixed in the King's crown.

The king's daughter stood in glory. The faithful Church is a pearl. And the martyrs in it are propitiatory sacrifices.

Within the ports of the daughter of Sion. The martyrs saw a pearl in Sion. And ran and bought it with the blood of their necks.

Thou art fairer than the children of men. The rose in the gardens is beautiful to behold. But more beautiful were the martyrs when they were killed.

Behold, how good and joyful a thing it is. Precious stones and beryls. Are ye, O martyrs, in the crown of the Son of the King.

Praise the Lord upon the harp; sing to the harp with a voice of thanksgiving. I heard the voice of the martyrs singing praises. With the harps of David (going) round Paradise.

His praise is above heaven and earth. Praise to that voice which said to the martyrs. Mingle your blood with my blood, and my life with your life.

O hear ye this, all ye people. The martyrs were sheaves of corn and the kings reaped them. And the Lord placed them in the garner of his kingdom.

He shall doubtless come again with joy. The martyrs and holy priests go out. To meet our Lord in the day of his coming.

And your prayers be on all of us. Holy martyrs, ask mercy for us. That by your prayers we may receive forgiveness.

I spake of peace. Peace to thee, Mar Pithiun, the chosen of Christ. Who didst bear all sufferings for the truth of thy Lord.

He reproved even kings for their sakes. How fitting is it for the boy Cyriac. When for him (God) reproves the unjust king.

And to be a joyful mother of children. The faithful Shmuni encourages her sons. O, my beloved sons, depart in peace.

Seek of the Lord, and pray before Him. Ask for us from thy Lord, O martyr George. Clemency, mercy, and forgiveness of trespasses.

Kings of the earth and all people. All races call blessed. The Virgin Mary, mother of Christ.

Glory be to the Father, and to the Son, and to the Holy Ghost. Peace be with you, holy Martyrs. Sowers of peace in the four quarters of the world.

From everlasting to everlasting. Thy memorial, O our Awa, is on the holy altar. With the just who conquered, and the martyrs who were crowned.

Let all the people say Amen and Amen.[1] By thee, O God, whose mercies are great. Let us be corrected and not by men. * Come, O my Lord, to help us and strengthen our weakness. For in thee is our hope by night and by day. * Christ who neglectest not all who call on thee. By thy mercy reject not the request of them that worship thee. * For on thee their eyes hang, and on thee they look. That thou mayest forgive their trespasses and wipe out their sins * O our Lord, by thy right hand overthrow Satan. Who inebriates without wine, and causes to slip without mud. * With the Publican we ask mercy. Pity us and have mercy upon us. * Thy cross hath saved us, thy cross doth save us. May thy cross be a wall to our souls. * May wars be brought to nought, and disputes laid to rest. And may thy peace rule in the four quarters of the world. * O our Lord, keep us, for we are as sheep. Among serpents who are worse than wolves. * O our Lord, sow thy peace and tranquility in the world. And take from us the rod of correction. * O our Lord, bless and keep the congregation. And make thy peace and tranquility to dwell in it. * O our Lord, give peace in the four quarters of the

---

[1] Ps. cvi. 46, Syriac. Thus the Gloria very frequently ends in these anthems.

world. And bring to nothing the persecutors who oppose (us). O our Lord, shut the mouth of the unjust, that they speak not wickedness against the sons of the Church.

The service is ended by a series of collects, one or more of which is said by each priest who is present, with extended hands, and with the sign of the cross at the end; and by the blessing said by the principal priest, who turns to the people with extended hands. He signs them with the sign of the cross, and they come and receive the kiss of peace, as at the beginning (though if the blessing be a very long one, the kiss of peace is given while it is being said), and the Nicene Creed ends the whole service.

The following three collects always precede the blessing:—

Of Mary. May the prayer, O my Lord, of the holy Virgin, and the petition of the blessed mother, and the beseeching and intreating of her who is full of grace, St. Mary the blessed, and the great power of the victorious cross, and divine help, and the petition of St. John Baptist, be with us always at all seasons and times, O Lord of all, Father, Son, and Holy Ghost, for ever. *Amen.*

Of the Apostles. May the prayer, O my Lord, of the holy Apostles, and the petition of the true preachers, and the beseeching and intreating of the brave warriors, preachers of truth and evangelists of righteousness, sowers of peace in creation, be with us always at all seasons and times, O Lord of all, Father, Son, and Holy Ghost, for ever. *Amen.*

Of Awa. May the prayer, and petition, and beseeching, and intreating of our pure and holy father, St Awa, Catholicos, St. Stephen, the firstborn of the martyrs, the giant of strength St. George, the brave martyr, blessed St. Augin, and all his spiritual band, Shmuni and her sons, and all the martyrs and saints of our Lord, be ever with us, a high wall and strong refuge, That thou mayest save, and deliver, and liberate us, and keep our bodies

Q

and souls from the Evil one and his hosts, at all seasons and times, O Lord of all, Father, Son, and Holy Ghost, for ever. *Amen.*

Throughout these services, wherever the name Awa (*lit.* father) occurs, that of the patron saint is often substituted; as *Awun* may either mean "O our father," or "O our Awa." And in this last prayer, the names of other saints are often added, according to local use. The concluding blessing is often an ascription of praise to God, followed by a prayer in the first person. "By the prayers of the just and elect, who pleased Thee from the beginning, absolve our sins, etc." But it is sometimes in the second person. Thus, the Sunday and festival blessing in the Liturgy, after a long prayer in the first person, ends, "and in the living sign of the Lord's cross, be ye sealed and kept from all that may hurt you, seen or unseen, now and always, and for ever and ever. Amen." The word for the blessing may be rendered either "the conclusion," or "the sealing." While it is being recited, the people bow their heads and beat their breasts.

The service described above is always what is with us called "first evensong," *i.e.* that of the evening before. No day, not even the greatest festival, has two evensongs; and on what we call the evening of Easter Day, the Syrians use the Monday service. It will be seen that there are no lections from the Bible in the daily offices. These only occur in the Liturgy.

Except that the deacon puts on girdle and stole (but not albe or surplice) for the litany, no vestments are used at the daily offices. Perhaps this is only on account of the poverty of the people. The canons say that priests and deacons are not to perform the service without priests' clothing (vi. § 6, Canon 2). But possibly this only refers to the sacraments.

A curious feature is the farcing of the Psalms. The short Psalm called *Shuraya* is always farced, and the psalms in the Liturgy and Baptismal Service, generally, as are all psalms on feasts of our Lord, Sundays, and saints' days. A clause is thrown in, after the first clause of the Psalm, and after the Gloria. Thus at the Liturgy, on ordinary days, they say Psalm xv. in the following manner:—

Lord, who shall dwell in thy tabernacle: or who shall rest upon thy holy hill? With pureness of conscience make me to stand, O our Lord, before thy altar. Lord, who shall dwell.... Whoso doeth these things shall never fall. Glory be, etc. From everlasting to everlasting, Amen. With pureness of conscience make me to stand, O our Lord, before thy altar. Lord, who shall dwell in thy tabernacle: or who shall rest upon thy holy hill? How beautiful and glorious is the house of thy holiness, O God, who hallowest all.

The "service of the night" and "service of the morning" are in practice said together, if, indeed, the former is not omitted altogether; it is seldom, at least, attended by the laity. This is an instance of the rule that if too heavy a burden be laid on people, the law remains a dead letter. It would be vain to expect people, in the midst of all their avocations, to attend a service which consists of one-third, at least, of the Psalter, and of several long anthems. The Psalms are divided into twenty portions, each called a *hulala* (corresponding to the

Greek *kathisma*), and a twenty-first hulula is made up of certain Old Testament canticles. The subdivisions of the *hulali* are called *marmiatha*. In each hulala there are two, three, or sometimes four such subdivisions. Besides the psalms sung at evening and morning prayer, the whole Psalter is recited at the night service once in three days. On Mondays and Thursdays are said the first seven hulali (Psalms i.–lviii. inclusive). On Tuesdays and Fridays the next seven (Psalms lix.–ci.). On Wednesdays and Saturdays the last seven (Psalms cii.–cl., with the twenty-first hulala). On Sundays ten hulali are said, in two portions, seven in the usual place, and three after the anthem called " Motwa." On feasts of our Lord, the whole Psalter is appointed to be said, with *giuri* or farcings. On saints' days ("memorials") three hulali are said, with farcings (Psalms lxxxii.–ci.).[1] Before each hulala is said an appropriate collect, and after each, " Hallelujah (*thrice*). Glory be to thee, O God. O our Lord, have mercy upon us. *Deacon.* Let us pray. Peace be with us."

NIGHT SERVICE.

Glory be to God in the highest. Kiss of peace. Our Father (farced). Collects, etc.

The Psalms, followed by a collect.

The Motwa, so called because all sit while it is being sung (from the verb *yát-iw*, to sit). This anthem varies according to the season, except on Wednesdays, when there are here special anthems commemorating all the saints. There is one for the week "before," and one for the week "after," but the ending is invariable.

Daily anthem, invariable, and collect.

The numbering of the English Prayer-book is followed throughout.

Shubakha, or short psalm, varying according to the day of the week (farced).

Tishbukhta, or hymn of praise, varying according to the day of the week.

Short litany, said standing (invariable).

Morning Service.

(The whole is invariable, except the " Martyrs.")

Two Collects.

Ps. cx. (farced), and collect.

Ps. xci. (farced) and collect.

Ps. civ. 1-16 (to "sap"), and Ps. cxiii., both farced, but with no Gloria.

Ps. xciii., cxlviii., cxlvi. (not on Sundays or feasts of our Lord, but on ferias and saints' days), cl., cxvii. All said simply, under one Gloria; and at the end: For ever, with every breath, let us praise the Lord. Christ the Light, we praise thee. *Or*, Praise the Lord, the whole earth. O Lord who givest light: we praise thee.

Deacon. Let us pray. Peace be with us.

Collect and "Lakhumara," farced with "My voice shalt thou hear betimes, O Lord: early in the morning will I direct my prayer unto Thee and will look up" (Ps. v. 3).

Collect and Ps. li. 1-18 (ferias only), farced.

Tishbukhta, or hymn of praise, by St. Ephrem.

Collect.

Deacon. Lift up your voices and worship the living God, all ye people. *All repeat:* Holy God, etc. (farced with the Gloria).

Two collects.

Anthem of the "Martyrs," varying according to the day of the week.

Two daily anthems.

Several collects, blessing, kiss of peace, Nicene Creed, as at evensong.

The services on Sunday, festivals of our Lord, and saints' days, are on the same model, but there are some portions from the *Khudhra*, or book of proper anthems, etc., for the whole year. On Sundays at evening prayer the same three psalms are always said, except from Advent to Epiphany, viz.: lxv., lxvi., lxvii. A song of incense is added. Incense is not ordered on ferias in the daily offices (though in some mountain churches it is used at every evensong). But on Sundays and saints' days the deacon takes the censer to the priest, who puts incense in with the sign of the cross, and the deacon then censes the people. There are two special anthems in lieu of the evening anthem, one called "the royal anthem," and another variable one. Instead of Psalm cxix. is a third *Shuraya* (short psalm), and the "martyrs' anthem" is not in practice used. At the Sunday night service, three extra hulali are recited after the "Motwa," and the hymns are special, according to the season. At the Sunday morning service, psalm li. is omitted; a hymn for Sundays, the Benedicite, and Gloria in excelsis are added; the "martyrs' anthem" is not in practice said. The service for festivals of our Lord and saints' days is similar.

The form of the Gloria in excelsis is as follows:—

Glory to God in the highest. * And on earth peace * And a good hope to mankind. * We worship thee. * We glorify thee. * We exalt thee. * Being who art from eternity. * Hidden nature that cannot be fathomed. * Father, Son, and Holy Ghost. * King of kings. * And Lord of lords. * Who dwellest in the glorious light. * Whom no man hath seen. * And cannot see. * Who alone art Holy. * And alone Mighty. * And alone Immortal. * We confess thee * Through the mediator of our blessings. * Jesus Christ. * The Saviour of the world. * And the Son of the Highest. * O Lamb of the living God. * Who takest away the sins of the world. * Have mercy upon us. * Who sittest at the right hand of the Father. * Receive our request. * For thou art our God. * And thou art our Lord. * And thou art our King. * And thou art our Saviour. * And thou art the forgiver of our sins. * The eyes of all men hang on thee. * Jesus Christ. * Glory to God thy Father. * And to thee, and to the Holy Ghost, for ever. Amen.

The Benedicite is shortened, thus:—

O all ye works of the Lord, bless ye the Lord. O ye Heavens of the Lord, bless ye the Lord. [*Say the first proper farcing and repeat the above.*] * O ye Angels of the Lord, bless ye the Lord. O ye waters that be above the Heavens, bless, etc. * O all ye powers of the Lord, bless, etc. O ye Sun and Moon, bless, etc. * O ye stars in Heaven, bless, etc. O ye rain and dew, bless, etc. * O all ye winds, bless, etc. O ye fire and heat, bless, etc. * O ye night and day, bless, etc. O ye light and darkness, bless, etc. * O ye cold and heat, bless, etc. O ye snow and ice, bless, etc. * O ye lightnings and clouds, bless, etc. O all the earth, bless, etc. * O ye mountains and hills, bless, etc. O all that bring forth upon the earth, bless, etc. * O ye seas and rivers, bless, etc. O ye springs of water, bless, etc. * O ye fishes and all that moveth in the waters, bless, etc. O all ye fowls of Heaven, bless, etc. * O all ye beasts and cattle, bless, etc. O ye sons of men, bless, etc. * O ye sons of men, bless, etc. O ye house of Israel, bless, etc. * O ye priests of the Lord, bless, etc. O ye servants of the Lord, bless, etc. * O all ye spirits and souls of the righteous, bless, etc. O ye perfect and humble men of heart, bless, etc. * O Ananias, Azarias, and Misael, bless, etc. O ye apostles and prophets, bless, etc. * O ye martyrs of the Lord, bless, etc. O all that stand in the house of the Lord, bless, etc. * *Repeat the first farcing;* then, Glory be, etc., *and* From everlasting, *with the second farcing. Repeat* O all ye works, etc. O ye Heavens, etc., *and say the third farcing.*

The daily offices thus have a very great amount of variable portions, and they are extremely rich. But this has to be paid for by a loss of simplicity, and by an intricacy which is worse than that of "the rules called the Pie." Frequently the service has to be stopped in order that a discussion may take place as to what ought to come next. And matters are made worse by the multiplicity of books, all of which, of course, are in manuscript, the words crowded up together without paragraphs, the leaves blackened with age, several leaves often wanting, and, worst of all, the pages not numbered. Often the first few words only of a prayer or anthem are given, without any reference, and one has to hunt over the book till the place can be found. No two books agree together. It is not wonderful if there is confusion. It is only modified by the prodigious capacity all show for learning by heart.

Almost all the daily services are contained in the *Psalter* or *Dawidha* (which also contains the collects proper to the hulali), and the *Qdham D'Wathar*, also called in full *Daqdham Wadhwathar* (before and after), which, as its name denotes, contains the services proper to the first and second weeks, also the selections of psalms for evening and morning prayer, and the various fixed psalms and anthems. The litanies are generally to be found in the Dawidha. The collects, however, except those proper to the hulali, are, as being said by the priest only, prefixed to the *Takhsa*. This is the priest's book, and contains also the three liturgies, less the variable portions and litanies, the baptismal service, several minor offices, such as the lesser consecration of churches, absolution, office for the Leaven, the longer benedictions, occasional prayers, etc.

The portions of the service which vary according to the season are found in the *Khudhra* ("cycle") if for Sundays and holy days, or the *Kashkul*

THE DAILY SERVICES. 233

(*lit.* "containing all") if for ferias. The *Geza* ("Treasury") and *Werda* ("Rose") also contain variable hymns and anthems. These are all immense volumes, especially the Khudhra and Geza.

Other service books are, the *Burakha* or marriage service, the *Kurasta* and *'Anidha* or burial services for priests and laymen, the *Siamidha* or Ordinal, book of the (Liturgical) Gospels, and books of the Apostle and Lections (but these are extremely rare). All this is a contrast indeed to our little Prayer-book.

Of the daily service, certain portions are confined to the priest, certain to the deacons, certain may be said by laymen. The priest only may say the collects, which hence are called "priestly prayers." The deacons say the litanies, and "Let us pray, peace be with us," and similar exhortations. Laymen may not say these "lest they be like Korah and Uzziah" (Sunhadus, v. § 4). But they may say the Lord's Prayer, Holy God, the *Lakhumara*, and all the psalms and anthems. Laymen are especially bidden to learn the intercessory psalms by heart, that they may be able to pray when alone; and old men, workmen, shepherds, and sailors, when far from a church, if they do not know any psalms, should mark a cross upon a wall, and make short ejaculations, such as "Make me a clean heart, O God," say Our Father and Holy God, and prostrate themselves to the earth, making the sign of the cross (Sunhadus, v. §§ 4, 5).

Besides the three services mentioned above, a fourth, corresponding to Compline (*suba'a* = satisfaction), is mentioned in the Sunhadus as necessary for all men. This is now in most places obsolete, except on a few nights in the year, when it is added to evening prayer. And, with this exception, we have never heard it said. But a learned mountain priest writes to us: "There are many men who still say Compline either at home or in church. They begin after supper, before going to bed; they say the Lord's Prayer, a hulala, or at any rate a psalm, 'praises,' and the anthem of the day, a hymn and canon [a sort of doxology], Holy God, collects, and the blessing. The Compline proper to holy days is written in the Khudhra." The name *suba'a* is derived from the custom in monasteries of having the only full meal of the day at bedtime. The Sunhadus orders that one *hulala*, an anthem, *shuraya* (short psalm), hymn, and litany, should be said. "Evening and morning prayer may not be increased or decreased by anybody, but Nocturns and Compline are according to the rule of each monastery; for laymen (seculars?) there is no fixed limit," *i.e.* as to length or shortness. "At Nocturns there should be five or seven *hulali*, an anthem, *shuraya*, praise, and litany" (v. §§ 2, 3).

In old times when there were monasteries, all monks and nuns, including novices, prayed seven times a day; the higher grades recited three *hulali*, or about twenty-three psalms at each hour of prayer (§ v. 1).

There is no fixed rule in practice about lights. There are always some at the Liturgy, and at the daily offices on great occasions, but ordinarily they are only used for the purpose of giving light. The twelfth of the Cautelae missae in the Takhsa says that a light of olive oil is to burn before the altar in the sanctuary, night and day; and the "Book of Heavenly Intelligences" says that this perpetual light in the holy of holies is kept up always as a symbol of the next world, and of the law of Christ, which has no end; whereas the lamp in the nave, which is to be lighted before prayer and extinguished afterwards, is a symbol of this world, and of the old law, which have both beginning and end; so also the nave is like this world, the sanctuary is like the next (*s.v.* "Churches and Candles," at the end of the book).

The prayers are said during winter in the nave of the church. No one ordinarily enters the sanctuary, except for the Eucharist and part of the baptismal service; but in summer they are said outside. Most churches have a summer chapel for this purpose, on the south side, where is also the entrance to the church. A *quasi*-altar for the cross is fixed to the east end, and the service proceeds as in the church. If there is no outer chapel, prayers are said in the churchyard, and an erection is made there for the cross.

The Syrians always pray to the east; for our Lord will, they say, appear there at his second coming. "As the lightning cometh out of the east, and shineth even unto the west; so shall also the coming of the Son of man be (St. Matthew xxiv. 27). Also tradition says that when our Lord led his disciples out as far as Bethany, and he lifted up his hands and blessed them, at his Ascension, he faced west. And the disciples worshipped him, turning towards the east (St. Luke xxiv. 50, 52). This is the origin of the practice" (Sunhadus, v. § 8). In a composition on Jonah, one of the mission scholars remarked that the whale turned to the east in order to give the prophet greater facilities for praying!

No pictures are allowed; it is doubtful if they ever were used. There is no mention of them in the Sunhadus and similar books. No doubt the influence of Mohammedanism would have brought about their disuse, even if they had ever been introduced. The Syrians are more liable to such Mohammedan influences than their neighbours the Armenians, who are powerful enough to withstand them, and who also have more contact with Europe. But probably pictures never were used in East Syrian churches. Their place is taken by the cross to which the people pay the greatest veneration. They kiss the cross on the lintel of the door on entering a church,[1] and the cross in the church before and after service. The women have often a special cross at the bottom of the church, so that none may fail to kiss it through modesty and bashfulness. The Syrians never tire of using the holy sign on themselves; they sign everything that is to be consecrated, and also the bread they eat at meals, and indeed think a man a very Mussulman or heathen who does not use the sign. They put their fingers to their mouth and say, *In the name;* then to their forehead and say, *of the Father;* to their breast at *and of the Son;* to the right shoulder at *and of the Holy;* and to the left shoulder at *Ghost;* thus reversing the Western method.

The Syrians, like other Orientals, pray standing. The tradition of kneeling is almost lost. The

---

[1] See below, chapter xv., and above, page 215.

canons indeed say that from Whitsun Even to Easter Even there is kneeling, except on Sundays and festivals, when it is not suitable, because it typifies grief and sorrow.[1] But in practice the Syrians only kneel for a few moments before the Invocation in the Liturgy, and at the special litany of the fast; and even then it has degenerated into sitting down. With those who have the habit of sitting on their heels, on the ground, this is perfectly natural. But it is a little unfortunate that the most solemn parts of the service should now be connected with the easiest and most comfortable attitude. The laity frequently prostrate themselves during the service, uttering reverent ejaculations.[2] In this way they make up for not being able to join in the anthems and psalms.

Among the special characteristics of the East Syrian services we may note their touching prayers for their oppressors, such as the following: "We also beseech thy mercy, O Lord, for all our enemies and all that hate us; for all that devise any evil against us: not for judgment or vengeance, O Lord the mighty God, but for pity and salvation, and the remission of all their sins; because thou willest all men to be saved and turn to the knowledge of the truth. For thou hast taught us, by thy beloved Son Jesus Christ our Lord, to pray

---

[1] v. § 8. See Smith and Cheetham, "Dictionary of Christian Antiquities," *s.v.* Genuflexion. Standing is enjoined by Canon 20 of Nicaea, but perhaps only for "the Lord's Day and the days of Pentecost," *i.e.* from Easter to Pentecost. Hefele, Concilien-geschichte, § 42.

[2] Prostration seems to have been an early form of kneeling. "Dictionary of Christian Antiquities," as above.

for our enemies and for them that hate us, and for them that rule over us with unrighteous oppression."[1]

Another characteristic, the devotion to the martyrs, has been referred to above. Nor will the Syrians yield to any one in devotion to the Blessed Virgin, though the language they employ is singularly staid and wanting in the rhetoric which is such a striking feature in Greek offices. The following are examples:—

Come and hear, and I will tell you. Hear and wonder, ye wise. A maiden brought forth in Bethlehem. The light of the whole world. And her memorial is celebrated with processions. In all four quarters of the world. And in heaven by the angels ("Martyrs," Monday morning).

Glory be, etc. May the strength that came down from on high. And sanctified her and adorned her with honour. That she might bear the true light. And hope and life to created things. Be among us. . . . * May we who have taken refuge. In the prayer of the Blessed one. Mary the holy Virgin. Mother of Jesus our Saviour. Be kept by it from the Evil one. And conquer all his wiles. * And in that great day of examination. When the good are separated from the evil. May we be worthy to have our joy with her. In the bridechamber of the kingdom on high. . . . (Motwa for Wednesday Commemoration of all Saints).

A striking feature of the Syrian services also is the variety of their intercessions, not only for their own church, for their own patriarch, metropolitan, and bishop, who are mentioned by name at least twice daily in the litanies and elsewhere, and for their own particular needs; but also emphatically

[1] From the Great Intercession of the so-called Liturgy of Nestorius. See the form of prayer drawn up by the Archbishop of Canterbury for his Grace's Mission Association.

for all the "sons of the holy Catholick church in this and every country," for their oppressors, as we have seen above, "for priests and kings and rulers, that they may be established in the peace of the churches, and in the safety of all the corners of the world;" and also for "all the departed who are separated from us and have departed among us," (Great Intercession for the Dead in the Apostles' Liturgy), they make continual prayer and offer special Eucharists.

The invocations of the saints in their service-books are also remarkable for their sobriety and freedom from rhetoric. They take three forms: (1) a direct prayer to God that the saints may pray for us; (2) a wish that they may pray for us; (3) and a direct appeal to them. The following are specimens of all three kinds:—

Glory be, etc. O Mary, mother of the King, the King of kings. Beseech Christ, who rose from thy bosom. That he may have pity on us by his grace, and make us worthy of his kingdom (second anthem, Monday evening "before").

From everlasting to everlasting. O Christ our Saviour, by the prayer of thy saints. The prophets and apostles and martyrs and all the just. Keep the company of thy worshippers from all harm (*the same*).

And let all the people say, Amen and Amen. Our holy Awa, be our guide. In good deeds which please thy Lord. That by thy prayers we may be helped, and with thee we may have joy (*the same; see page* 226).

And may your prayers be on all of us. May the prayers of Gadai, and Maccabeus, and Tersai. Hebron, and Hipson, and Bacchus. And Jonadab, the seventh son. And of their teacher, Eleazar. And of their mother, the faithful Shmuni. Be a wall to us (Monday morning, "martyrs"; see 2 Macc. vii.).

May [the martyrs], O my Lord, pray and beseech for us to thy

Majesty in the great and glorious day when thy justice shall be revealed from heaven . . . (Morning collect at the end of the service).

Their sound is gone out into all lands. Matthew, Mark, Luke, John. May your prayers be a wall to our souls (Motwa of first Wednesday).

Seek the Lord and his strength. Ye martyrs, ask mercy for the world. Which has its true refuge in the strength of your bones (Motwa of first Wednesday).

THE METHOD OF DIVIDING THE PSALTER.

I. *Psalms at the Night Service.*

The dashes show the subdivisions, or *Marmiatha*, of the *Hulali*. The numbering of the English Prayer-book is followed.

	HULALA.	PSALMS.
Monday }	1	i., ii., iii., iv.—v., vi., vii.—viii., ix., x.
Thursday }	2	xi., xii., xiii., xiv.—xv., xvi., xvii.—xviii.—xix., xx., xxi.
	3	xxii., xxiii., xxiv.—xxv., xxvi., xxvii.—xxviii., xxix., xxx.
	4	xxxi., xxxii.—xxxiii., xxxiv.—xxxv., xxxvi.
	5	xxxvii.—xxxviii., xxxix., xl.
	6	xli., xlii., xliii.—xliv., xlv., xlvi.—xlvii., xlviii., xlix.
	7	l., li., lii.—liii., liv., lv.—lvi., lvii., lviii.
Tuesday }	8	lix., lx., lxi.—lxii., lxiii., lxiv.—lxv., lxvi., lxvii.
Friday }	9	lxviii.—lxix., lxx.
	10	lxxi., lxxii.—lxxiii., lxxiv.—lxxv., lxxvi., lxxvii.
	11	lxxviii.—lxxix., lxxx., lxxxi.
	12	lxxxii., lxxxiii., lxxxiv.—lxxxv., lxxxvi.—lxxxvii., lxxxviii.
	13	lxxxix.—xc., xci., xcii.
	14	xciii., xciv., xcv.—xcvi., xcvii., xcviii.—xcix., c., ci.
Wednesday }	15	cii., ciii.—civ.—cv.
Saturday }	16	cvi.—cvii., cviii.—cix., cx., cxi.

THE DAILY SERVICES.

17 cxii., cxiii., cxiv., cxv.—cxvi., cxvii., cxviii.—cxix., 1–89.
18 cxix., 69—cxx., cxxi., cxxii., cxxiii., cxxiv., cxxv.—cxxvi., cxxvii., cxxviii., cxxix., cxxx., cxxxi.
19 cxxxii., cxxxiii., cxxxiv., cxxxv.—cxxxvi., cxxxvii., cxxxviii.—cxxxix., cxl., cxli.
20 cxlii., cxliii., cxliv.—cxlv., cxlvi., cxlvii., 1–12.—cxlvii. 12., cxlviii., cxlix., cl.
21 Exodus xv. 1–22.—Isaiah xlii. 10–14.—Deut. xxxii. 1–23.—Deut. xxxii. 23–44.

Feasts of our Lord, the whole Psalter.
Sunday "before." Hulali 5–14 inclusive.
Sunday "after." Hulali 12–21 inclusive.
Saints'-days. Hulali 12, 13, 14.
The Gloria is said after each Marmitha.

Rules as to weeks "before" and "after." If the Sunday is "before," so also is Monday, Wednesday, and Friday, the first choir beginning the service; but Tuesday, Thursday, and Saturday are "after," the second choir beginning, and *vice versa*. But there are three services for Fridays; one is called "the middle Friday."

II. *Psalms at the Evening Service.*

Sunday.	(1) Advent to Epiphany, special.
	(2) At other times lxv., lxvi., lxvii.
Monday.	xi., xii., xiii., xiv.—xv., xvi., xvii.
Tuesday.	xxv., xxvi., xxvii.—xxviii., xxix., xxx.
Wednesday.	lxii., lxiii., lxiv.—lxv., lxvi., lxvii.
Thursday.	xcvi., xcvii., xcviii.—xcix., c., ci.
Friday.	lxxxv., lxxxvi.—lxxxvii., lxxxviii.
Saturday.	cxlv., cxlvi., cxlvii. 1–12.—cxlvii. 12., cxlviii., cxlix., cl.

Daily, in addition. cxli., cxlii., cxix., 105—113., cxvii.

Shurayi (short psalms) at Evening Service, with the "Letter" psalm.

Week "before."
Monday.   xii. 1–7; xv. 1–5; cxix. 1–17.

THE DAILY SERVICES.

Tuesday.	xvii. 1–6 to "hear me"; xxi. 1–5; cxix. 17–33.
Wednesday.	xxiii. 1–5; xxiv. 1–6; xlv. 14–17.
Thursday.	xxv. 1–5; xxviii. 1–8; cxix. 49–65.
Friday.	lxxv. 1–5; lxxxii. 1–5; cxvi. 11-13 to "people."
Middle Friday.	xcv. 1–8; cxxxix. 1–5; xl. 7–10 to "me."
Saturday.	xxx. 1–5; liv. 1–5; cxix. 65–89.

Week "after."

Monday.	xlii. 1–5; cxxiii. 1–3; cxix. 89–105.
Tuesday.	lxvii. 1–6; xl. 16–20; cxix. 113–129.
Wednesday.	lxxii. 1–5; ci. 1–10; Ex. xv. 20, 21 to "gloriously."
Thursday.	cxix. 41–49; cxix. 121–129; cxix. 145–161.
Friday.	cxlv. 1–7 to "kindness;" cxlv. 18 to end; xxxi. 21–24.
Saturday.	cxxiv. 1–6; cxxv. 1–3; cxix. 161 to end.

All these *shurayi* are farced, and the Gloria follows them. On Sundays and holidays the *shurayi* vary with the season.

III. *Psalms at the Morning Service (invariable).*

cx. with Gloria; xci. with Gloria; civ. 1–6 to "sap;" cxiii., xciii., cxlviii., cxlvi. (on ferias and saints' days only), cl., cxvii. with Gloria, li. 1–18 (ferias).

CHAPTER XI.

HOLY COMMUNION.

Infrequency of the celebrations — The three liturgies — Their antiquity—The preparation of the elements—Legend of the holy leaven—Baking the holy loaves—Mixing the chalice—Description of the service—The lections and their system—Difficulty of finding places—Expulsion of catechumens, offertory, and creed—Form of Sursum Corda and cherubic hymn—Communicating the people—The children and infants—The Antidoron—Communion of the priests—Reservation—Vestments—A Syrian sermon on Holy Communion—The rest of the Takhsa—Confession—Office of absolution.

ALTHOUGH, from a theological point of view, baptism comes before Holy Communion, in the Syrian services the order is reversed. Baptisms always take place after the Liturgy is completed; and in the *Takhsa* or priest's book, the baptismal office comes after the three liturgies. We may therefore follow the Syrians, and describe first the Order of Holy Communion.

Unfortunately the Liturgy is only used on comparatively rare occasions; usually only on the principal festivals of our Lord and popular saints' days; especially on Christmas Eve, Christmas Day, the Epiphany, Wednesday of the Rogation of the

Ninevites, three times in the fast, Palm Sunday, Maundy Thursday, Easter Even, Easter Day, Ascension Day, Whitsunday, Holy Cross Day, (Sept. 13); and perhaps St. Thomas (July 3), St. Mary (August 15), Mar Shimun Barseba'i, and one or two others, and the day of patron saint of the church. Very many village churches do not have communion so often even as this; but, on the other hand, some churches in the mountains keep up a regular Sunday Liturgy, according to the command of the Sunhadus (v. § 7). The hour is always an early one, except on fast days, when there is a late communion, often in the afternoon, in order that all may fast till then; for it is a matter of course that no one will touch food until he has communicated.[1] There is a rule that the evening, night, and morning services must have preceded; no priest or deacon is to take any part in the service unless he has also assisted at these three services (Cautelae Missae, in the Takhsa. No. 27). But in practice, that there may not be a long break between the end of the morning service and the beginning of the Liturgy, the celebrant and one deacon are baking the bread and preparing the chalice while the rest are saying the morning prayer.

As a rule there may be only one celebration in a church in one day. But sometimes in the Great Fast, in Tiari, there are two celebrations, one early for children, who cannot go long without food, and another in the afternoon for grown-up people, who are thereby secured against tasting bite or sup till the proper time. A priest who has to serve several

[1] See below, chapter xv.

churches, may, at any rate in the mountains, celebrate two or three times in a day on such occasions as Easter or Christmas, once in each village.

The East Syrians have three Liturgies, ascribed respectively to "the Apostles"—Mar Adai, one of the Seventy, and Mar Mari his disciple, who were the "converters of the East"—to Theodore the Interpreter, and to Nestorius. It is extremely unlikely that the two last should have been written by those two authors; for they contain no allusion to Nestorianism, and, moreover, are purely of the East Syrian family, and differ greatly in plan from the Liturgies used at Mopsuestia and Constantinople. It is true that the third liturgy has much evidence of Constantinopolitan influence. But this may be accounted for by supposing that some East Syrian author had before him the Constantinople Liturgy when composing this one, and was much influenced by it. In the early ages even the distant East Syrians had many dealings with the Greeks, as seen by the extraordinary number of Greek words, especially ecclesiastical words, in their language. And this was not merely in the very first ages, but at a time when such words as *patriarch, metropolitan, archdeacon, subdeacon (hiupatiaqna)*, and others could be introduced. Probably during the fourth or early in the fifth century, therefore, some learned Eastern Syrians, one of whom at least had access to Greek liturgies, composed those offices which go by the name of Theodore and Nestorius. It is extremely unlikely that they are later in date than the rise of the Nestorian heresy, and almost impossible that a patriarch of Constantinople, who as far as we can tell, knew nothing of the liturgy of Seleucia and Ctesiphon (the "Apostles' liturgy"), should have composed a portion of a liturgy on that model, which was so different from what he was accustomed to. But the resemblance of the third liturgy to that of St. Basil may account for the reputed authorship. The popular account is that the third liturgy is the original work of Nestorius, and that the East Syrians, finding it so like their own, at once decided that its author must be orthodox, and cast in their lot with him.

This bit of history is on a par with the popular theory of the origin of the different liturgical uses. Each of the Apostles is believed to have written a different liturgy for his own sphere of labour, and there are therefore twelve nations of Christians. In the last days the Apostles or delegates from the churches will all meet again in Jerusalem and will compare their liturgies, and whichever is found to be best will be the liturgy of the world! It is not difficult to guess to which it is thought the prize will be given.

The old liturgy of the Christians of St. Thomas, or of Malabar, belongs to this family, and is indeed but a recension of that of the Apostles. Thus the early missions of Seleucia were borne witness to. But Mar Shimun no longer has adherents in India; these interesting Christians being either Roman Catholics or Jacobites. The present Mar Shimun consecrated a bishop, or metropolitan as he was called, for India. But it is not known what became of him.

Of the three liturgies, the first, of the Apostles, is

used on all ordinary days; in fact, always except on the Sundays from Advent to Palm Sunday inclusive, when the second liturgy, ascribed to Theodore of Mopsuestia, is used; and on five days in the year, when the third, ascribed to Nestorius, is used: viz. Epiphany, St. John Baptist, the Greek doctors, Wednesday of the Rogation of the Ninevites, and Maundy Thursday, all of which fall between Christmas and Easter.

The Eastern Syrians are especially careful in preparing the elements for the Holy Communion. They emphasize the continuity of the Eucharist by the unity of the bread used; each time it is baked it is leavened not only with some dough from the last baking, as is the case with all bread, but also with a small portion of the holy leaven which is handed on from age to age in each church. There is a curious legend connected with the leaven, which is believed to have been handed down from the founders of the church, Mar Adai and Mar Mari. The following is abridged from the Iskuliun (Scholium) or Commentary of Priest Isaak of Ishbad,[1] a rare manuscript now in our possession:—

<small>At our Lord's baptism St. John caught the water that fell from his body in a vessel, and before his death gave it to his disciple, John the son of Zebedee, to keep till it should be required. At the last supper our Saviour gave one loaf to each of the disciples, but to St. John he gave two, and bade him eat one and keep the other for the holy leaven. When the soldier pierced the side of our Lord on the cross, there came out water and blood, and John saw them; the blood the sign of the mysteries of the body and blood which are in the church, and the water</small>

[1] Dr. Badger gives this also from a different text, from the Scholium of Yukhanan Bar Zobi ("Nestorians and their Rituals," vol. ii. p. 151).

the sign of the regeneration of those who believe. John alone perceived the separation of the blood and the water, and took the blood in the loaf which he had kept from the Passover, and the water in the vessel which the Baptist had given him. After the descent of the Holy Ghost, the disciples remembered that the Lord had commanded them in the forty days to prepare the leaven which they took from his body; and they took the baptismal vessel and mixed it with olive oil, each taking a horn of it for the oil of baptism; and the loaf which had received the Saviour's blood they ground in pieces and mixed in flour and salt, and divided amongst themselves, that it might be the leaven of the body and blood of Christ in the church.

This leaven is renewed from time to time with a special office by a priest and deacon on Maundy Thursday; what remains in the vessel is mixed with dough, salt, and olive oil, and leavens the whole; and no Eucharist can be celebrated without it. The Syrians say that the reason why the "Westerns" hate Nestorius is that, when he fled from Constantinople, he took away the holy leaven and left them without! Some writers count the leaven a sacrament, or, as the Syriac expresses it, a mystery. But there is no consensus of opinion as to the number of the sacraments. The writer just mentioned counts two, Baptism and Holy Communion. Others count seven, and add to these two great sacraments of the gospel Holy Orders, the Holy Leaven, Absolution, Unction, and the Sign of the Cross. But it is thought that these writers borrow the number seven from Western Christianity. Confirmation is counted an integral part of baptism, and it would not be likely that a Syrian writer would make it a separate sacrament. The sacrament of the Holy Communion is generally spoken of in the plural as the "mysteries," perhaps on account of its several mystical significations.

The elements are generally prepared during the recital of morning prayers by the celebrant, vested in albe, girdle, and stole, and assisted by the deacon.[1] No layman may mix the dough (Cautelae Missae, No. 3); this is properly the function of the sacristan (*Qankaya*), who must be a priest or deacon ("Heavenly Intelligences," *s.v.* "Sacristans.") But generally the celebrant himself, saying some collects and the first thirty Psalms, or as many as the time allows, takes fine flour and olive oil and warm water, mixes them together, pouring in (ordinary) leaven from the last baking, and a little salt; he then presses the dough in five places with a stamp, covers it well, and leaves it to rise. He then takes away a portion for the *antidoron*[2] from the top and for the leaven of the next occasion, and a portion for the priest's loaf from the middle, making in it a square hollow in which he puts a little olive oil, saying part of Psalm cxIv. He then goes and brings the vessel with the holy leaven from the sanctuary, and taking a little in two fingers signs the dough and the olive oil with it, and returns the vessel to its place saying part of Psalm xxiv. He kneads the dough well, saying Psalms lxxxii to ci. inclusive, and goes to the special oven in the ground or wall either of the baptistery or of a special chamber (as at Qudshanis), and, after sprinkling a little incense on the fire, bakes the

---

[1] There are not many copies of the Order for the Preparation of the Elements in use. This account is taken from a MS. of the district of Jilu.

[2] See below, page 260.

loaves (of which there *must* be at least three, and there should be at least seven: Cautelae Missae, No. 16) against the sides of the oven, saying appropriate anthems. When all is done he takes the paten, which is a tray about a foot in diameter, and puts it in a recess in the sanctuary, saying part of Psalm xcvi. The loaves themselves are about half an inch thick or less, and about two inches in diameter; each is pressed with a wooden stamp. None but the finest flour and purest water and olive oil may be used; and no part of the holy bread must be used for any other purpose (Cautelae Missae, Nos. 3–6). Each loaf is called *bukhra*, or " the firstborn."

The priest then prepares the cup; he pours in a little wine in the form of a cross, mixes water with it in the same way, and then pours in the rest of the wine, reciting St. John xix. 34, 35. The chalice is usually a large copper bowl without any stand, about eight inches in diameter. No spoilt wine may be used. The water should be in equal proportion to the wine; or, if there is a scarcity of wine, not in greater proportion than two to one, or at the very most three to one (Cautelae Missae, Nos. 24, 25). As a matter of fact, wine is plentiful in the plain of Urmi and in the southern districts of Kurdistan; but in some places, as at Qudshanis, wine has to be brought from a distance, and the scarcity of it perhaps is one cause of the infrequency of the celebrations. In some cases priests have been known to use the juice of raisins soaked in water.

Meanwhile the deacon sweeps out the sanctuary. This is very necessary; as the reverence which dictates that it shall only be entered by the clergy, and by them only when fasting, involves a considerable amount of dirt. The sacristan is ordered to clean the sanctuary every week before the sacrament (Cautelae Missae, No. 10). Altars, however, which are made of sun-dried bricks or stones plaistered over with mud, may not be washed with water when once fixed, except for the purpose of renewal; but they may be anointed with spices and sprinkled with rose water; and in all places, in times of peace, the altars and altar slabs are to be kept in good order (Nos. 1, 2). These slabs, which are frequently mentioned in the service-books, are not now used.

When all is ready the semantron is beaten and the people are summoned. But they often do not assemble in the church till the service has been well begun, and this is perhaps the reason why the Gospel is so often, if not always, removed from its proper place when few are present and read just before the communion of the people, when also a little sermon or explanation of the gospel is often given. The other lections have in practice almost entirely disappeared. The books containing them in full are extremely scarce; and the clergy have therefore to refer to the khudhra, where the ancient section (*skhakha*) is given with the first few words and the ending. But it takes a long time, even then, to find out the proper lection, and it is no wonder if only the Gospel has in consequence survived. Even in the case of the Gospel the priest often reads any one which he pleases, finding the proper one so hard to discover. It is not uncommon for a long discussion to take place in the most solemn part of the service as to what is the

Gospel for the day, and a prolonged turning over of manuscripts often produces no result. It is hoped that the lectionary lately published by the Archbishop of Canterbury's mission may remedy this state of matters after a time.

The number of lessons provided for each celebration makes up, in theory, for the absence of them in the daily services. They are four in number. Two, called particularly "the lections," are from the Old Testament and Acts of the Apostles; sometimes both from the former, sometimes one from each. The Epistle, or "Apostle," as it is called, is always from St. Paul, and the tradition remains of saying after it, "Glory be to the Lord of Paul." The unity of the Gospel narrative is emphasized by the expression "one Gospel, four preachings;" the Syrians never talk of "the four Gospels;" and the Gospel is therefore given out thus: "The holy Gospel of our Lord Jesus Christ, the preaching of Matthew (Mark, Luke, John)." After the Gospel the people answer, "Glory be to Christ our Lord." Before both Epistle and Gospel are appointed short psalms and also *Turgamas* or anthems explanatory of what is about to be read.

In the "lections" Genesis and Isaiah preponderate, though Deuteronomy, Joshua, and Acts are very frequently read. The following books are not read at all—Ruth, 2 Samuel, 1 and 2 Chronicles, Ezra, Nehemiah, Esther, Job, Psalms (as lections), Proverbs, Ecclesiastes, Song of Songs, Hosea, Obadiah, Nahum, Zephaniah, Haggai, Malachi, all the Apocrypha except the Song of the Three Children which is read on the Confessor's Day (the memorial of the martyrs under King Sapor), and Ecclesiasticus xliv., which is read on the Friday of the dead, Philemon, the General Epistles, and Revelation. It is noticeable that on Maundy Thursday (the "Passover," as it is called), Exodus xii. is read. This is curious, as their strong views about leavened bread would point to the opinion that our Lord ate then an anticipatory passover with leavened bread, and that the true passover was on Good Friday. On Easter Even and Easter Day they read Abraham's trial, Jonah, Isaiah lx. 1-8, and the prayer of Hannah.

An esteemed correspondent writes of the system of lessons:—

"I think the East Syrian lectionary the most admirable, on the whole, with which I am acquainted. (1) It seems to have preserved the original and primitive customs better than any other extant lectionary. In the Apostolic Constitutions we find accounts of two systems: in Book II., two Old Testament lessons, Psalms, Acts, Epistle of St. Paul, Gospel; in Book VIII., the Law, Prophets, Epistle, Acts, Gospel. Of these that in Book II. is undoubtedly the earlier account, though that in Book VIII. is probably Ante-Nicene. In these the Law and Prophecy of the Synagogue are supplemented by New Testament lessons. The East Syrian scheme seems a survival of the same kind of system. Acts would naturally be appropriated to Easter-tide, and the natural desire for uniformity would be quite sufficient to effect the omission of a lesson from the Law when Acts was read, so as to have *four* lessons. The ancient character of this lectionary is also borne out by the fact that it retains the Jewish reckoning of the Prophets, beginning with Joshua. (2) The scheme is complete, designed for the whole ecclesiastical year, and it is of a piece throughout; not like the Roman, which has been supplemented and patched by the addition of incongruities. (3) It is so full, giving the most useful parts of Scripture, and nearly the whole of the New Testament, except the Catholic Epistles and Apocalypse. If we compare the Gospels together we find that almost the whole of the narrative is given; the most striking exceptions being the parables peculiar to St. Luke. Genesis, Deuteronomy, Joshua, and Isaiah are given, practically in their entirety, and there are selections from other books. St. Matthew and St. Luke are given nearly entire, if we except narratives which are common to both of the Gospels. St. John, Acts, Romans, 1 Corinthians, Galatians, Ephesians, Colossians, Philippians, 1 Timothy, and Hebrews are given nearly entire, and the other Pauline Epistles are well represented. (4) The particular selection of lessons is admirable, especially those for the Sundays of Advent and the Gospels for Holy Week."[1]

The lections are read from the *bema* or raised platform outside the sanctuary wall, between it and the dwarf wall which is parallel to it. The lections from the Acts and Old Testament are assigned to the readers, the "Apostle" to the deacon; but the priest himself reads the Gospel.

During the service the people stand reverently in the nave, the women in the background, the men in front. The singers group themselves on the south side round the *quasi*-altar on which are the books,

[1] From a letter of the Rev. W. C. Bishop, M.A.

HOLY COMMUNION. 255

opposite that of the cross. The huge *khudhra* is before them, and they sing the proper anthems of the day, while the deacon is saying a litany, or the priest is saying prayers in a low voice. The deacons are in the sanctuary, one swinging the censer, one clanging the cymbals at the conclusions (called "Canons") of some of the longer prayers. There are generally not more than two deacons, but the number may be increased. One goes to the bema and says a litany, another gives the kiss of peace to the people, somewhat as at the daily services, except that the celebrant first kisses the altar and the deacon takes his hands between his own and kisses them, and then goes out to the sanctuary door and gives the peace to the person of highest rank, and then to the next, and so on. The deacons also have to open or shut the veil which is hung over the opening between sanctuary and nave, to snuff the candles, make the proper responses and the curious ejaculations such as "Pray in your minds, peace be with us!" "Glorify the living God!" "How dreadful is this place!" Thus at the invocation in the third liturgy the deacons say, "O how dreadful is this hour, and how fearful is this time, when the priest calls on the Spirit and he descends from on high and does his will and hallows the heavenly Eucharist.... In quietness and dread, in trembling and fear, stand ye and pray. Peace be with us."

In the plain of Urmi the deacons generally write out their part, called the *shamashutha*, from the Takhsa, with the directions in the vernacular, and learn this by heart.

We have, however, anticipated somewhat. After the

long litany and some prayers have been said, the priest censes the *ma'apra* or outer vestment, which has hitherto been lying on the altar, and puts it on; and the deacons dismiss the catechumens, saying:—

Let him who hath not been baptized depart; let him who doth not receive the sign of life depart; let him who doth not accept it depart. Go ye hearers [1] and watch the doors.

The offertory follows, consisting of anthems, during which the holy vessels are put on the altar, but there is no collection of alms. After other anthems and some prayers the Creed is said thus:—

We believe in one God, the Father Almighty, Maker of all things visible and invisible. And in one Lord Jesus Christ, the only begotten Son of God, the firstborn of all creatures. Begotten of his Father before all worlds and not made. Very God of very God. Son of the nature [2] of his Father; by whose hands the worlds were fashioned, and everything was created. Who for us men and for our salvation came down from heaven, and was incarnate by the Holy Ghost, and became man, and was born of the Virgin Mary. He suffered and was crucified in the days of Pontius Pilate. He was buried, and the third day he rose again, as it is written, and ascended into heaven, and sat down on the right hand of his Father. And furthermore he is ready to come to judge the dead and the quick. And in one Holy Ghost, the Spirit of truth, who proceedeth from the Father, the life giving Spirit. And in one holy Apostolick and Catholick Church. And we confess one baptism for the forgiveness of sins, and the resurrection of our bodies, and the life for ever and ever. Amen.

The Sursum Corda takes different forms. The Apostles' Liturgy has:—

---

[1] In allusion to the class of penitents who were allowed in old days to be present at the Eucharist but not to communicate.

[2] This is the Syriac way of expressing "of one nature." See below, chapter xiv., On the Syrian language.

Lift up your minds. *Ans.* Unto thee, O God of Abraham, Isaak, and Israel, O Glorious King.

The Offering is being offered to God the Lord of all. *Ans.* It is meet and right.

But in the other two liturgies the priest's part is very much expanded. In the baptismal service, where the Sursum Corda also occurs, we have it as above, except that the third clause has: "Let us confess, worship, and glorify God, the Lord of all."

The Cherubic Hymn is said by all. It is as follows:—

Holy, holy, holy, O Lord the mighty God. Heaven and earth are full of thy praises and of the nature of thy being, and the excellency of thy glorious splendour. Hosanna in the highest. Hosanna to the Son of David. Blessed is he who hath come and who cometh in the name of the Lord. Hosanna in the highest.

A very large part of the service is said by the priest in a low voice; the intercessions are all thus said, and are divided into "prayers of beseeching," said kneeling,[1] and "prayers of inclining" said with bowed head. As is well known, in the Apostles' Liturgy the words of institution are not written. It is considered probable that they were always said, though a motive of reverence forbade their being written. Unfortunately, it is not uncommon now for the more ignorant priests altogether to omit this essential part of the sacrament. Both the other liturgies contain them; and if they had not been recited in the oldest liturgy the absence of them would certainly have been a matter of accusation against the Syrians. In all three liturgies the great inter-

[1] This is the direction. As a matter of fact, the priest often squats on the floor. See above, page 237.

cession for the living and departed precedes the invocation of the Holy Spirit upon the elements. The Apostles' Invocation is unique. "And, O my Lord, let thy Holy Spirit come and rest upon the offering of thy servants, and bless and hallow it, that it may be to us,[1] O my Lord, for the absolution of trespasses," etc. The other two liturgies have different forms. The second has, "May the grace of thy Holy Spirit come upon us, and upon this offering, and dwell upon and overshadow this bread and this cup, and bless and hallow and seal them in the name of the Father, and of the Son, and of the Holy Ghost; and may this bread become through the power of thy name the holy body of our Lord Jesus Christ, and this cup the precious blood of our Lord Jesus Christ, that whosoever with true faith eateth of this bread and drinketh of this cup, they may be to him unto the forgiveness," etc. And the third liturgy has, "May the grace of the Holy Spirit come and dwell and rest upon this offering which we offer before thee; and bless it and hallow it, and make this bread and this cup the body and blood of our Lord Jesus Christ. Change thou them and hallow them by the operation of the Holy Ghost, that the taking of these glorious and holy mysteries may be (effectual)," etc.

After the fifty-first psalm has been recited, there is an elaborate ritual for the signing and breaking of the elements, up to which time there have been no manual acts. One of the holy loaves is dipped in the chalice. And at this time also a loaf is

---

[1] Or "become [effectual] to us." The word for *to be* and *to become* is the same.

dipped for the communion of the children. Meanwhile the deacons sing anthems and a litany, and the Lord's Prayer, said simply, but with its doxology, is repeated by all, who thus ask God to give them a good communion.

While anthems are being sung in the nave the people communicate. The deacon who read, or ought to have read, the Epistle goes up to the priest, who puts a veil round his shoulders—a sort of humeral veil—and gives him the paten. The deacon who gives the kiss of peace likewise receives the cup. This is said to be the function of the sacristan ("Heavenly Intelligences," *s.v.* "Sacristans"). The priest then proceeds with the first deacon to the door of the sanctuary, where the deacon stands holding the paten, with the veil of the sanctuary wrapped round him; and the priest, taking portions of the holy loaf, communicates the people. To a priest he says, "The body of our Lord to the discreet priest for the absolution of trespasses." To a deacon he says, "To the deacon of God," and to a layman, "To the circumspect believer." The people receive either in their hands or in their mouths. There is no rule on this point in the Takhsa. Meanwhile the other deacon proceeds to an opening in the dwarf wall on the north side, and administers the cup, saying, "The precious blood for the absolution of trespasses, the spiritual feast for everlasting life to the discreet priest, *or* to the deacon of God, *and to every one according to his degree.*" All devoutly wipe their lips after reception on a coloured napkin held by the deacon. The men receive first, then the women.

It is a touching sight to see the little children coming to receive the Holy Communion, those hardly able to walk led up by their parents or brothers, the babes held in their mothers' arms, in obedience, as the Syrians believe, to the command of him who said, "Suffer little children to come unto me and forbid them not." These children are communicated in both kinds at one time by the priest with the loaf dipped for the purpose, and do not receive from the chalice.

Not so edifying is the scene on great festivals and popular saints' days, when the crowd is too great for the church, and when there is often much confusion and even sometimes a struggle for precedence. But it must be said that the people are in their own way very reverent, although their reverence does not always show itself, as ours would, in a solemn silence; and a stranger is much struck and surprised by the beauty of the service.

As the communicating takes a long time, the thanksgivings are generally sung when it is going on. It is rather unfortunate that most of the communicants leave the church before the service is over. Directly they have received they partake of the *antidoron* or blessed bread, which is administered by a priest or deacon at the nave entrance to the baptistery, and leave the church. The practice of giving the *antidoron* is not very common now; but in some churches the communicants take a piece of ordinary bread which is given them as they leave the church. The *antidoron* is not to be given to heathen, magi, those of other faiths, or even to Christian children (Cautelae Missae, No. 11).

After a few prayers and the blessing, the kiss of peace is given, and the veil drawn; the priest and deacons then make their communions. This is probably an error, arising from the absence of any direction for their communion in the Liturgy and from the directions for consuming what is left of the holy Sacrament after the blessing. This is ordered to be done by two persons (Cautelae Missae, No. 18), the priest and the sacristan ("Heavenly Intelligences," *s.v.* "Sacristans"). At this time also several late comers, especially women, who owing to the press, or to bashfulness, or because they have been kept by home duties, or for some other reason, have not received before, are communicated.

Reservation is not now practised by the Syrians, and if a person is ill there is no means of giving him the holy Sacrament. The author of the "Heavenly Intelligences," however, perhaps remembering how in Justin Martyr's account the deacons carry the consecrated gifts to the sick, arranges that in villages where there is no priest, the deacon is to go to another village where there is one, and bring the Sacrament thence (*s.v.* "Deacons"). This is not now done. The Cautelae Missae forbid a priest to leave the holy gifts on the altar until the next day, because in the "old law" manna might not be left till the morrow, and neither the old nor the new law commands the Sacrament to be left more than a day (No. 19).

The East Syrian vestments are a rather difficult question. In practice they wear an albe, called *sudra* or shirt, which is of cotton, and has three crosses embroidered on the shoulders in red or black. This albe is girded, and a stole is worn over it, by deacons over the left shoulder ("Heavenly Intelligences," *s.v.* "Deacons") and tied as with us, by priests over both shoulders and crossed, the ends confined by the girdle, and by bishops over both shoulders not crossed. Thus this custom seems to be a very ancient one. The priest during the celebration puts on an outer linen vestment which they call the *ma'apra*, which is like a square sheet, with a few crosses embroidered on it (*pluviale*). It is usually worn on the shoulders like a cope, though it has no morse, and is very liable to fall, but it is at various parts of the service put over the head. The bishops in Persia usually wear Russian vestments. In some parts of the mountains the albes are very short, and linen breeches are worn.

It is not, however, very easy to understand the meaning of the various vestments in the books. The following are mentioned in the "Heavenly Intelligences":—[1]

Biruna, a sort of mitre, or episcopal headdress worn by all bishops (βηριόν). "It is like the hood worn by shepherds.".

Martuta, the pallium, worn by patriarchs.

Qandarin, an episcopal vestment worn above the pallium, spread beneath the *kwantha* or hood. "It is the sign of honour given by the Arab power to the patriarchs."

The above vestments, with the pastoral staff, and (special?) sanctuary shoes are only patriarchal or episcopal. The staff "is a shepherd's symbol, like

[1] At the end; and also under the different orders of the priesthood.

those of Moses and Aaron; its head is of crystal, like the almonds which Aaron's rod yielded" (Numbers xvii. 8).

The *ma'apra* is assigned to all clerks, except perhaps readers, in the "Heavenly Intelligences." But whether the long *pluviale* mentioned above or something of the nature of the modern amice is intended, is not quite certain. It is mentioned as sometimes put over the head, sometimes cast back on the shoulders, sometimes wrapped round the neck. "It is like the veil (*sudara* = sudarium) worn by blessed Moses on his face when speaking to the children of Israel." We may compare the word *amictus*, which was originally a long garment, and was afterwards used for the short linen vestment worn on the shoulders or on the head.[1]

The *kwantha*, worn by bishops and priests, was a sort of hood "like the wings of angels, because high-priests and priests are earthly angels." But if it is the same as the *gultha*, it was also worn by all clerks. The *gultha* is in another passage identified with the *ma'apra* (*s.v.* "Archdeacons").

The *urara* or stole was worn by subdeacons, as well as by deacons at the litany, folded round their necks. Deacons at other times wore it (as now) on the left shoulder. It is not mentioned how the other clergy wore it.

The *zunara* or girdle, worn by all clerks, is a sign of service, and separates the earthly from the heavenly.

The habit of monks was black, "partly as a sign of grief, and to distinguish them from the world,

[1] Smith and Cheetham, D.C.A., *s.v.* "Amice."

and because of the scarlet robe which the Jews put on our Lord."

The following sermon is the unassisted effort of a young Syrian deacon, and may be of interest.

On the Holy Offering.

(1) First let us ask what is the Offering? The answer is: That it is the offering of a sacrifice before God. (2) Let us see since when this has been done. We read that it has been done ever since Adam; for the Bible says, "They made them aprons of skins and put them on."[1] Also Noah made an offering after the flood; also Abraham and all the fathers till the time of the children of Israel, as is quite manifest. For we read that they offered a lamb quite pure and without blemish. This they did twice; and some others were called everlasting sacrifices [meaning?]. This the priest did for an atonement, and sprinkled with its blood those who had sinned. But this could not save men completely, for it was a type of us, given that men might not be idle [without sacrifices] till Christ came; and Christ came and changed it to his body and blood; and he was that perfect sacrifice which was sacrificed upon the cross.

Our Lord, in the night that he was betrayed, took bread, blessed it, and brake it, saying, This is my body of the New Testament in my blood (*sic*) which is broken for you. And also the blood, that is the wine; he said, This is my blood of the New Testament which is shed for you. This be ye doing for my memorial. And so the Apostles ever did, for St. Paul said, When ye eat this bread and drink this cup, ye do show the Lord's death till his coming. So we offer this sacrament for our sins, that they may be washed away. (3) Let us ask, Where must the offering be made? The answer is, In the church, which has been consecrated with apostolic consecration [*lit.* laying on of hands]. (4) Who must offer it? Bishops and priests who have been consecrated with apostolic consecration. (5) What things must be done? Very clean flour of wheat and wine of the grape must be used, as it is written, "I will not drink of this

---

[1] That is, probably the animals had first been sacrificed. This appears to be a reminiscence of a Bible lesson.

fruit of the vine, till I drink it new in the kingdom of God." (6) Who consecrates the sacrament? God the Holy Ghost. Two signs descend on the sacrament, one the invisible grace which is not seen, and one which is seen, for it changes from bread and wine to the body and blood of Christ. And I believe that a man, if he takes it with a pure heart and with faith will not receive judgment, but will be removed from death unto life. It is necessary that Christians should have preparation for this sacrament, and repentance from sin. Amen.

The Rest of the Takhsa.

Besides the three Liturgies and the baptismal service, the *Takhsa* contains the collects said at the daily offices, called the "priestly prayers," and several other minor offices, prayers, etc. There are occasional collects, long blessings which may be used at the Liturgy and other times, the lesser consecration of churches, an office for the leaven, and an office of absolution to be said over any person who has committed a grievous offence. Auricular confession is not now practised by the Syrians, though there are frequent references to it in the service-books, such as the following, "Our Lord has committed the medicine of repentance to learned physicians, the priests of the church. Whomsoever therefore Satan has cast into the disease of sin, let him come and show his wounds to the disciples of the wise physician, who will heal him with spiritual medicine."[1] The office of absolution consists chiefly of anthems and a litany, after which a prayer for absolution is said over the head of the penitent.

[1] From the Khudhra, Monday of the Ninevites, qu. by Mar Audishu in the "Pearl" (Marganitha). See Badger, vol. ii. appendix, for a translation.

One who has "voluntarily apostatized" is signed with oil. Penitents are admitted to Holy Communion on Easter Even. Dr. Badger gives a full translation of the office in his second volume.

CHAPTER XII.

BAPTISM. BURIAL OF THE DEAD.

Likeness of the Baptismal Service to the Liturgy—Description of the service—The holy oil—Invocation on the oil—Anointing the child—Confirmation by imposition of hands—Absence of kiss of peace, of communion after baptism, and of interrogations — Godparents — Swaddling clothes — Salting infants—Private baptisms not allowed—Signing a sick child—Deacons and deaconesses baptizing — Names — Surnames — Burial of the dead—The coffin—The mourning—The cemetery—The funeral procession and service at the grave—Washing after the funeral—The parting kiss of peace—Memorials—Gravestones—Rams.

THE East Syrian baptismal service appears to be of later date than the Liturgies, on which it is closely modelled. There is an invocation on the oil and on the water; and an anointing and baptizing to correspond to the communion in two kinds; and the general order and structure of the service are nearly the same in both cases.

The baptismal service begins, like the Liturgy, with the Invocation of the Trinity, Lord's Prayer, collect, etc. The Psalm "O how amiable" (lxxxiv) is said with its farcing, and a collect and "prayer of the laying on of hands" follow. Each infant is then signed with the holy oil by the priest between the eyes in the form of the cross, with the words, "N. is signed with the oil of anointing, in the name of the Father, and of the Son, and of the Holy Ghost, for ever." They then enter the baptistery, with censer, lights, cross, and Gospels, and recite some anthems, a collect, etc., and Psalm xlv., "My heart is inditing of a good matter," with its proper farcing. The litany is said by a deacon, and another collect is followed by Psalm cx., "The Lord said unto my Lord," a long litany, said kneeling, another collect, and Psalm cxxxii., "Lord, remember David," farced.

The *Lakhumara*, as in the Liturgy, is said by all, and the priest repeats its appropriate collects; then all join in the hymn, "Holy God, Holy Mighty, Holy Immortal, have mercy upon us," with the Gloria Patri. They meanwhile pour enough water into the font to cover the child entirely, and put a veil and the cross and Gospels on the font.

There are no lessons from the Old Testament and Acts at baptism; but the "Apostle" (1 Cor. x. 1–14) is read by the deacon, who says, "Paul, the apostle, the Epistle to the Corinthians. My brethren [pray ye], Bless, O my Lord." A hymn called *madrasha* takes the place of the *zumara* and *turgama* of the Liturgy, and the Gospel follows relating the discourse of our Lord with Nicodemus (St. John ii. 23—iii. 9). The deacon says the same litany, "Father of mercies," as in the other service, and in the same way also the priest says in a low voice "a prayer of the laying on of hands." This is followed by the expulsion of the catechumens; and the rest of the service corresponds to the *Missa*

Fidelium. Anthems are sung, and ordinary olive oil is put into the vessel called *laqna* by the priest, who places it on the altar in the sanctuary and covers it with a veil. Another priest stands by with the horn of the holy oil or "oil of anointing" in his hand. This corresponds to the offertory; and we may notice that in baptism there are two oils, as there are two leavens in the Eucharist. In the latter ordinary leaven is used in the first instance, and a very minute portion of the holy leaven, believed, as has been said, to have descended from St. John the beloved disciple, is added to it afterwards. So in baptism, ordinary olive oil is used, and a very small portion of the holy oil, also descended from St. John,[1] is added from the horn, which is specially reserved for it.

The Creed and a litany follow, and the priest proceeds to consecrate the oil at the altar; he prays to be made worthy, recites the Sursum Corda (in a different form from that in the Liturgy), and says a "prayer of inclining" over the oil, making an invocation in these words: "May the grace from the gift of the Holy Ghost, who is of thee in his perfect Person, and sharer in thy being and the attributes of creation, come and be mingled with this oil, and give to all those who are anointed with it the earnest of the resurrection," etc. The triumphal hymn is then said, and another prayer, after which the priest signs the ordinary oil in the *laqna* with the holy oil in the horn, and covers the *laqna* with a veil. There is nothing here corresponding to the words of institution, or to the Great Inter-

---

[1] See the description on page 247.

cession, though after the invocations comes a prayer corresponding to the recital of the work of redemption, with special reference to the oil. They then go to the font in the baptistery on the south side of the sanctuary, and proceed to consecrate the water, putting the cross and gospel on the east of the font. The priest says, "The grace of our Lord," and a prayer which corresponds to the recital of the work of redemption, and refers to Christ's command that we should in baptism cause a new and spiritual birth to them that believe, and which ends with the invocation, "Let the same Spirit come, O my Lord, even on this water that it may receive strength for the help and salvation of those who are baptized in it." Here also there is nothing answering to the words of institution and Great Intercession.

The Sancta Sanctis is given in another form from that in the Liturgy. "The holy thing is right and fit to a holy nature," and they answer "One holy Father, one holy Son, and one holy Ghost, for ever and ever, Amen." The deacon says, "Glorify the living God."

While those in the nave are singing a hymn or *madrasha* from the ones appointed for the Epiphany (which deal with the baptism of our Lord), "in order that they may not be idle," the deacons undress the children and bear them, each wrapped in a linen cloth, on their shoulders to the priest in the baptistery; the congregation meantime waiting in the nave, out of sight. The deacons ask the names and tell them to the priest, who anoints the children on the breast with three fingers in the form of a cross, saying, "N. is signed in the name of the Father, and of the Son, and of the Holy Ghost, for ever," to show that the knowledge of the Trinity is fixed in their hearts. They are then anointed all over and brought to the priest, who stands at the font, the children's faces being turned to the east.

The priest dips each child three times, saying at the first time, "N. is baptized in the name of the Father" (*Answer*, "Amen"), and at the second, "In the name of the Son" (*Answer*, "Amen"), and at the third, "In the name of the Holy Ghost, for ever, Amen" (*Answer*, "Amen"). The priest dips the child into the water up to his neck, and lays his hand on his head, and gives him to the deacon, who wraps him in a white robe, and carries him to his sponsors, who clothe him, but do not cover his head until the child is confirmed.

The priest proceeds to the confirmation. He goes to the great door of the sanctuary, accompanied by the deacons, with the book of the Gospels, the censer, lights, and horn of the holy oil, and they bring near to him the children who have been baptized. The Venite (Ps. xcv. 1–8, P.B.) is recited, and two collects, as a thanksgiving, and then two prayers of laying on of hands, said aloud, the latter being of the nature of a blessing: "The earnest of the Holy Ghost which ye have received, and the mysteries of Christ, which ye have taken, ... keep you from the Evil one and his hosts," etc. The priest is directed to lay his right hand, at least during the first of these prayers, on them; "he makes his right hand to pass over the heads of all of them." We may compare the use of the right hand only in ordination. The priest then signs the children between the eyes with the forefinger of the right hand, saying, "N. has been baptized and perfected in the name of the Father, and of the Son, and of the Holy Ghost, for ever" (*Answer*, "Amen"). He also puts crowns of coloured threads on them, as in the marriage service.[1] It is remarkable that among the Eastern Syrians, (1) the apostolic laying on of hands at confirmation has survived; (2) there is no anointing at this time; (3) the minister is the priest, who does not use oil consecrated by the bishop, as Greek priests do. The learned Dr. Bickel, however, is of opinion that oil was formerly used at confirmation in this ritual. ("Zeitschrift für Katholische Theologie," Innsbrück, 1877, No. 1.)

The priest and deacons then re-enter the baptistery; and, while anthems are being sung, the ordinary oil in the *laqna* is poured into the horn containing the holy oil, which is thus perpetually replenished; and if any remains in the *laqna*, it is poured, with the *laqna* itself, into the font. Four prayers are said, and the blessing given. A collect follows for "unloosing the water from its consecration;" the *laqna* is cleansed, and all wash their hands in the font, and pour away the water into a place where men do not tread. The water may not be twice consecrated, and without consecration baptism is impossible, except for one near death. This last part of the service answers to the "ordering of the Mysteries," or consumption of what remains in the Eucharist.

[1] See above, page 151.

It is a little curious that there is no kiss of peace at the baptism, considering the similarity of the service to that of the Liturgy, and the importance assigned to the ceremony itself by the Syrians. The kiss of peace at baptism is mentioned by St. Cyprian, St. Augustine, and St. Chrysostom,[1] but it is not found in the Syrian baptismal office. Yet in the place where it should occur on the analogy of the Liturgy, we have the words: "Peace be with you." *Answer*, "And with thee and with thy spirit," as in the other service; and perhaps it is intended that the peace should be here given, though there is no direction to that effect. Another omission is the communion of the newly baptized and confirmed children. The Armenians communicate them with the reserved sacrament, directly after the service is over, though the baptism may be at any hour of the day; the Syrians, however, do not communicate them, although one would expect that they would do so from the position of baptism directly after the Liturgy. Perhaps this is an ol custom which has dropped out.[2]

It will be noticed that there are no interrogations administered to, or promises made by the godparents, though the Creed publicly recited is the profession of faith. There are, however, sponsors. Each child has one godfather and one godmother, and these godparents are also sponsors at his or her marriage. A woman who marries gives up her own godparents, and takes her husband's. This goes on from father to son. Thus, if A and his wife are

---

[1] Smith and Cheetham, D.C.A., *s.v.* "Kiss."
[2] See below, page 276.

T

sponsors to B (a boy), they will also be sponsors to B's children; or if A and his wife die, A's son and his wife will be godparents to B's children, and so on. Thus the godfather and godmother are always of the same family, though in practice they are not always husband and wife. Also, both by custom and by canon,[1] the relationship of sponsors to their godchildren is treated as one of affinity, and therefore a bar to marriage. The relationship between godparent and godchild is most close, and lasts all their lives; and the name in the vernacular for a sponsor means "one who is near."

In passing, it may be remarked that the Syrians always wrap their babes in swaddling clothes, or *bands* as they appropriately call them. On the child's head is put a little skull cap. It certainly cannot be said that they know how to make their babes look pretty. A curious custom is that of salting the infants, which is said to be very good for their health, and is mentioned by Ezekiel in connexion with swaddling (Ezek. xvi. 4).

No private baptisms are now allowed; though the rubrics in the Takhsa seem to be less rigorous than modern custom, in case a child is near to death. But the practice is rigid; baptisms can only be celebrated in a consecrated church, after Holy Communion. If the village has no church, the child must be carried to another village which has one. Also some churches are not used for baptism, as, for instance, the old church at Iyal on the Perso-Turkish frontier; the children being taken

[1] Ashitha Sunhadus. This is not in the ordinary copies, but it is universally held to, at any rate in Kurdistan.

down the valley to the great church of Mar Bishu (see page 295). Thus there are often difficulties in the way of children being baptized; and it is to be feared that there are many cases of infants dying without receiving this sacrament. There is not, however, much danger of a child growing up unbaptized, so great is the regard of the people for baptism. Such cases do, however, occasionally occur, through some accident, and if this is discovered, the child will be baptized when grown up. But, under ordinary circumstances, all baptisms are in infancy. A fairly learned priest, when asked what he would do if an unbaptized child were dying, and there were no church available, replied that he would sign him with the sign of the cross in the name of the Holy Trinity. And there is a regular form used on such occasions, though it is doubtful if it is to be found in any book. It consists of the Lord's prayer, several collects, the *Lakhumara*, Holy God, and a litany. The priest takes a basin of water, and signing it with the sign of the cross, says, "In the strength of our Lord . . . may this water be blessed; in the name of the Father, and of the Son, and of the Holy Ghost, for ever;" and he signs with the water a cross on the child's forehead. The water is then given to the nurse, who bathes the child in it. If afterwards the child recovers, he is taken to the church and baptized. If not they "trust to the mercy of God."

In some places children are signed a few days after birth, even when there is no danger. This ceremony is considered most important, and the child's name is given to it at this time.

This signing is thought to have great efficacy; not, indeed, like baptism, but still as a *quasi-sacramental* rite. The Mussulmans of the Urmi plain, who greatly reverence and often covet the old Christian churches, occasionally bring their children to be signed on a feast day; not with the idea that they may become Christians, but because they look on the signing as a sort of charm which will probably be useful to the child.

Probably the Syrians would consider a person baptized by a layman not validly baptized, and would rebaptize him. But, like all Easterns, they seem to confuse the words "valid" and "canonical." The question, however, does not seem to have been decided by them, one way or the other. As baptism must follow the Eucharist, there is not in practice any fixed age for it. Eight days seems to be considered the proper age, but the sacrament is often or generally postponed till a festival, when there will be a celebration of the Liturgy. The Sunhadus says that those who serve at the altar are not to eat till the ninth hour (3 p.m.), lest an unbaptized child should be near death and need their services (vi. § 6, Canon 5).

In practice, deacons are not allowed to baptize. According to the book of "Heavenly Intelligences," however, they may do so in cases of need (*s.v.* "Deacons"). If a deacon is far away from a priest, he is to mix the water, and take the oil of anointing, consecrated by a bishop or priest, and sign the water with it, without calling on the Holy Spirit. He then baptizes those who are in urgent need of baptism in the name of the Holy Trinity, and gives them the holy gift, consecrated by a priest (brought from another village). But he may not consecrate the oil. Dr. Badger quotes a canon forbidding deacons to baptize (vol. ii. p. 140). This is not in the copies of the Sunhadus seen by the present writers.

In the same book even a deaconess is allowed, for decency's sake, to anoint and baptize women. The priest merely puts his hand behind a curtain and sign them with the sign of the cross ("Heavenly Intelligences," *s.v.* "Deaconesses").

One of the mission teachers, who strongly objected to deacons in the West being allowed to baptize in the absence of the priest, and being confronted with the example of St. Philip the deacon, said he must certainly have been ordained priest before he was sent down to Samaria.

Most of the men's names given are biblical. When softened down in their Eastern pronunciation they are most musical. Auner, Awishálum, Zakbárya, Erémya, Yonan (Jonah), Yukhánan, Gauriel, Múshi (Moses), Awîmelk, Ishai (Jesse), Ishu (Jesus, Joshua), Benyámin, Rúil (Reuben), Iskhaq (Isaak), Yósip, Shlímun, (Solomon), Shîmun (Simon), Túma (Thomas), etc. The preponderance of biblical names has given Dr. Grant an argument to support his theory that the Syrians are the ten lost tribes. A few other names, derived from Christian saints, are also common, such as Giwérgis (George), Húrmizd (a famous monk), and a few Mussulman names, such as Réshid, Mánsur, Ablakhat.

Among the names taken from East Syrian fathers are the very common compound names like

Khnaníshu (Clemency of Jesus), Sauríshu (Hope of Jesus), Audíshu (Servant of Jesus). Less common are Dadíshu (*lit.* Uncle of Jesus), Ishuyáw (Jesus gave), with which we may also compare, Yawálaha (God gave = Matthew or Theodore, or Deusdedit or Dieudonné). The name of our Lord, Ishu (Jesus, Joshua), is one of the commonest of the men's names, and it is not thought at all irreverent to use it. In some districts a man born on a festival receives the name of that day. Thus, one born on the Lord's day, is called Khoshába (= Sunday or First Day), or Yomáran (Day of our Lord); on the Epiphany, Dínkha (Sun-rising, the mountain and ancient name for that festival); on Palm Sunday, Oshána (Hosanna); on the Transfiguration, Giliána (Revelation), and so forth.

In the books we find many curious compound names, such as "Glory to Jesus," "Glory to God," "Glory to our Lord," "God hath sought out," "Son of the Church," "Son of the Monastery," "Son of the Martyrs," "Jesus had pity on her," "Jesus is our hope;" and the like. But these are now obsolete.

The women's names are mostly Mussulman, and denote flowers or the like; but the commonest of all is Máriam, after the Blessed Virgin; and we have also Elíshwa (Elizabeth), Sára, Répqa (Rebekah), Rákhil (Rachel), and a few others, from the Bible.

When a boy has the same name as his grandfather, he is not, in the plain of Urmi at least, called by his own name during the old man's lifetime, but Bába; and this name will often cling to a man all his life, and becomes the commonest of all names in common use. But it is not a baptismal name.

A son never has the same name as his father. Surnames are not ordinarily used, and if two men of the same name have to be distinguished from one another, they say, "Son of So-and-So," or give the name of his trade or village, as was done in Europe in the Middle Ages. But the name of the father or of the trade has not developed into a surname. A Syrian, on hearing that all members of a family in Europe had the same name, said, "But how can you distinguish between them?" When it was explained to him about Christian names and surnames, he thought that very confusing; and when told that some people had half a dozen names or more he thought it utter foolishness!

In a few cases in the mountains a whole family or clan is distinguished by some name. Thus in a village of Tkuma the members of the priestly family—for that office is mainly confined to it in that case—are called "So-and-So of the house of the Priest (*d' Bi Qasha*)."

Burial of the Dead.

The funeral service of the Syrians is of a most dramatic and striking kind—wonderfully impressive to those who can follow the Syriac, and yet very unlike what we are accustomed to in the West. It is contained in two books called the Kurasta, and the 'Anidha, the former of which is very large; but the whole is not recited at one burial. There are separate services for patriarchs, metropolitans, bishops, priests, deacons, laymen, women, children; though for the most part the shorter services are contained in the longer. The office for the clergy, if recited in full, takes at least five hours, though during some of this time the body is being prepared for burial.

The funeral must necessarily take place in a hot country as quickly as possible after the death. Messengers are at once sent to call all the friends of the deceased; the carpenters are set to work to make the coffin, which they do in a few hours; or, if it is in the neighbourhood of the town of Urmi, a coffin is bought ready made from the bazaar, only distinguished from those of Mussulmans, by a little cross in silver paper on the lid; but in the mountains, in the case of the poorer people, coffins are often dispensed with; slabs of stone are placed in the grave, to line the bottom and lower parts of the sides. In this stone tomb the body is laid, decently shrouded and covered with cloths, and while the service is going on, other stone slabs close it in, and the earth is thrown on and the grave is filled in.

Usually there is a delay of a few hours while preparations are being made. And during this time the scene in the house is an agonizing one. The women have crowded in and are wailing and tearing their hair with grief. Even strong men give way to the loudest lamentations. With us it is thought right to restrain oneself. Not so with the Syrians. Loud wailings are a tribute to the departed; and a people who are by nature impulsive, on such an occasion as this give way to the most passionate sorrow. It is a very real trouble to them at the time, though they may not have greatly loved the deceased in his lifetime. Their feelings are strong, and the present woe causes the most reserved of them to shed tears. One can picture the scene in the house of Jairus—the minstrels, or pipers, and the people making a noise (St. Matt. ix. 23),—a scene of confusion, which was not fitting for the miracle our Lord was to work. One is tempted to think that the people have not quite learnt the meaning of Christian death: "The maid is not dead but sleepeth." The same loud weeping no doubt existed from the earliest times. Abraham came to mourn for Sarah and to weep for her (Gen. xxiii. 2). It was not merely that he was in grief and could not restrain himself. He *came* to weep and mourn, as a tribute to his departed wife. And when he himself died, and his sons Isaak and Ishmael came to bury him, no doubt there was the same mourning. Such, too, was the lamentation of David over Saul and Jonathan (2 Sam. i. 17), and of Joseph and the Egyptians for Jacob, which gave a name to the place, Abel-mizraim (Gen. l. 11). But such manifestations of grief may easily pass into an unmeaning show, and it was found necessary to make canons in early ages against its abuse. The Syrian Sunhadus forbids women to bring in heathen weepers to mourn for the dead under pain of excommunication; nor are men to allow this to be done (v. § 24).

Rules are laid down for the washing of the bodies of the dead. In the case of monks, nuns, bishops, metropolitans and Catholici, only the heads, hands and feet are to be washed; but in the case of secular priests and the laity, the whole bodies are to be washed (v. § 23). The body of a patriarch must be washed by bishops ("Heavenly Intelligences," *s.v.* "Patriarchs"). A layman's body is washed by "grey beards" of noted gravity and goodness; a woman's body by aged women of honour and reverence.

The coffin is carried on a bier out of the house. In the case of a layman there is not usually a service in the church; and one can well understand that when the only door is some three feet square, and sometimes approached by a ladder, it is very inconvenient to take the body inside. There is usually only a celebration at the funerals of the clergy, though the Sunhadus apparently contemplates one in all cases, as it orders the lections from the prophets to be read over all laymen and lay brothers and sisters; and in the *'Anidha* a communion hymn is appointed for all cases. For deacons and deaconesses the Sunhadus says the "Apostle" is to be read, and for priests and higher degrees, the Gospel (v. § 23). But ordinarily the lections are read in the house. They differ for the different degrees. Thus for baptized children the story of Bath-sheba's child is read (2 Sam. xii. 15–24) and of the widow of Zarephath (1 Kings xvii. 17–end); for women the death of Sarah (Gen. xxiii. 1–8 and 19) and of Tabitha (Acts ix. 36, *sqq.*), and so on. The procession then moves directly to the grave, the priests and deacons going in front and chanting anthems antiphonally; many of them compositions of great beauty. The cemetery is usually outside the village, and, especially in the plain of Urmi, does not usually adjoin the church. In the church itself no one may be buried, except the martyrs, whose bones are to be "put in the churches to help those in need" (v. § 12). But in the summer chapel which is attached to the church "bishops may be buried, and monks may be buried in the special cemetery inside the monastery" (v. § 25), such as the beautiful little chapel in the Jacobite monastery of Mar Matai (St. Matthew) near Mosul, where the bones of the great Gregory Bar Hebraeus rest.

In Urmi there is much in common between marriage processions and funerals. At both the drums beat, and the sad horn sounds; perhaps the same instrument as is referred to in the account of the weeping at the death of Jairus's daughter. Great branches of trees are carried, adorned with handkerchiefs and apples. At a burial, the deceased's horse follows, carrying his clothes on the empty saddle. At the grave, it is common to see a man jump into it, beat himself on the breast, and utter the most piteous cries. When the coffin is lowered, it is covered with stone slabs which rest on ledges left in the sides of the grave on purpose to receive them, all cast in a handful of earth, and the sextons and young men at once fill the grave. The priests and deacons are meanwhile singing the anthems of the burial service. At the end, stones are placed, one at the top and one at the bottom, and these are signed by the priest with his book in the form of a cross. In Tiari every one signs a cross on the gravestone with a little stone. It is forbidden to bury gold or silver in graves (Sunhadus, v. 24). When all is done, the near relatives stand on one side, and all present give them their condolences or "heal their head;" it is somewhat like the procession at the kiss of peace. Each of the bystanders passes by, touching the hands of the bereaved relatives, and saying, "May your head be pleasant" (or healed).

In many places there is the curious custom of washing after the defilement of touching—only metaphorically—a dead body. On leaving the grave, all go down to a stream hard by; and after a considerable number of prayers, the water is blessed with the sign of the cross, and all wash their face and hands. This is uncommon in the plain of Urmi, though traces of it are found. After the funeral the people often go and eat at the deceased's house; and again "heal the heads" of the relatives.

At the funeral of the clergy, the body is usually taken into the church, and there is sometimes a celebration of the Holy Eucharist. The bier of priests is put in the centre of the nave, and only that of a patriarch may be brought into the sanctuary as far as the lamp. It is carried by bishops and priests. According to some, the bier of a metropolitan may be brought into the sanctuary, but not so far as that of the patriarch. All members of the threefold episcopate are to be buried in their ecclesiastical vestments (Sunhadus, v. § 26; "Heavenly Intelligences," *s.v.* "Patriarchs and Metropolitans").

The service itself is most dramatic, and consists chiefly of anthems, many of which are dialogues between the departed and the company of those who are already in Sheol, or between the departed and the congregation of mourners. The following hymns *or madrashi* may be given as specimens of the service. There are many such in the '*Anidha*, for the various degrees and conditions of the departed; different ones are appointed for patriarchs, bishops, monks, virgins, priests, teachers, deacons, old men, for "all men," for rich men, murdered men, drowned men (these two are a sad comment on the life of the people), strangers, bridegrooms, young men betrothed, an only son, young men, lads, for use at Holy Communion, for women, young women, brides, and children. The following is for bishops.

Tune.—*The just judgment.*

Antiphon. O our holy father, beseech Christ. That by thy prayer, mercy may be showed us.

Verses. May the Father whom ye have loved comfort you. And the Son by his grace be to you a wall. O my sons, grieve not. For grief is not necessary. For the way which all men go. * May our Lord be to you the treasure of the Spirit. And may his love and his will govern your lives. With tears of his mind Joseph wept for his father. With tears and groans we will weep for thy decease.

The following is one of several appointed for priests:—

Tune.—*Pity me in thy mercy.*

Antiphon. O my brethren, and ye who love Christ, I beseech you in our Lord, that when ye stand before him, ye remember me in love.

Verses. Alas for thee, O discreet priest. Friend of the glorious bridegroom. Let it not grieve thee that thou hast departed from trouble to life. * In thy death, O our brother and companion. The leaven of our lives is buried. In the day when thy Lord comes. He places thee on his right hand.

There is a short service appointed to be read at the burial of unbaptized infants, who have been signed with the sign of the cross in the manner described above.[1] From this Dr. Neale has inferred that the East Syrians deny original sin (note 29 in Badger, vol. ii.). But this can hardly be maintained

---

[1] See page 275.

in the face of the very definite language concerning the corruption of our old nature in the baptismal service and elsewhere. If the Syrians err in this matter, it is not in the denial of original sin, but in the opinion that this "signing" has a sacramental efficacy for the bringing of children born in sin into the new covenant. Dr. Neale mentions that Mar Saurishu (Sabarjesus), in the synod of A.D. 596, condemned the doctrine of original sin. But this is not the case with the Syrians as a whole. Their rituals and books plainly affirm it. The *'Anidha* says that in the case of unbaptized children who have been signed no lections are to be read, but one *motwa* (or anthem sung sitting) is to be recited, and a few short anthems until they finish the burial, after which he gives the blessing. If the infant had not been signed, there is to be no service, but a priest is to walk in silence before the bier, "out of respect to the parents." He is to take earth and sign it, and say, "May the Power that fashioned thee from the dust quicken and raise thee, now and at all times, for ever and ever. Amen" (Rubric at the end of the funeral service in the 'Anidha). There is no more here than a pious hope that God, who is not tied to his sacraments, may extend his infinite mercy to the uncovenanted also, who, from no fault of their own, have not received the sacrament of baptism. Dr. Badger gives another rubric, directing that unbaptized children of less than ten days are to be buried by women; but over those who live to six months without being baptized, if in the meantime the mother has "partaken of the sin-forgiving body and blood, which shall have mingled with the milk which he has sucked, one *motwa* shall be said, and in consideration of his parents, one priest shall attend his funeral" ("Nestorians and their Rituals," vol. ii. p. 321). But this is not in the copies of the 'Anidha seen by the present writers, and the arrangement given above is far more in accordance with Syrian ideas.

One of the most striking features of the funeral services is the parting kiss of peace. This is a very ancient custom, mentioned by St. Ambrose, and is preserved by the Greeks to this day.[1] But it is now seldom practised by the Syrians, except at the funeral of priests and bishops. Just before the body is laid in the grave, all take their leave of him. The priests, deacons, and laymen all pass by the bier in turn, and kiss the dead priest's hand, or sometimes a cross laid on his breast, and then stand in a line at the head of the grave while those who are behind come up, and the kiss of peace is passed round in the usual way. The ordinary "healing of the head" of the relatives is perhaps the same custom, a little altered.

For the second and third day services of "consolation" for the mourners are appointed; and on other days also "memorials" are very commonly made of the dead. The Holy Communion is celebrated, alms are offered by the relatives, and, after the Liturgy, all who attend are entertained by the mourners. The Sunhadus says that these memorials had, in old times, been made on the third and ninth days, and, according to the Apostolic Canons, on the thirtieth day, and at the end of the year. But it

---

[1] Smith and Cheetham, Dict. Chris. Ant., *s.v.* "Kiss."

says that the usual custom was that they should be made on the third and seventh days (v. § 27). The martyrs must have a memorial every year (v. § 12). Memorials of departed friends and of the saints may be made on any day, whether Sunday or not, even if there are several memorials together, except only on the festivals of our Lord: Christmas, Epiphany, Palm Sunday, "the Passover" (Maundy Thursday), Easter Day, Ascension Day, Pentecost, and Holy Cross Day; and also on the two festivals of the apostles (the Seventy, and the Twelve, the seventh Friday and Sunday after Pentecost) and the "Hallowing of the Church," the last Sunday but three before Advent (v. § 28).

The gravestones used by the Syrians are often mere rude blocks laid flat on the grave. But the richer people put beautifully carved square stones in the shape of a box, but solid. These are common enough in the plain of Urmi. The inscriptions are generally in the Estrangêla character, and almost always in classical Syriac. They do not very often have more than the name and degree of the deceased and the day when he "rested," as they beautifully express it. Perhaps they added the age as far as they know it: "about 25," or whatever they may guess it to be. They have no registers of births, deaths, and marriages, and hardly any knows his own age accurately, or that of his children, even when they are young.

Another form of gravestone is the ram, which is also found in ancient Christian monuments elsewhere. St. Ambrose (Ep. lxiii.) says it is used as a symbol of the Word, even by those who deny the coming of

BURIAL OF THE DEAD.

Christ, and finds in the fleece of the ram a symbol of the "clothing upon" of Christians (2 Cor. v. 2); in his defence of the flock against the wolf, a symbol of Christ's victory over Satan; in his leading the flock a symbol of the Divine guidance; in his substitution for Isaak a symbol of the one sacrifice; in his dumbness before his shearers (Is. liii. 7) a symbol of the meekness of Christ.[1] The ram is also found occasionally in Mussulman burying grounds in the plain of Urmi, but the Syrians say this is only in cases where the burying ground was originally Christian. They do not seem to have any tradition as to the meaning of the symbol, and they do not now make gravestones of this kind; but they regard it as a mark of great esteem, and preserve the proverb, "I will put a ram on your head," which means, "I will pay you great honour."

[1] Smith and Cheetham, "Dict. Christ. Ant.," *s.v.* "Ram."

CHAPTER XIII.

THE CHURCHES OF THE EAST SYRIANS.

Description of Mar Shalita at Qudshanis—Creeping through the doorway—The metropolitan church—Great church at Mar Bishu—Reason of small doors—Entrance, feet foremost—A cave church—Churches in the mountains before Tamerlane—Hangings—The absence of outward signs of Christianity—Churches in Persia—Mart Mariam at Urmi—The tomb of the Magi—Shimun Safa at Mosul—Mar Sergis—Dedications—Consecration of a church—Restoring old churches.

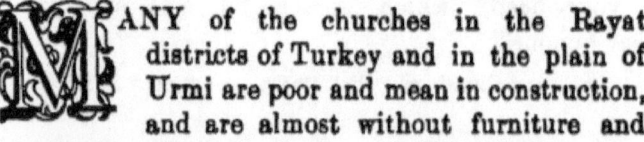ANY of the churches in the Rayat districts of Turkey and in the plain of Urmi are poor and mean in construction, and are almost without furniture and hangings, and their books are dilapidated. But there are others which date from before Mohammed, and which are much more substantial structures. Some of these, though not in districts technically Ashiret, yet had the protection of the semi-independent mountaineers, their neighbours, of Kurdish chiefs of tribes, or of their own half Ashiret parishioners. The patriarchal church of Mar Shalita at Qudshanis may be taken as a typical church as to form and arrangement; but it differs from most others in being perched upon a rock as well as partly built into its side, and in that its body, as

distinguished from later additions, is of hewn stone. The body of the church is a rectangular parallelogram whose long sides run east and west, and is entered by a low door about three feet high from the raised threshold to the lintel, near the west end of the south wall. The westernmost part (two-thirds or more) forms the nave; and the eastern

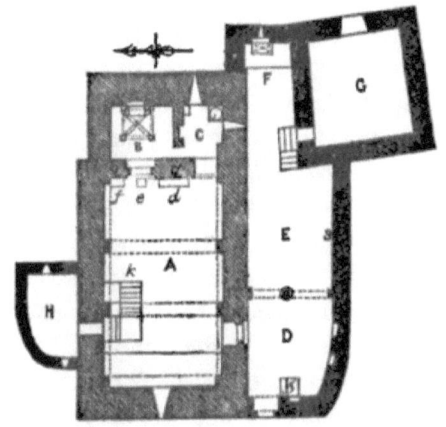

GROUND PLAN OF THE PATRIARCHAL CHURCH, QUDSHANIS.
From a drawing of the Rev. Dr. Cutts.

A, the nave; B, canopy and altar; C, baptistery and font; D, covered part of outer court; E, open court, for the summer prayers; F, raised pace, with *quasi* altar for the Cross; G, room formerly inhabited by the Raban Yonan; H, room used for baking the holy loaves; d, e, f, *shkhinta*; K, entrance, with ladder; k, staircase leading to H.

third, separated from it by a solid stone wall, is divided into a smaller room on the right, which is both baptistery and sacristy, and a larger on the left, which is the sanctuary, and contains the altar under a stone canopy, supported by the east wall and by two pillars in front. This canopied space raised on a footpace is the holy of holies. On the altar are the cross and two candlesticks and the

Book of the Gospels; and in recesses in the sanctuary walls are the chalice and paten and the holy oil. The censer hangs on a nail close to the exit to the baptistery, and on the right of the altar below the holy of holies is a wooden stand which is carried forward to the chancel arch, or rather sanctuary arch, to be used as a book-rest for the reading of the Gospel for the day.

The sanctuary is called by various names. It is usually referred to in the books as *madhbkha*, *i.e.* the sacrificing place, a name which is also given to the altar. Another common name is *qanki* (which corresponds to *cancelli?*); but in some districts (though not in the books) this name is now given to the baptistery, and not to the sanctuary. The name "holy of holies" is also often applied (though not so properly) to the whole sanctuary, and not only to the part under the baldachino. The altar itself is called *madhbkha*, or else the "throne." The name *bim* or bema is not given by the Eastern Syrians to the sanctuary, but to the raised place outside the sanctuary wall, between it and the dwarf wall mentioned below. The Cautelae Missae in the Takhsa say that altars are not to be washed with water, when once fixed, except for purposes of renewal, when the consecration service would be used again. They may be anointed with spices, or sprinkled with rose-water.

The sanctuary arch is only some five feet wide. At Qúdshanis, and at most other places, it is closed by a curtain, which is drawn on one side during the greater part of the Communion Service. But in some places there are also doors which are fastened

between one celebration of the Liturgy and
another. In front of the arch are three steps down
to the nave, but in the middle of the lowest, stands
a *quasi*-altar on which the cross is placed. It is
called the *shkhinta* (a feminine form of Shechinah),
and is vested in various calicoes and silks, Russian
chalice veils, and stoles, which partly cover a book of
the Gospels, and in front form the resting-place of
the cross. From the north wall of the church, a
low wall runs towards the altar of the cross, and
to within a few yards of it. To the south of the
altar of the cross, a similar gangway up to the
sanctuary is left by a low wall which runs to
opposite the doorway from the nave into the
baptistery. In front of the northern dwarf wall is a
lower wall, or altar, whereon are placed books, and
in the case of Qudshanis a second cross. In front
of the southern dwarf wall is a similar solid table,
on which rest a lamp-stand, and, after a deacon has
censed the congregation, the smoking censer, and in
front of it those who are readers gather with any
clergy who are in the nave to sing the people's part
of the Liturgy and other services. On the low wall
or ledge running along the eastern half of the north
wall of the nave are several volumes of service-books,
each protected from dust by a sort of pocket; and
where the ledge ends a solid stone staircase leads up
to an opening in the wall of the church proper,
through which access is had to the chamber where
the bread to be used for the Sacrament is baked by
the celebrant before service. In almost all other
churches this takes place in the baptistery. West
of the staircase is a cross for the women to kiss,

that they should not have to forego this act of reverence from the impossibility or impropriety of their forcing their way through the crowd of men who are in front. In the Qudshanis church is another low wall in which the patriarchs are buried.[1] There is only room for one more coffin. Outside the south wall is a court whose east and west ends are roofed over. Under the eastern roof is a rude "altar of the cross," in front of which are said the daily services in the summer half of the year; and at the southern part of this *quasi*-chancel is a room which was for many years the cell of the Raban Yonan. Underneath this cell is another which is reached by stairs opening in the floor under the western roof of the court and by a passage. The west wall of the summer chapel is pierced by a doorway of about three feet in height, through which and over its high threshold access is gained to the ladder which leads down to the churchyard. This is the only exit from and entrance to the church. The south side of that part of the courtyard which is not roofed over is bounded by a wall between three and four feet high, pierced near the ground by one large and two small apertures. The whole courtyard bears some resemblance (except for the lofty wall of the church proper) to the deck of a ship, with raised forecastle and quarter-deck, and with two small ports and one large one for a gun in the bulwark. The resemblance is increased by the presence of a ladder, by which men go up to the roofs to repair

[1] This seems not to be contemplated by the Sunhadus. See above, page 282.

them or to sweep away the snow. It should be understood that the church itself is built upon a large rock, and the courtyard is raised to the same level, being built upon a lower storey, because the ground slopes rapidly away to the south.

Most churches are on the level of the ground at the entrance. In Tiari and Tkhuma there is an upper storey which is used (except the part over the sanctuary) for storing corn and other produce of the church land, if there be any, or the produce given by the villagers to the Qankaya or sacristan, who is responsible for the performance of divine service. Nearly all the churches in the mountains are of stone and are vaulted. Most of them have a double nave, the exterior or southern chamber being a sort of ante-chapel. The metropolitan's church in Shamsdin, has three of these parallel naves. The outermost is used as the summer chapel for daily prayer; and in it are stored some few possessions of the church, as lamp oil, wax for candles, etc., and the black tents of neighbouring Kurds, who leave them there, as of right, when the summer is over, just as they ask the metropolitan for présents of sheep and other edibles when the humour takes them. This church is almost or quite unique in having a tall and wide entrance door, but this is because it forms one side of the courtyard of the metropolitan's residence.

The great church of Mar Bishu on the Turco-Persian frontier, is almost as lofty as the metropolitan's church, and has eight chambers or "temples" as they are called. The outermost (*i.e.*

that by which entrance is gained), runs north and south, and this is the chapel for daily prayer. The eastern parts of the next two temples, the "chapel of the dead," and the "chapel of the women," open into its west side. The wall which forms its north end, and the north side of one of these two shorter chambers is pierced by two apertures which

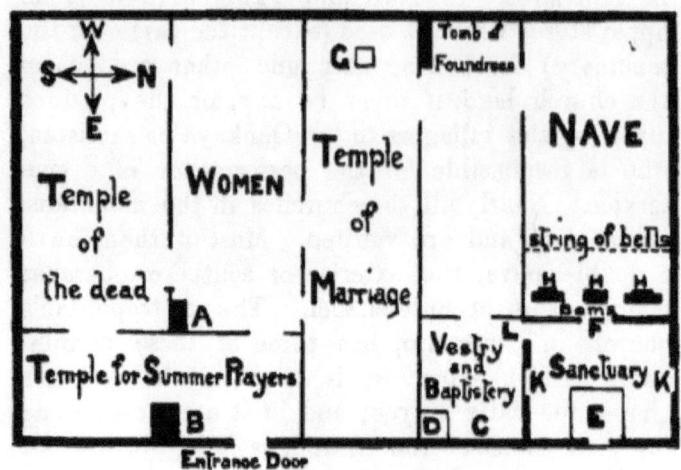

GROUND PLAN OF THE GREAT CHURCH OF MAR BISHU.
From the authors' sketch.

A, tomb of Mar Khazqi'il (Ezekiel); B. tomb of Mar Yukhanan (John); c, the place for baking the holy loaf is above, on an upper storey, approached by an inside staircase of stone; D, font; E, altar and canopy; F, great sanctuary doors; G, lectern where marriages take place; H, H, H, the low dwarf wall, pierced with openings to allow a passage to the sanctuary, with projections for cross, books, etc.; K, K, recesses; L, door from baptistery to sanctuary.

give access to the fourth chamber, the "temple of marriage." This contains a lectern, at which marriages are performed. From the temple of marriage, an opening in the north wall towards the west end leads to the fifth chamber, the temple of the tomb of the foundress, a king's daughter who built at least the four innermost chambers. At the east end of this fifth chamber is the vestry and baptistery (the sixth temple). This contains the font, and above it, on a second storey, which is approached by an inside staircase of stone, is the place for baking the holy loaves. In this baptistery, all the children not only of Mar Bishu, but of the neighbouring village of Iyal, which is about an hour up the valley, are baptized. From the temple of the tomb of the foundress a doorway in the north wall, near the west end, leads into the seventh chamber, which is what we should call the nave, and to which the name "temple" is often confined. At the east end of this is the eighth chamber, the sanctuary, separated from the nave by a wall pierced by a great doorway with large wooden doors. All these chambers are connected by doorways; but the three outer chambers are peculiar in being connected by large arches, and are thus open to one another. Usually each chamber might be regarded as a separate church. In the nave is the usual dwarf wall, and the *quasi*-altar of the cross is in the middle, in front of the sanctuary doors, as at Qudshanis. About a third of the way down the nave, a vast number of bells are strung across the church, which are plucked by any one entering. These bells are brought from Russia.

It is fortunate that in buildings built almost entirely of stone or mud, fires are practically unknown, for the only means of egress from these churches is by a little door, usually on the south side, often not more than three feet high. The church of Tis, in Shamsdin, has a door two and a half feet by fourteen inches, and the only way an unaccustomed visitor could enter was by sitting down and putting in his feet first. These small doors are sometimes at a considerable height above the ground, and can only be approached by a ladder. The reason of the smallness of the doors is said to be (1) that all may bow their heads on entering God's house; (2) that the Kurds and other Mussulmans may not put their cattle into the church. Probably the latter is the true reason. It need hardly be said that in these churches no cross appears on the roof to offend a Mussulman eye; and the only sign of Christianity about the outside of the building is a very little cross over the door, which is devoutly kissed by those who enter. In the mountains the churches are sometimes built against the side of a hill, so that one wall is solid rock; and in the old church above Duri in Southern Berwer a cave is utilized for the nave and sanctuary, so that the baptistery and outer chamber are the only parts artificially built. It is dedicated to a Syrian hermit called Raban Qayuma. The name means "one who stands," but it is not known if he was an ascetic who never sat down. It also means "one who is firm or steadfast."

We believe Dr. Badger to be in error in stating that there are no architectural or monumental records which argue a longer residence of "Nestorians" in Kurdistan than Tamerlane's time ("Nestorians and their Rituals," vol. i. p. 257). There are several churches, some said to be built by kings, which claim to date from before Mohammed, as Mar Giwergis (George) of Khananis, and two churches in the district of Diz or Dizin. These were probably built before the immigration of refugees from the south.

Every church is supposed to contain a part of the body of the saint whose name it bears. Some have tombs of one or more saints in them. Generally these are in a wall at the east end of the nave.

A curious feature about the churches, both in Turkey and Persia, is the quantity of hangings in the nave, sometimes garments, sometimes many yards of calico or even common cotton handkerchiefs. These are votive offerings. In some churches, however, as in Gagoran, in the plain of Gawar (in Turkey), almost an hour away from the garrison village of Diza, there is not even a sanctuary curtain at all, or the sanctuary curtain and the cross and all else are removed except at Communion time, because the Kurds would help themselves to them.

Probably most of the churches in the plains, and in the districts which are neither Ashiret nor even semi-Ashiret, are comparatively modern; and most of them are mean to the last degree. They would be only known in the distance not to be sheep stables or some such buildings, because they are either whitewashed outside, or are somewhat loftier. No European could guess what they were; none could learn that they were churches without being terribly shocked, nor would such a traveller see even the better sort without having borne in upon his mind something of the meaning of Christ's people and

Christ's religion being under the heel of Mohammedans unaffected to any great extent by Western (that is, in fact, Christianized) civilization. He would reflect, too, that where the church buildings are so poverty stricken and unworthy, it is not to be wondered at if the Church have lost some of its moral beauty and dignity and worthiness; and that its members should not be too severely judged if they should be found, in too many ways, to fail to be worthy of their vocation and to have suffered from the moral atmosphere which is compounded of the example of the dominant race and of their own extremity and fear. This was borne home to the present writers by nothing so much as by seeing the contrast, on their return to a Christian country, between the open profession there of our religion in the houses of God, and the shame with which in Persia and Turkey the churches hide their heads. Nothing struck them on re-entering Russia so much as seeing a great cross lifted up on the dome of a church in the first town they came to.

In the plain of Urmi the churches are usually built either of sun-dried bricks or of layers of mud like the houses; they are not vaulted, but are covered with the usual composition of mud and straw laid on wooden beams. The larger doors bear witness to a greater freedom from persecution than in the mountains. There are nearly always four chambers, with perhaps the addition of a porch; on the north side the nave and sanctuary, on the south the "summer chapel" and the baptistery. The latter is not connected with the summer chapel, but has a side entrance to the sanctuary, and a diagonal passage in the thickness of the wall to the nave. Many of the sanctuaries have canopies. The altar is solid brick or mud, coated over with plaister and covered with a cloth; it sometimes projects as with us; but far more frequently is a recess in the east wall with which it is almost if not quite flush.

The old church of Mart Mariam (St. Mary) in the town of Urmi is by far the most interesting building

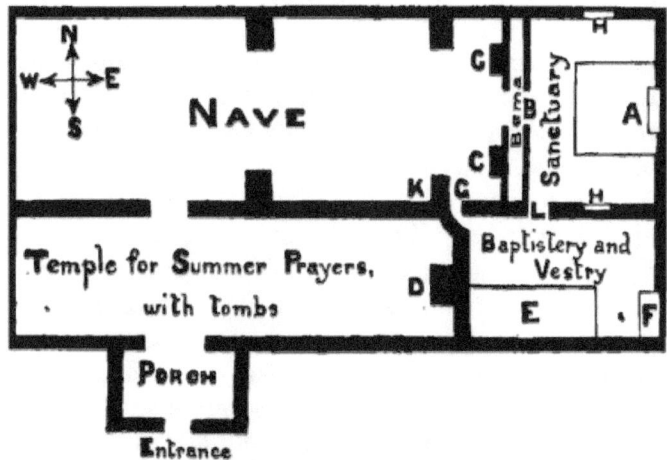

GROUND PLAN OF MART MARIAM, URMI.
From the authors' sketch.

A, altar and canopy; B, veil; C, C, dwarf wall, with projections for the cross on the north side, and for books, etc., on the south; D, projection for the cross, etc.; E, solid table, with oven for baking the holy loaves; F, font; G, opening to baptistery from nave; H, recesses in wall; K, reputed tomb of one of the Magi; L, entrance to sanctuary from baptistery. The projections in the walls of the nave are supports for the low domes, which are a peculiarity of this church.

the Syrians possess in Persia. It is said to have been built by the Magi,[1] and to contain the tomb of one of them. The entrance is by a comparatively modern porch, which gives access to the summer

[1] A famous church in the valley of the Zab, in Tiari, is dedicated to Mar Sawa, who is said to have been a descendant of the Magi.

chapel, in which are some tombs. This is considerably below the level of the ground, and when the snow is piled up on the outside, the whole church is scarcely visible.[1] A very low passage in the thickness of the wall leads from the summer chapel to the nave of the church. The worshipper gropes his way along in entire darkness, descending a little the while, and is lucky if by the time he reaches the nave he has not fallen headlong. Even when he has reached the nave he will see nothing until his eyes are accustomed to the dimness; then he will make his way to the north side of the dwarf wall, where, as in all the plain churches, he finds the *quasi*-altar of the cross, with the symbol of our redemption placed for him to kiss. If he has to take part in the service of the sanctuary, he will have to grope his way through another narrow and dark passage in the thickness of the wall, with many awkward turns, to the baptistery. The nave, unlike other Urmi churches, is vaulted; indeed the roof consists of a succession of domes. As everywhere else, the walls are covered with an immense number of hangings, which collect the dust to an alarming extent.

The church of Mar Sergis (Sergius), in the village of that name on the hills to the west of Urmi (but still in Persia), is also very old and very interesting. Here, strangely enough, the baptistery is on the north side of the sanctuary. On the north of the nave there is a curious cell in which mad men are

[1] A similar instance of a church once underground, though now the ground around it has been somewhat cleared, is Shimun Safa (Simon of the Mill) at Mosul, where St. Peter is said to have lodged and converted the miller who was his host.

shut up. This is thought to cure them of their madness. But lunacy is fortunately extremely rare.

The dedications are generally to Syrian bishops and monks, and often a church which seems to be dedicated to an Apostle is really named after a later saint of the same name. But Mart Mariam (St. Mary) is the commonest of all dedications. Another very usual one is to the sons of Shmuni, the seven martyrs of the second book of the Maccabees; and of other dedications may be mentioned Mar Giwergis (George), Mar Shalíta, Mar Sergis (Sergius), Mar Audishu (Ebedjesus), Mar Saurishu (Sabarjesus), Mar Quriáqus (Cyriac, the boy martyr), and more rarely Mar Mari and Mar Adai. The two most famous churches of Mar Audishu are at Termáni near Urmi, and in the mountain district of Tal (an old monastery), both the scene of many pilgrimages even by Kurds and Persians.

The consecration of a church is called, like ordination and confirmation, a "laying on of hands." There are two kinds, consecration with oil, and consecration without oil; the former is only for new churches, or for churches rebuilt, or when for some very grave cause the church has to be re-dedicated. The latter, which may be performed by priests commissioned by a bishop, is for more ordinary occasions. Consecration with the Syrians is not looked on by the Syrians so much as a "baptism" of the church, a formal dedication once for all to God which may not be repeated, but rather as a blessing on the building. There is really no reason why the lesser consecration should not be repeated every year—as a sort of service for a dedication festival. As a matter of fact, it is ordered in case of certain accidents or breaches of the church's law.

Both services consist almost entirely of a long series of anthems, sung mostly in the sanctuary by the bishop and his attendants, who face the four different walls in turn. The east wall is called the "House of the Altar;" the north wall the "House of the Treasury" (the Treasury is a recess in the wall for the sacred vessels); the south wall is the "House of Forgiveness;" and the west wall is the "House of the Door." Each wall, and the altar, and also the outer lintel of the sanctuary door towards the nave, are signed in the form of a cross with the oil in the greater consecration. The Liturgy then follows. The daily prayers may be said in an unconsecrated building, but baptism and Holy Communion may only be celebrated in a consecrated church. Thus the consecration service enables the people to receive all the ordinances of religion.

The Syrians look upon their churches with the greatest reverence, and the restoration of their village sanctuary is one of the very few things which will call forth their liberality. They are not at all utilitarian, and think it better to rebuild an old ruin in a place where there is not a single Syrian left, than to erect a new church in the middle of a large population. The Sunhadus says the same. "Restoring old churches is better than building new ones. New churches and new monasteries are not to be built without the bishop's consent, unless they are also endowed. Builders of churches or monasteries may not appoint their priests and heads except by command of the bishop" (vii. § 8).

CHAPTER XIV.

EAST SYRIAN IDEAS, THEOLOGY, LANGUAGE, AND CHARACTER.

Nestorianism—Relation of the Syrians to that heresy—Their unorthodox language—Their agreement with the Catholick faith when expressed in untechnical language—Their statements contradicting Nestorianism—The schism from the rest of Christendom—Hopes of conciliatory explanation—Ceremonial defilement—Dogs—Shell-fish—An experiment in lobster salad—The tortoise's freedom from house tax—Mosaic law—Asceticism—Externals in religion—Use of God's name—Punishing whole families for one man's faults—Parables—The deaf man—Open, Sesame—Riddles—The Bible—Uncertainty as to the Syrian Canon—Charms—The Syriac language—Their idioms—Note on falsehood.

ALTHOUGH this is not a theological treatise, a description of the life and customs of the East Syrian Christians would be incomplete without a short account of their relation to Nestorianism. Of Nestorius it is sufficient to say that he was a native of Antioch, who became Patriarch of Constantinople, and was condemned by the general Council of Ephesus in the year 431 for teaching, substantially, that there are two Persons in our Lord, one God and one a Man. His phraseology practically teaches that there are two distinct beings, the Son of God and the Son of Mary, the association between whom differs rather in degree than in kind from the association between the Divine Word and any saintly man. He had no personal connexion with the Eastern Syrians,[1] and the only question before us now is how far they adopted what is known as Nestorianism, viz. the doctrine that the Son of God and the Son of Mary were two separate Persons. There is always a difficulty in ascertaining the exact theological position of a modern Oriental, partly from his dislike of being questioned, and partly from a certain illogical tone about his mind which prevents him defining his ideas very accurately. An answer to our question can therefore only be obtained by discovering from their books whether their forefathers have definitely adopted what we know as Nestorianism, or whether they have only taken the side of Nestorius from a misapprehension and from not understanding the meaning of technical terms; and their traditional theology will aid us in discovering whether they *now* are Nestorians in fact and doctrine as well as in name. It may be remarked that the subject should not be approached, as has too often been the case, with a desire to pick holes in every loose theological statement, but in a spirit of charity which compares one thing with another, and where necessary presumes the better

---

[1] There is an opinion among some Syrians that Nestorius came to them and approved so much of the "Liturgy of the Apostles" that he adopted it himself. They all believe that he gave them their third liturgy; but this is probably an error; see above, page 245.

and not the worse interpretation of ambiguous language.

1. On the one side we have to put the fact that Diodorus, Theodore of Mopsuestia, and Nestorius are revered as saints,[1] and are the principal fathers commemorated on the festival of the "Greek doctors." Their names also occur in several of the litanies and bidding-prayers, and in some of the anthems at the various offices. This does not necessarily imply that the Syrians hold the doctrine taught by them, but only that they do not accept the judgment of Catholick Christendom with regard to them. Also the East Syrians reject the General Council of Ephesus and, therefore, the authority of all subsequent councils, and do not accept the watchword, Theotokos (Mother of God), by which the Ephesine fathers safeguarded the true doctrine of the Incarnation; nor will they allow the propriety of such expressions as "God died,"[2] nor the "Communicatio Idiomatum," that is, the attributing to Christ himself in his single Person, under the title belonging to one of his two natures, of the properties peculiar to the other; as when St. Paul says that the "Lord of Glory" (a Divine title) suffered crucifixion (which he suffered in his human nature) (1 Cor. ii. 8).[3] These methods of expression are explicitly rejected in the Syrian books and tra-

[1] But the prefix *Mar* put before their names does not imply the same thing as our *Saint*. It means " my Lord," and is given to any bishop, alive or dead, and, in fact, it is as if we were to talk of Monseigneur Nestorius. *Mar*, however, is given also to St. Stephen and St. Ephrem and one or two who were not bishops.

[2] See below, page 309.

[3] Liddon's Bampton Lectures, v. 5; Hooker, E. P., book v.

ditionally by the people themselves. If it were not for the books, one would be loth to depend on the floating ideas of the time in saying that the Syrians do not accept the "Communicatio Idiomatum." How many ordinary English folk, for instance, would stumble at phrases justified by it, until they were explained to them. And yet we accept the Council of Ephesus. The Eastern Syrians undoubtedly use unorthodox technical terms. This is in consequence of their not bowing to authority. Not accepting the expressions of the general councils, which are defined to have a certain meaning, they are led to adopt loose expressions of their own, which it is often difficult or impossible to reconcile not only with orthodox technical terms, but with their own untechnical language on the same subject. The commonest of these doubtful expressions is the attribution of two *Kiani*, two *Qnumi*, and one *Parsopa* to Christ. The word *Kiana* means nature. But no one can exactly explain *Qnuma* and *Parsopa*. The former is the word used for the Persons of the Holy Trinity; and also in untechnical language (in classical Syriac), for "oneself." The latter, the Greek πρόσωπον, is used in the old grammars for "person." The ordinary traditional commentary on this phrase is as follows: Two Kiani—Christ has two natures. Two Qnumi—Christ is perfect God and perfect man. One Parsopa—there is only one Christ; not one God and one a man. In this comment, either Kiana does not express the whole of what we mean by nature, or by a not uncommon instance of a mixture of the subtle and illogical in the Oriental mind, two separate words, Kiana and Qnuma, are used to express the same idea, while appearing to express different ones. Assemanni, however, says that by Qnuma the Syrians mean hypostasis, by Parsopa a nature as patent to the senses ("Bibl. Orient. De Syris Nestorianis," vol. iii. part i.). But he may perhaps be prejudiced against the East Syrians, as being a Roman Catholick Maronite. In any case the phrase is an extremely doubtful one. The Scholium of Priest Isaak of Ishbad says that "when the Synod of the 632[1] decided that there is one Qnuma in Christ, whereas there are two natures and a duality of Qnumi, this was because there is no difference in the Greek between Qnuma and Parsopa, and it was not intended to decide anything contrary to orthodox truth" (last part, § i.).

2. On the other hand, if the Catholick doctrine of the Incarnation is put in simple and untechnical language, all who know their old books will cordially and frankly accept it, and say that it is the same doctrine that their fathers taught. All would assent to such a statement as the following: It was the self same He who was from the first, as touching his Godhead, in the bosom of the Father, and who, as touching his manhood, in the fulness of time appeared on earth as Jesus Christ. Similarly, no difficulty is felt in assenting to such expressions as "God the Son died *in respect of his manhood*," while they would reject the simple statement "God the Son died," as conveying (to them) the notion of the Godhead dying. And doubtless the

[1] Perhaps Chalcedon, at which, according to some, there were 630 fathers (Hefele, "Conciliengeschichte," § 188).

term Mother of God—which even to some Westerns appears to convey more than Theotokos, and, until its meaning is explained, is a stumbling-block to so many in England who hear it for the first time—is liable to be confused by them with "Mother of the Godhead." But they would indignantly disclaim the idea that a rejection of this name entailed the assertion that the Son of God descended on the Son of Mary, and was united with him, or that God the Word descended on *a man* and in this sense only became flesh. They admit that as the magi worshipped the infant Christ as God, so angels could properly worship the unborn child. Perhaps in view of the inveterate habit in those who speak Syriac of mixing up—not merely in theology—the abstract and the concrete,[1] it would be better to use the original term, Theotokos, than the translation "Mother of God," in any explanation that might be offered. The Old Syrians have heard such extraordinary statements, teeming with Monophysitism, attributed (no doubt erroneously) to the Roman Catholick missionaries of Mosul, that they invariably connect the deadliest error with the translated phrase.

Again, in their books, and especially in their services, they use language which is not to be reconciled with Nestorianism. This is not merely in their three liturgies, which are probably older than the rise of that heresy. But, for instance, the baptismal service, which is almost certainly later, contains language which no intelligent holder of

[1] A man, meaning to say that there were a great many men assembled, remarked that "there was a great deal of human nature here."

Nestorianism could adopt. Thus: "We confess thee, O our Lord Jesus, who in thy manhood art from Abraham and David, and in thy being from thy Father" (farcing to Psalm cx.). Here we have an approach to the Catholick doctrine that the personality or "being" of our Lord resides in his divinity. So, "He hath promised to us a resurrection from the dead by the revelation of God the Word, the Saviour of all, who took the likeness of a servant, while he was the image of the Father," etc. (First Litany). "Let us confess the Son, who is of one substance with the Father, who . . . put on our flesh, and by it brought us near to him" (Second Litany). "Throughout the office the Saviour, Christ, is continually identified in the simplest and most absolute manner with the Divine Son, the Second Person of the Holy Trinity; and in order to express the theory of an *association* between the Son of God and the Son of Mary (as supposed by Nestorianism), it is not too much to say that the office would have to be reconstructed; *i.e.* supposing always that it was to be used in its simple grammatical meaning without disingenuous mental glosses in a sense contrary to that which the words convey."[1]

Much allowance must also be made for the un-technical character of the Syriac language. There seems little doubt that in many cases the translations of Greek theological terms into Syriac were not easily intelligible, and it is not surprising if

[1] From a letter by Dr. Bright, Regius Professor of Ecclesiastical History and Canon of Christchurch, Oxford, who stated that he only knew the office from a translation.

the Syrians sometimes misunderstood them. We may perhaps compare the difficulties that arose between the Latins and the Greeks over the word "hypostasis."

3. Nevertheless, although we may probably acquit the Eastern Syrians of holding, as a body, Nestorian doctrine on the Incarnation, yet we cannot acquit them of schism. And they cannot be in a thoroughly orthodox position until they accept the General Councils. Yet, bearing in mind the union which was effected two years after the council of Ephesus between the Catholicks and John of Antioch with his bishops by means of conciliatory explanations, and remembering the studiously charitable tone in which the "Westerns" are spoken of in books like the Sunhadus or Book of Canon Law, which only once refers to Nestorius, in a matter of internal discipline (vii. § 4), it is not too much to hope that the Eastern Syrians will one day accept the decrees of Ephesus, when duly explained to them, as expressing truly the faith once delivered to the saints, and as faithfully embodying their own belief.

Of course the wildest theology is sometimes heard from the lips of the unlearned among the Eastern Syrians. But this is as often Gnostic as Nestorian, and is due to pure ignorance of the ancient books of the nation. The same is only too often the case in England. Just as John of Antioch and others misunderstood and considered heterodox the language of St. Cyril and the Ephesine fathers, so it is more than likely that the still more remote Easterns thought that the language of the Council, which agreed with Cyril, meant something approaching to Monophysitism, and consequently rejected it. It will be remembered that they only knew of the proceedings of the Council through the report of partisans of Nestorius. It must, however, be admitted that the impatience which has too commonly accompanied controversy in early times, and the political interests of the day, were probably factors in warping the judgment, and misguiding the action, of the Syrians of that age.

With regard to the hope that much good may come from conciliatory explanations, the following words may well be weighed carefully. "The formula of reunion between Cyril and John of Antioch shows how mutual explanation did, in that instance, remove differences; Cyril agreeing to adopt language which he had not before used, *e.g.* as to the 'consubstantiality of the Incarnate with us as touching the manhood.' Thus far, the objections of the Syrians did great service to the Faith by leading Cyril to balance his language better. I always feel that his original Twelve Articles were not *throughout* judiciously worded; that they did, in one or two places, at least, invite misgivings on the part of the Syrian school of theologians, and that they needed complementary statements, such as the reunion supplied."[1]

Let us now leave the theological question, vital as it is to the Gospel faith, and turn to some of the other ideas of the Syrians.

---

[1] From a letter by Dr. Bright. See also Hefele, "Conciliengeschichte," §§ 155-157. We may venture to quote another suggestive remark of Dr. Bright to the writers: "It is your duty in this mission to *get behind words*."

The idea of ceremonial defilement is thoroughly alive among the people. To a Western mind it is most extraordinary to find that some things are considered essentially unclean, though physically they are perfectly clean. Thus, for instance, after a funeral, in many places, every one washes his hands and face, though all they will have done is to attend while the service is being read. The notion of physical defilement due to touching a dead body is extended ceremonially to every one who has assisted at the burial. The same notion prevents people from touching a dog. All through these Eastern countries the dog's best qualities, his fidelity and affection, are unrecognized; and though every householder keeps one as a watch for his courtyard, and shepherds keep dogs for their flocks, no one would dream of making a friend of them. Some of the mountain dogs are magnificent animals; and in the plain of Urmi the great khans keep greyhounds for purposes of sport; but the usual village dog of Persia is a miserable cur, and is not an inviting object. As he never receives anything but a blow, he is usually a great coward, and attacks any one when he thinks he can do it with impunity.

No doubt much of the notion of ceremonial defilement rests on a sound basis. Thus it would, from physical reasons, be unwise to eat pork in hot countries like Persia and Turkey. Yet the notion now is not so much that a pig is unwholesome eating, as that he is essentially an unclean animal. So with all shell fish. A Syrian was given lobster salad once in London, and thought it a most delicious dish. But when he heard that the chief ingredient was lobster, he could not eat another mouthful. One of the deacon scholars at Urmi was discovered torturing a tortoise. When remonstrated with, he said in a tone of great surprise, "But he is an unclean animal, Rabbi!" When pressed as to why it should be unclean, and, even if so, why it should be illtreated, he promptly replied: "It must be an evil beast, or God would not have punished it by giving it such a burden to carry." The obvious reply, however, that it could take about its house with it rent free, and had no house tax to pay, appealed to his mind forcibly, and made him almost doubt if he had not made a mistake. Shellfish and tortoises are mentioned as unclean in Lev. xi. 10, 29.

It would be interesting to know if any of this is a survival of Manichean dualism, which looked on some creatures as essentially evil. Neither Christians nor Mussulmans in these countries have got into their heads the teaching of Genesis that all God's works were good at first. "Behold, it was very good" (Gen. i. 31). The same thing accounts for the way in which the Mosaic law is looked on as almost, if not quite, in force now. The book of Leviticus will be known thoroughly by those who can hardly pass an examination in Gospel history. The old Syrian books constantly, like the Puritans of old, found a command or a canon on the Mosaic law. Yet this in no way makes for a Jewish origin for the people, for the Mussulmans around them have exactly the same ideas, and indeed it is probably through their influence that they are kept up.

Although the Syrians' fasts are rigorous, they are not a particularly ascetic people. Perhaps the prevalence among them in early ages of Manicheism led to canons being made against an asceticism which might savour of a notion that the things of this world are essentially bad. Thus those who fast on Sundays for ascetic reasons are anathematized (Sunhadus, v. § 11. See Chapter XV.). And over-asceticism is reproved in the book on monks. "Henceforward no one is to be shut up in houses, or to stand on pillars, or let their hair grow, or put irons on themselves" (vii. § 2, Canon 7).

The great respect paid to the externals of religion is very striking to a Western. For instance, they think far more of an ecclesiastical precept than of the moral law. If a man breaks the whole Decalogue, he comforts himself, and his neighbours, with the reflexion that he is a "son of man" or that "God is merciful." But if he breaks his fast, or does not pay the patriarch's dues, he is worse than a heathen. We in Europe are often ashamed of our religion, and do not profess all that we believe; with us many men do not care to be seen going to church or saying their prayers; and we do not think it right to introduce the name of God, except on rare occasions, into our conversation. The Syrian looks at things from quite a different point of view. Externals are to him of the greatest importance; and it is not profanity or hypocrisy that makes him interlard his conversation with references to God and his works, but a (to him) natural regard for the Christian religion. For instance, a conversation between two persons meeting in the streets, which in Europe would turn on the weather—a subject seldom discussed in the East—will among the Syrians run thus. "All hail to you." "You have come in peace." "Thanks be to God, your health is good?" "If you ask, praise be to the Lord, I am well." "If God prospers you, come to my house to-morrow," and so on. Similarly, no layman is ashamed of knowing about things ecclesiastical, and theological topics are frequently discussed. It is not wonderful if a man publicly professes his religion; the wonder would rather be if he did not do so.

This is by no means hypocrisy. A Syrian does not use God's name in this conversation in a spirit of cant, to make himself appear better in his neighbour's eyes than he is, any more than an ordinary Mussulman will say his prayers by the roadside for show. It is a natural part of his religion. And, indeed, there is much value in the custom, as the use of these phrases often reminds the heart of their true meaning. And so generally, whereas a European who does not try to keep the commandments will turn his back on God, and not attend church or Communion, the Syrian will go as far as being disobedient to his Maker, but not as far as open rebellion.

It is less pleasant to hear our Blessed Lord's name called on to attest a statement hastily made, and indeed often devoid of truth. "By Christ," is but little more than our "indeed." And in some districts to say, "By God, I will not go,' is hardly stronger than a simple negative future. A strong form of "indeed" in the mountains is, "By the habit of Mar Shimun;" or if the patriarch is addressed, "By thy holy habit," or "By thy head."

Perhaps the punishing of families for the sins of the individual can hardly be called a Syrian "idea." Yet, under a semi-barbarous government, it is the practice. A murderer's family suffers heavily for his crime, and frequently has to pay the blood-money. A whole village is often fined for the offence of a few of its members. "Those strange and monstrous forms of civil justice which were incorporated in the regular practice of the Eastern courts, and in extraordinary instances in the Jewish, were a sort of actual wild justice; in the first instance designed as a magnifying and expansion of the really guilty person, but beyond this aiming at a rough sort of instruction, at marking certain crimes by way of warning, and terrifying the people from the commission of them."[1] Thus Simeon and Levi spoiled the city of Shechem, and slew all the males (Gen. xxxiv. 25-27). The whole of the "men that appertained unto Korah" were destroyed (Numb. xvi. 32). At a later date, in the court of Darius, the families of Daniel's accusers were cast into the lion's den (Dan. vi. 24). Yet the Syrians themselves say, "They hang every sheep by its own legs;"—a man pays the penalty for his own misdeeds; as God had taught through Ezekiel, "The soul that sinneth, it shall die" (Ezek. xviii. 4). But the more enlightened precept is overborne by the Mussulman practice. For this reason, if a traveller is robbed, the whole village is responsible. The same thing is the case all over Asia. For

[1] Mozley, "Ruling Ideas in Early Ages," Lecture v.

instance, among the Tartars, says M. Huc, when a mule is lost from a caravan, the persons occupying the nearest encampment are bound either to find it, or to replace it ("Travels in Tartary, etc.," vol. i. chap. iii.).

Parables, riddles, and similes appeal strongly to the Syrian mind. The artifice of the widow of Tekoah or the parable of Joram find their counterpart in everyday life now. Yet one may hope that they have, as a rule, a clearer idea of the moral to be drawn from a parable than a little *natar kursi* or bishop elect, who at a Bible examination thought that the lesson to be learnt from the story of the Prodigal Son was that you ought to take your father's goods and go to a far country, and when they are all spent, to return for more!

The stories they tell are something of this nature. A deaf man went to see an invalid, and, as he could hear nothing, he made up his mind what he would say beforehand. He determined to say, "Peace be with you," and then, "How is your health?" The sick man would doubtless reply, "I am better," and he would answer, "Thank God!" He would then say, "What is your medicine?" and on receiving the reply, he would say, "May it be pleasant to you." Then he would ask, "Who is your doctor?" and when informed he would say, "May his coming be blessed." Fortified with this prepared conversation, he paid his visit, but unfortunately the answers did not fit in, and the following was the result:—"How is your health?" "I am dying." "Thank God! What is your medicine?" "Poison!" "May it be pleasant to you. Who is your doctor?" "The angel of death." "May his coming be blessed!" Further conversation was prevented by his forcible ejection.

They tell a variation of the "Open, Sesame," story with regard to a chamber supposed to exist in the rock of the Castle of Semiramis, at Van, full of treasure. A shepherd lying outside dreamt that the word which would open the rock was told him. He said it, entered, took the treasure, repeated the word, and passed out. But, finding he had left his staff behind him, he used the word a third time, and re-entered. On trying to come out he found he had forgotten the word. He is still inside, and his cries can plainly be heard. Curiously enough the Syrians do not read the Arabian Nights, and seem never to have heard of them.

The riddles are chiefly Biblical, such as the following.

Living I walked not; when dead I walked; and when I walked it was not on earth and not in heaven. Answer: Noah's ark.—Who was it who went to hell because he did not tell a lie, and who if he had told a lie perhaps would have gone to heaven? Answer: Herod, because he kept his word and put St. John Baptist to death (the assumption may be noted).—A birth where there will be no burial, a burial where there has been no birth. Answer: The east has a birth and no burial, the west a burial and no birth.—Two went into judgment and three came out convicted. Answer: Adam, Eve, and the serpent.

We may here notice the intense love of the Syrians for the Bible. We have already described somewhat fully their lectionary, with the lessons appointed for the Holy Eucharist; the fulness of which makes up to a great extent for the absence of lessons from the daily services. There does not seem to be any authoritative statement in the East Syrian books as to the Canon; the lectionary contains no lessons from the General Epistles and Revelation, but it also contains none from several books which are contained in the Pshitta.[1] It has two from the Apocrypha. The catalogue of Mar Audishu, however, contains all our canonical and deutero-canonical scriptures except Ruth, the prayer of Manasses, and Revelation; Ezra, Nehemiah, and (perhaps) the two apocryphal books of Esdras are comprised under the one name Ezra. The Catholic Epistles are called "the three Epistles of James, Peter, and John." The catalogue also contains Josephus, Tatian's Diatessaron, and other books.

The Sunhadus, quoting an "apostolic canon," lays down as a course of instruction for schools, the Pentateuch, Joshua, Judges, Samuel, Kings, Proverbs, Ecclesiastes, Song of Songs, Ruth, Job, sixteen Prophets; for little boys Bar Sirach and the Psalms; from the New Testament, the fourfold Gospel, Acts, three General Epistles, and fourteen of St. Paul (vi. § 2).

A popular idea of the Syrians is that charms are beneficial, to avoid the evil eye, or to cure a disease, or for some such thing. This idea they share with the Mussulmans. Animals and children habitually wear talismans. Charms are written on long slips of paper, often beautifully illuminated

[1] The Peschitto. See above, page 252.

and enclosed in cases. The writers, unfortunately, are as a general rule priests. This is several times strenuously forbidden in the Sunhadus; no one may resort to wizards, and all conjurers and astrologers themselves are to be entirely deposed, if of the clergy, and excommunicated if laymen (v. § 22; vi. § 6, Canon 18). The charms themselves usually consist of a long prayer in Syriac. The Mussulman charms are taken from the Koran, and are in Arabic.

In Kurdistan many think that some priests can write a document which will bring lingering illness and death, or madness or other disasters, on the people against whom they are written. One lad used to walk in his sleep. A priest wrote a document which would prevent this as long as he retained it; but as they would not agree on the price (a few shillings) it was not tested.

The Syrian Language.

The vernacular used by the Syrians is a form of Syriac, not directly derived from the classical language, which is substantially the vernacular of Edessa or Urhai, but (probably) from the Aramaic dialects spoken in Christian times in Mesopotamia, Babylonia, and Assyria. It is an exceedingly interesting language, showing a genuine development of an ancient tongue on analytical principles; the old synthetic forms having given way to freer methods of expression, as in modern European languages. It is only marred by the very large number of foreign words employed, which differ in the various districts. In the plain of Urmi the

Turkish and Persian are chiefly borrowed from, in the mountains, the Kurdish or Arabic, in the plain of Mosul, the Arabic. Each district, almost each village, has a dialect of his own, sufficiently different to make it difficult for a man of, say, Urmi to understand a man of Tiari, but sufficiently close, especially in structure, to show the common origin of all. This difference of dialect makes it exceedingly difficult or almost impossible to print books in the vernacular which can be understood by everybody. Hitherto the Syrians have overcome this difficulty by always writing in classical Syriac. The only books written in the vernacular, before the present century, are a few in the Alqosh (Elkosh) dialect—that of the plain of Mosul. These are written in a purely phonetic manner; among others there is a book of the liturgical Gospels, which would naturally be read in the vernacular, as now.[1] Since the establishment of printing presses, the vernacular dialects have been regularly reduced to writing, and the late Dr. Perkins and others did much good work in this way. But it may be thought that his method was too phonetic, and it accorded with the use of one dialect (that of Urmi) only. There is now no standard of spelling, and different people write in different ways. But it seems desirable to print so that the books may be understood by the largest possible number; and this may be done partly by paying regard to the classical Syriac and to etymology—for a word written etymologically may suit two quite different

[1] In the town of Mosul they are read in Arabic, written in Syriac character. This is called Carshunic.

pronunciations—and partly by eschewing words used in one district and not in others.

The Syrians have very few verbs; one way of overcoming this is by forming (as in the classical language) causatives to almost all verbs, so that the number of meanings is doubled. Thus "to make to read" is to teach; to "make to learn" is to instigate, and sometimes to teach, "to make to remember" is to remind, and so on. One has to be careful in the use of these causatives. For instance, one must not say St. Paul wrote an epistle by the hands of a scribe; but "caused it to be written." Another way of multiplying verbs is to use "to eat," "to draw," "to strike," and a few other verbs, with nouns (of which there are an enormous number), and this produces some curious results. One "eats" trouble, a schoolboy "eats" sticks, a judge "eats" bribes, an embezzler "eats" money, an angry man "eats" threats, a person convicted of lying "eats" (as with us) his words. So one "draws" a photograph, a disease, one's arm (when one signs a deed), tobacco, trouble. One "strikes" almost everything: musical instruments, one's knees (when one kneels), a plough, a sickle, with the evil eye, strength (when one makes an effort). On the other hand, the wind, lightning, thunder, locusts, storms, all "strike." Thus a great variety of ideas are expressed. One "pours" a slander or a gun; if one is a judge, one "pours" offenders into prison; one "pours" a person on the road when one sees him off. Ones "holds" an excuse, one's ear (when one pays attention), or a man's hand (when one helps another), a man's neck (when one restrains him), and so on.

The Syrians are very fond of diminutives, but often these are not used now in a diminutive sense. They always speak of "a little old man" (for a grandfather), a little brother, a little daddy (this is familiar, but used by sons), and generally of a little uncle. A shortened form of these diminutives gives titles. A bishop, in Persia, is called Little Uncle; and any old man has the same prefixed to his name, as "Little Uncle James;" and similarly an elderly lady is spoken of as "Little Aunt Mary," "Little Aunt Elizabeth," and so on.

A great many ideas are expressed by "son of," "daughter of." Inhabitants of a place are its "sons," a man's fellow countryman is the "son of his country," "my namesake" is the "son of my name." Two men of the same name will address one another, in the mountains, as Barshi, which is a corruption of this. If you ask how old a man is, you hear he is the son of so many years. A seed is now called "the son of seed;" a thimble is the daughter of the finger; an echo, of the voice; a bolt-socket, of the bolt; a glove, of the hand; the daughter of the sun or moon is the halo often seen round them; the latter is also a child's disease, supposed to come at new moon; the daughter of hail is quartz, and so on. The original idea of these expressions is that the derived noun has the nature of the other. A man calls himself a "son of man," to denote that he is human; "human nature" is in Syriac *barnashutha*, which we may render "son-of-mannishness." Hence even an uneducated Syrian can well comprehend (as did the Pharisees of old) what our Lord meant when he called himself the "Son of God." An uneducated Western might think, that because he was the "Son of God," therefore he was not God. Not so the Syrian. A mere child would understand that this name meant that our Lord was of one substance with the Heavenly Father, just as he himself, a "son of man," is of one substance with his earthly father.

A paucity of adjectives leads the Syrians to prefix to nouns the words, "lord of." They then get an epithet. A watery road is "lord of water," an expensive thing is "lord of price." A married woman also is "lord of a husband!"

Note on the East Syrian Character.

Although no liberality in making allowance for circumstances can make wrong right or even neutral, nor can save vices from being essentially hateful, nor render sins tolerable, yet, unless all the circumstances (including the moral atmosphere, which so greatly affects the sensitiveness of conscience to this or that appeal or shock) are weighed, it is impossible to have an other than unfair estimate of the character of a person. Falsehood in England is reckoned ungentlemanly, and most well-bred people are no more really tempted to lie, than they are to wear their hats in a drawing-room, or to dye their beards red with khena. But no one would deny the epithet of really good and pious to some at home who nevertheless are frequently guilty of Satan's own sin of pride, which sometimes breaks out into open manifestation. So, in the case of an

Oriental, who has inherited the disposition to make things easy by a falsehood, and who has grown up in an atmosphere wherein practically falsehoods are (like some of the deceits of English society) ordinary efforts of policy, and does sometimes, under what seems to him pressure or "necessity," swerve from the truth, it ought to be allowed that the fact of his so sinning does not destroy all claim to his being reckoned (by us, his fellow-sinners), to be on the whole a good man, who has set his mind to do God's will. The present writers, who have suffered greatly from such falsehoods, have learnt to make allowance for their perpetrators in proportion as they realized the life and surroundings of the Syrian people.

A great many of the faults of the Syrians, which most damage themselves and displease the average Western, such as lying, slandering, envy, and the intriguing which exercises these three, as it often provokes them, are those to which the mass of Englishmen have much less temptation, or temptation to which is overbalanced by some practical consideration. All wickedness is sin in every climate. But if only the guiltless are to throw stones at the guilty, it is permissible to direct our countrymen to self-examination, before they turn down their thumbs against the Syrians, who need rather the sympathy of their fellow-sufferers under the deceits of the god of this world.

CHAPTER XV.

THE KALENDAR. FASTS AND FESTIVALS. SUNDAYS.

Beginning of the year—The Era—Blessing the months—Shwat, or February—Easter—Shawu'i—Vigils—A festival of our Lord—Village festivals — Dancing—Sacrifices—Epiphany — Mart Mariam, Urmi—Ascension Day—Holy Cross Day—Veneration of the Cross—Saints' days—Legend concerning St. George's martyrdom—Sundays—How reckoned—Sunday bathing forbidden—Fasts—Sunday fasting—Animal food forbidden—Wednesdays and Fridays—Fasting Communion—Soma—Table of holy-days and Sundays, with some account of saints commemorated—How to find Easter.

THERE seems to be considerable doubt among the Syrians as to when the year begins. The kalendars usually start with October, and in lists of months October, or First Tishrin as it is called, is given as the first. But in the Khudhra, or book of proper services for Sundays and holy days, the year begins with Advent. And popularly the Epiphany is often held to be the beginning of the year. The Julian kalendar is used in reckoning the months, and in all the books, and still in the mountains, the "era of Alexander" (or "of the Greeks"), *i.e.* the era of the Seleucidæ, for the years. This is reckoned from 311 B.C. In letters the Christian era is now more commonly used in the plain of Urmi, but it is not easy to say if it was ever employed until of late years, or whether its use is due solely to intercourse with Europe.

The years are numbered by letters, not by Arabic figures, which have only lately been introduced by Western influence. They will, even in speaking, put vowels to the consonants which represent the numerals and form a short word for each year, instead of saying its number in full. Thus, 1888 is appakh; 1889 is appat, and so forth.

On the first day of every month, at the evening service, a long anthem is recited, to "bless" the month. "May —— [the month] come with joy," they say, "And be received like the Request. Of Elia and the son of Amram. May their prayer be a wall to us. * Bless, O my Lord, the months of the year. The seasons and weeks and days. Bless the vineyards and plants. Bless the seeds and the fields. Bless, O my Lord, —— which has come. And may it be furnished with all blessings. And let there not be in it confusions. Nor sorrows, nor afflictions," and so forth. But February is not blessed. It is "the month of afflictions," and they only pray "let there not be confusions in it" (anthem of the months in the "Before and After"). Therefore this service is omitted on February 1. In popular belief Shwat or Ishwat (February) is a sort of hobgoblin. The boys sometimes personate him, and go about the village singing a sort of Hogmanay.

In Qudshanis and in each village in Tiari, and probably in other places in Kurdistan, Shwat is jestingly supposed to be a personal being and to spend one day at each house as guest. Of course in Qudshanis he begins at Mar Shimun's house. If it rains or snows on a day it is because his host for that day had not treated him with due honour. The host will try to prove that it is not his fault, but that Shwat had not got over the bad temper he was put into by neglect at his former host's house. The exchange of banter at any rate lightens the effects of February's gloom in the Ashiret country. The poor Rayats have had all the humour for badinage crushed out of their dull lives.

The fasts and festivals depend far more than with us upon Easter. Most of the saints' days are movable feasts, and fall on Fridays, which depend on Easter.[1] This seems to be a unique feature. Between the first Sunday after Christmas and the Great Fast, or Lent, every Friday is a saint's day according to the list given below. And even some of the saints' days which go by the months are not on fixed days of the month, but on fixed days of the week. Thus the first Wednesday in March is sacred to St. George, and so forth. Easter itself agrees with that of the Greeks, and is determined according to the table at the end of this chapter. There is sometimes as much as five weeks difference between theirs and ours, and occasionally, because of the use of the old style, theirs falls later than ours can possibly fall, as in 1888, when it was on May 5th, new style. Also the Syrian Easter may be nearly a fortnight after the full moon.

[1] Albiruni (A.D. 973-1048), qu. in Smith and Wace, "Dictionary of Christian Biography," s.v. "Nestorianism," says that the Nestorians and Melchites agree in keeping Lent, Christmas, and Epiphany, but disagree about other feasts and fasts.

The year is divided into periods of about seven weeks each; each period being called a *shawu'a*, from the Syriac word for seven; but some have only four weeks. These periods are: Advent, Epiphany, the Great Fast, the Resurrection, the Apostles, Summer, Elia,[1] Mar Mushi (Moses),[1] and the Hallowing of the Church. Their arrangement is given in the table annexed.

Only festivals of our Lord are properly called "feasts;" saints' days are called "memorials" or "commemorations." Of the feasts, Easter is naturally considered the queen, being called in Urmi emphatically the "Great Feast," in contradistinction to Christmas which is the "Little Feast." On these two days the Liturgy is said very early in the morning, indeed soon after midnight; but it is considered essential that every one should have gone to bed first, if only for an hour or two. This is the only relic in the plains of Urmi of the vigils, or all-night services, but in Kurdistan they are frequent; and the Sunhadus (book vii. § 4, Canon 11) orders that, on days before feasts and Sundays which have a vigil, no work is to be done in the monasteries, lest prayer be interrupted by sleepiness. The Christmas and Easter liturgies over, the people proceed to one another's houses to "bless their feast;" or if any member of the community has lost one of his family since the last feast, they visit him to "heal his head." "May your head be pleasant," they say. In Tiari, on the occasion of one of these visits of condolence, the visitor drinks a little wine, then pours out a little more into

---

[1] These are the Old Testament fathers.

which he puts some silver coin and gives it to the bereaved person, saying, "Glory to God, may your head be healed." The bereaved then begins again to drink wine, which he had given up during his mourning.[1]

At every house at these festival visits tea or coffee, sweets and cakes, and often wine and spirits are partaken of; the tea served in little glasses, a few drops of strong tea poured in first, and boiling water added from a samovar or urn, with perhaps a little lemon juice or other flavouring (but not milk), and sugar in abundance. The more sugar put in, the more love is shown; so one must not churlishly refuse it, but learn to drink cup after cup of sugar water flavoured with tea. Sherbets are also sometimes served round, and rose water poured over the hands and head of the guest. In these visits much good will is shown; old enmities are often reconciled—this is generally the bishop's office; he brings the disputants and gives them a little lecture on the follies of quarrelling, and says, "Now agree together." So they—literally—kiss and make friends, after which they go and kiss the bishop's hand. At Easter coloured eggs are presented, generally red, but often with ingenious devices scratched on them. The Syrians love to make these eggs fight by knocking their ends one against another; whichever egg is not broken is the conqueror, and the owner wins the broken one.

---

[1] See page 107. A similar ceremony takes place at a Tartar wedding. Presents of money are placed in a jar of fermented milk. The father of the bride drinks the wine and keeps the money. (Huc, "Travels in Tartary, etc.," vol i. chap. viii.).

The feast is indeed blessed if rain falls on it; and greatly are the Mussulmans incensed if rain falls on the Christian festival and not on theirs; rain is indeed a gift of God (Prov. xxv. 14) at all times in so thirsty a land, and nothing is more desired as a sign of God's favour on the feast day.

The village festivals are a great feature of the Syrian life. They fall on the feast of the patron saint of the village church, and if the church is much venerated, people will flock to it from all parts. They begin with the Qurbana (Eucharist), to which the people often have to come in detachments, the church being only large enough to hold a fraction of those who have come to the feast. One set will receive the Holy Sacrament, and leave the church to allow another set to enter, and so on. On these occasions, even Mussulmans sometimes come and make offerings to the church, and have their children signed with the sign of the cross.[1] After the Qurbana, games and dances will be kept up all the day, ending too often, unfortunately, in drunkenness and fights between Christians and Mohammedans. But the abuse does not take away the use; and if these festivals were somewhat reformed, they might be made the servants of religion. The Syrians are a warm-hearted people, and much good feeling is called out on these occasions. The dancing is peculiar, but stately and pretty. Of course in a Mussulman country there is no such thing as the "lasses and lads" "tripping it" together; the men dance by themselves, and perhaps in the background the women by them-

[1] See above, page 276.

selves. A ring is formed with joined hands, and with a slow step to the music of a sort of fife and a drum, they move round, with many gesticulations and waving of handkerchiefs. Of course these festivals are great opportunities for the dancers on the tight rope, and all that race, who do a thriving trade.

On these occasions (and also on other days), at the more revered churches, it is common for the villagers to bring, often from a great distance, sheep to be sacrificed. Some popular churches get as many as two hundred sheep in a year. These, however, are not given to the church, or to the priest; but a feast is made, and all partake, a little blood having been sprinkled on the church door. It is in fact a picnic, though regarded as an act of piety and devotion.

The festival of the Epiphany is a great day among the Syrians. They do not, however, commemorate then the coming of the Wise Men, but the baptism of our Lord. The name in the plain of Urmi is the "New Waters," for this reason. The mountain name, which is also that of the books, is "The Sun Rising." In the night, before the Qurbana, it is the custom to plunge into a generally hard-frozen pool, with much shouting and singing of religious hymns. It is curious that the Syrians do not lay more stress on the commemoration of the Magi, since they devoutly believe that they come from their own country, and point to the old church of Mart Mariam in Urmi, built by the Wise Men on their return from the Holy Land, and containing the grave of at least one of them; in it, the Syrians still make their offerings of prayer and praise to the Babe of Bethlehem (see page 301).

On Ascension Day, the little girls go round their village dressed as brides, singing and asking for pennies; whence the day is popularly known as Bride-Ascension.

The festival of the Cross, observed on September 13 (not 14), is one of the greatest days in the East Syrian kalendar, and is nearly always marked by a celebration of the Liturgy. It is a day on which no work is done, and all go to church; it is generally an occasion for a great communion, especially in the mountains. It appears, however, to commemorate the Invention rather than the Exaltation of the Cross; the allusions are to Constantine and Helena, who are constantly mentioned in the old books. It will be remembered that all through the East there is only this one festival of the Cross. But in Tal (in Kurdistan), there is a festival of St. Helena in September, on which no work is done. The veneration paid to the cross seems to be a set-off for the absence of pictures. The cross is placed for every one to kiss on entering the church; it is signed with oil on the church in different places at its consecration; and the people cannot understand how any one can be a Christian who does not "rub his forehead" with it, as Tertullian expresses it. In the Sunhadus the following account is given of the veneration paid to the cross (v. § 9). "Tradition says that when our Lord blessed the Apostles on the Mount of Olives, he stretched out his hands in the form of the cross, as typifying that by the cross he must come to the glory of his ascension (Phil. ii. 8, 9). When they saw the type they fell down and worshipped him. This is the beginning of the veneration of the cross. The first church was the upper room, the second at Antioch. The Apostles said they did not worship wood or gold or any common substance, but Christ, who is the cross. The signs and miracles done by the cross drew men to honour the wood and sign of the cross, and to venerate it."

Unreflecting persons, without knowledge of Oriental habits, have thought that the kissing of the cross on entering a church savoured of superstition. But Mussulmans as well as Christians kiss the hands of their superiors on entering their presence-chambers, just as with us the Queen's hand is kissed. Orientals kiss the print of the seal (which stands for a signature) on the letter of a superior, and touch it with their foreheads; so in England, in taking an oath, the New Testament, the letter or written word of God, is kissed, as representing the unseen Lord whose new covenant is revealed in it. The church is the house of God, and the cross is the sign and seal of our Lord. To neglect to kiss the seal of Mar Shimun or the sign of the Redeemer, would, to the inhabitants of these eastern regions, argue disloyalty. There seems to be no thought of worshipping the cross itself among the Syrians, but they treat it as we treat the Bible, reverently, not as the rival of God, nor idolatrously, but as belonging to and reminding them of Him. Dr. Grant, one of the first of the American Presbyterian missionaries to this people (a most religious, single-minded, and God-serving man, and a worthy example of missionary zeal and love) testifies to the absence of superstition in the Syrian's reverence for the sign of our Lord.[1]

Of the saints' days, only the Fridays mentioned above, and a few others, as St. Thomas (July 3), Mar Shimun Barseba'i, the sons of Shmuni (the martyrs mentioned in 2 Maccabees vii., who are held in very great veneration, and to whom many churches are dedicated[2]), and St. George, have a proper service in the Khudhra. Many other days, however, are kept holy, especially as village festivals, among which the memorials of the boy saint, Mar Quriaqus (St. Cyriac, July 15), Mar Audishu (Ebedjesus), and Mar Shalita are particularly observed. On St. Thomas's day (July 3), the Urmi people all make an excursion to the sea, and bathe there. On the festival of Nusardil, the memorial of the twelve Apostles (the seventh Sunday after Pentecost), the people have the custom of sprinkling one another with water. The Twelve do not, as a rule, have separate memorials, but are all commemorated together on this day. The service for St. Mary, given in the Khudhra for the Friday after the first Sunday after Christmas, also does duty for the other memorials of the Blessed Virgin. Perhaps the most popular of the saints is St. George, who is commemorated on April 24 (not 23), and also in March and November. Between Superghan and Urmi is a

---

[1] See his book, "The Nestorians," p. 63.
[2] Their names are given in the books as Gadai, Maccabeus, Tersai, Hebron, Hipson, Bacchus, and Jonadab. Their teacher was Eleazar (anthem of the martyrs for Monday morning).

very interesting place, now quite deserted. It is one of the many hills[1] which rise suddenly out of the plain, and is called Baqchiqal'a. It is said to have been the site of the city of Zardusht (Zoroaster) who was a native of this plain. There are some remains of a fort on it, and a causeway leading over the marshy ground towards the sea, still used as a road for some distance in wet weather. Here is said to have taken place the martyrdom of St. George. According to Syrian histories he was a merchant, who came to Urmi in pursuit of his trade, became converted to Christianity, and was martyred at Baqchiqal'a by the local chieftain. The church at Superghan, like many others, is dedicated to him, and for this reason the mission high school there is named St. George's School. On the sea shore at Superghan is the holy well of St. George, a mineral spring, which is said to heal all lepers who bathe in it. Perhaps this St. George has no connexion with the patron of England.

The Wednesday commemoration of All Saints has the following anthem in praise of him.

From everlasting to everlasting. The divisions and orders of the Spiritual ones. With the priests in the church, are singing praise. For a memorial of the holy martyr. Mar Giwergis, who did brave deeds and conquered and was crowned. * He suffered and bore troubles. Fire and the sword and stoning. The persecutors inflicted on him. Many and various torments. He put the wicked king to shame. Who persecuted the good servants. He brought low the excellency of his power. And the gods which he worshipped. Zeus and Apollo and Artemis. The work of men's hands. * The giant of strength Mar Giwer-

---

[1] Many of these are great ash heaps, and are said to be relics of Parseeism.

gis cried. And said to the nobles of the king. Ye shall not worship idols. Carved and wrought by artificers. Lo, Christ is the King of kings. And Lord of all gods. He giveth an inheritance to all that fear him. A bride-chamber and good things that pass not away. He clotheth with glory in his kingdom. The pure martyrs who believed in him.* Kneeling in prayer before his Lord, he besought and made request, saying. Take away by thy grace. From all who keep the commemoration. Of this day of my persecution. Hail and famine and pestilence. Locust, young locust, and caterpillar. The blast that destroys the fields. And the terrors of the night. And all evil confusion. And keep all the inhabited world. By the great strength of thy Godhead.

Sunday is strictly observed, as far as abstaining from work is concerned. In Tiari there is a great objection to Sunday travelling. In the days of the former Malik, any one making a journey on Sunday was fined. Now what is called "necessity" leads to some work being done. Most of the Syrians are not very careful to abstain from travelling on that day. And except in some mountain districts, where the Liturgy is said weekly, the Eucharist is not often celebrated then, as a popular festival or saint's day usually has the preference. Hence the curious result that in practice the Liturgy is said more often on Friday than Sunday. Still the law of the Sunhadus (book v. § 7) is emphatic: On Sunday there must be service, reading of holy Scripture, and the Offering;[1] and in some places this is still observed.

"Sunday," says the Sunhadus (v. § 7), "begins at sunset and ends at sunset. We must honour the risen Lord with processions, praises, and alms.

[1] This is the usual name for the Eucharist; Qurbana (Corban).

There must on this day be no quarrels or law suits." Hence, as with us, the service on Saturday night is that of Sunday; but that on Sunday night is the evensong of Monday. But the rule of no work begins at the evening prayers on Saturday night, "the ninth hour of Saturday," and ends at dawn on Monday.[1] On one occasion, when the deacon-servant of the mission was requested to cut the hair of one of the missionaries on Saturday night, he replied, "Very well, Rabbi; I will not say my prayers till after that, so that it may not be Sunday!" Sometimes the Sunday for all purposes is held to end after evening service, and people have been known to put the prayers very early on Sunday afternoon, so that they might turn to some secular occupation.

Both by popular custom and by the Sunhadus it is forbidden to bathe on Sunday. Hence Saturday is the great washing day. "Christians may not bathe on Sunday before or after the Sacrament, for the day is holy, and has in it nothing of the flesh. If a man bathes after the Sacrament, he counts it as an unclean thing." Here is another instance of the notion of ceremonial defilement, still so strongly kept up in all matters. But, on the other hand, "on Sundays and feasts of our Lord we must wash ourselves and put on special clothing, and cleanse our souls from sin" (Sunhadus, v. §§ 7, 14).

The fasts of the Eastern Syrians are very severe. But it is curious that they are longer in practice.

[1] See the curious epistle on keeping Sunday at the end of the 'Anidha or Burial Service.

than in the canons of the Sunhadus. In practice, every one fasts in Advent, twenty-five days; Lent, fifty days; the Rogation of the Ninevites, three days at the end of winter, a fast instituted in commemoration of the preaching of Jonah at Nineveh, and most strictly observed; and Wednesdays and Fridays throughout the year, not excluding Christmas Day, are days of abstinence. Also, most people fast for fifteen days before the "memorial of St. Mary," on August 15. Sundays are included in these fasts. But the Sunhadus expressly forbids fasting on Sunday, as being a Manichean custom. "The Manicheans denied the Resurrection, and fasted on Sunday because they said the world would come to an end on that day, after nine thousand years. . . . No one may fast on Sunday under pain of anathema" (book v. § 11, Synod of Gangra). The Ashitha Sunhadus, however, quotes from the same synod a saving clause, "If it is not from an evil and Manichean intention, a man may fast on Sunday." And the reason, doubtless, why at the present time men fast on Sundays in Lent and Advent, is that if they had meat, butter, milk, etc., in the house for that one day, there would always be the temptation to eat up the remains on the other days of the week. The Sunhadus also expressly makes Advent a voluntary fast, except for monks, as also the seven weeks of the Apostles and Elia (book v. § 19). It does not mention the fasts of St. Mary and of the Ninevites, but makes *forty*[1] days of Lent compulsory for all (by implication),

---

[1] vii. § 3, Canon 5. But in the Khudhra fifty days fast are allowed for, if the Sundays are reckoned in.

and Wednesday and Friday explicitly; the former in memory of the conspiracy of the high priests on that day against our Lord, and because our Lord then revealed his sufferings to his disciples; the latter because of the crucifixion (v. § 10). Monks also are ordered to abstain till evening, with the exception of a "taste" at midday; and compline (a service now almost obsolete) is called "satisfaction," because said at the time of the only full meal of the day (v. § 3, vii. § 2, Canon 6).

In the fasts no meat, fish, butter, eggs, or, indeed, any animal produce may be eaten; and to obey the laws of their church in this respect is a very severe matter; yet, especially in Kurdistan, they are most strictly kept. The mountaineers, and the stricter Urmi men, will not eat, or drink, or smoke, until midday during the Great Fast or Lent, except on Sundays; but at other seasons they merely do not eat meat, butter, etc., and may take of other things as much as they please. The Wednesday and Friday fast, however, is no great hardship to any one. Almost everywhere, it only begins in the morning, and ends with evening prayers. Thus, at the evening meal on what we call Wednesday and Friday night meat may be eaten; of course theoretically at the evening meal on what we call Tuesday and Thursday night only fast food should be eaten; but this is almost never the case. And in many districts, especially from Easter to Pentecost, butter, milk, and eggs may be eaten on these two days. The principal food in the fast consists of bread, red haricot beans, black beans (a very small variety), rice cooked with walnut or other vegetable oil, "dolma" or vine leaves stuffed with rice and raisins and cooked in vinegar, treacle, fruit, raisins, and walnuts. We need not look on this strict adherence to the letter of the laws of fasting as a slavish adherence to the externals of religion; it is not the least Pharisaic, but is a severe discipline, cheerfully accepted by all, even by children. One of the smallest of the mission scholars, who, when at death's door, during the fast, was bidden by the doctor to drink some broth, exclaimed indignantly, "Am I a Kurd, that I should eat meat?"

Fasting before communion is strictly observed; the Sunhadus lays down that no clerk who takes any part in the service of the Eucharist or baptism, or ordination, is to eat or drink anything beforehand (book vi. § 6, Canon 3). No rule is laid down for laymen, but the custom stringently binds all. The Cantelae Missae, in the Takhsa, say that priests and deacons must fast before entering the sanctuary. Only if no Sacrament is there, and necessity calls, he may go as far as the outer lamp; but in no case if he has drunk wine (No. 26). This canon refers to Leviticus x. 9, as an authority, and says this is forbidden both by the old and new law. We may notice here the very great influence the Mosaic law has on the Syrians. They like to prove everything by the Old Testament, the New Testament, and the Fathers.

During the Great Fast, the people sometimes hang up in their homes a turnip or some such thing, which they call Soma[1] (Fast), with a feather stuck in it for each week of the fast. These

---

[1] Soma is often made a bogey to frighten children with.

feathers are plucked as the weeks go by. A similar custom still obtains in Southern Italy. "Those who are keeping Lent strictly in Sorrento hang a black doll outside their windows. This doll has six feathers stuck into it, one of which is pulled out at the end of each week's fast."[1]

On what we should call Sunday evening, but which is the evening of the first Monday of the Fast, in Qudshanis and some other parts of the mountains, a young man disguises himself beneath a huge mask cut out of a large pumpkin or gourd, made horrible with an immense nose and fearsome teeth and with beard of goat's hair all shaggy and black. Of deathly visage and altogether calculated to produce an obstupui-steteruntque-comæ-et-vox-faucibus-hæsit impression on the simple minded; obese as Jack the Giant-killer before he ripped up his waistcoat and let the porridge out, and bearing in his hand a wooden dagger as big as a sword and far more murderous-looking;—Soma, attended by a few satellites, visits the houses. He speaks not; but sounds like violent whispers, which precede the bursting of a storm, give token of reserved strength and threatening passion, should he perceive reluctance to comply with the demands he makes for the observation of the holy season. Apart from this, however, he is polite enough; bows as he receives your welcome in return for his companions' salute. His best man interprets that he has come to bid you fast for seven weeks and that you must not eat meat, cheese, milk, eggs, nor any product of animal life. On the present writer asking until when he must

[1] *Guardian*, September 30, 1891, p. 1559.

fast, Soma's hand pointed to the horizon at sunrise and described the course of the sun to about three or four in the afternoon; but he yielded to protest and pointed to the zenith as the limit of fasting. The very mention of any kind of zuhma, *i.e.* food cooked with butter, excited a fit of anger. When all has been amicably arranged, his attendants receive a contribution of raisins, walnuts, beans, or corn. Soma goes to another house and the children come out from behind their "last line of defence," their mothers, in a scared way. The apparition of that evening is the subject of conversation for several days, and a threat of his anger will avail well through the fast to choke the petitions of the little people who find the lenten *régime* not to their taste.

The middle Wednesday of the fifty days of Lent is called in Urmi *Palu, i.e.* the division. It is often marked by some entertainment, but the fast is not broken. This is the case also in the mountains, though this name is not there used.

There is a little confusion as to the exact time when a fast ends. The usual rule for Advent and Lent is that if a man has communicated at the Liturgy on Christmas or Easter Even, he may end his fast after the evensong; but otherwise not till after the Liturgy on Christmas and Easter Day. In the mountains this only applies to Christmas Even. The Liturgy on fast days is said late, often one or two hours after noon, in order that all may remain fasting till then.

The *Takhsa* has a rule that if a man for any reason does not communicate on Easter Even, Easter Day, or Maundy Thursday, or in the days following

Easter, he is to remain a "Nazarite," *i.e.* not eat meat, for a month; but he need not abstain from other things. If, however, he communicated on Maundy Thursday, but not on Easter Even or Easter Day, he may end his fast after fifteen days (Second Canon in the Takhsa).

The East Syrian Kalendar.

The following holy days and fasts are taken either from the Khudhra, or from a manuscript attached to a copy of the Kashkul, or book of variable ferial anthems, of the date May 14, 1443, A.D. Besides the saints noted below, this manuscript contains the names of several local fathers, whose days never had a proper service appointed for them, and which are never now observed. A very few days given below are from well-established local tradition, as Mar Audishu on New Sunday, and St. Mary on May 15th and August 15th.

Old Style.

Dec. 1. The Advent fast begins.

Four Sundays in Advent (*Subara* = Proclamation, or Annunciation).

Dec. 25. Christmas Day ("The Nativity" or "The little feast").

Friday. Mar Yaqu (James), the Lord's brother (obsolete).

First Sunday after Christmas.

Friday. St. Mary.

Second Sunday after Christmas.

Monday, Tuesday, and Wednesday. Rogation of Mar Zaya (very rarely observed).

Jan. 6. Epiphany ("The Brightness" or "Sun rising;" also "The New Waters") commemorating our Lord's baptism.

Friday. St. John Baptist.

First Sunday after Epiphany.

Monday, Tuesday, and Wednesday. Rogation of the Virgins, observed in Qudshanis and some other places by girls.

Friday. St. Peter and St. Paul.

Second Sunday after Epiphany.

Friday. Four Evangelists. Also the "memorial of the one hundred and fifty bishops who excommunicated Macedonius." But the latter is obsolete.

Third Sunday after Epiphany.

Friday. St. Stephen.

Fourth Sunday after Epiphany.

Friday. The Greek doctors (especially Nestorius, Diodorus of Tarsus, Theodore the Interpreter, etc.).

Fifth Sunday after Epiphany.

Monday, Tuesday, and Wednesday. Rogation of the Ninevites, which is always twenty days before the Great Fast. This is in memory of the preaching of Jonah whose reputed tomb is in a mosque close to the mounds of Nineveh.

Thursday. Forty martyrs who were frozen to death [at Sebaste] (obsolete).

Friday. The Syrian doctors, *i.e.* those of the "Church of the East," not of Antioch; especially Mar Nersai who lived *cir.* 520 A.D. (Assem., B. O. iii. pt. i. p. 611). Also Memorial of Mar Saurishu of Bith Garmai, "who instituted the Rogation of the Ninevites on account of a great plague."

Sixth Sunday after Epiphany.

Friday. Mar Awa Catholicos, A.D. 536-552 (Assem., B. O., vol. iii. pt. 1, p. 611), or "One Person" (the Patron Saint).

Seventh Sunday after Epiphany.

Friday. The forty martyrs [of Sebaste] (see above). The lections are as on the Confessor's Day (below).

Eighth Sunday after Epiphany. Memorial of all the "Eastern Catholici."

Friday. Memorial of the dead.

Sunday before (*lit.* across) the Great Fast, fifty days before Easter.

NOTE.—If there are eight Sundays after Epiphany, the above order is followed; if seven, the memorial of the forty martyrs is dropped; if six, the Evangelists and St. Peter and St. Paul are joined together; if five, also the Greek and Syrian doctors; if four, also St. Stephen and Mar Awa. In these cases the services are partly of the one and partly of the other. The Sundays are joined in the same way. (Rule in the Khudhra.)

The great fast begins on the Monday which falls forty-nine days before Easter. But in the mountains, and often in Urmi, the Sunday before that Monday is reckoned a fast.[1]

The first, fourth, and last weeks of the fast are called the weeks of the Sacrament, and have lections appointed in the Khudhra for each day, except for the Saturdays.

Monday, Tuesday, and Wednesday in the first week of the fast. Rogation of the Archangel Gabriel (very rarely observed).

Five Sundays.

Palm Sunday (Feast of Hosannas). On this day the Syrians use the branches of a red species of willow as palms. This tree is called by them the Hosanna tree.

The Passover (Maundy Thursday).

Friday of Suffering (Good Friday).

On this day the Syrians do not celebrate the Liturgy.

The great Saturday or Sabbath; or the Saturday of light.[2]

Easter Day ("Feast of the Resurrection," or "The Great Feast"). See table below. Easter week is called the week of weeks.

Friday after Easter. The "Confessors" under King Sapor.

Low Sunday ("New" or "Red" Sunday). In some places observed as the memorial of Mar Audishu (Ebedjesus).

Saturday. Mar Khnania (Ananias) "of the wolves."

Second Sunday after Easter.

Monday. Raban Hurmizd of Shiraz (see Sept. 1). This saint is buried in the old monastery called by his name near Alqosh (Elkosh), where also in a Jewish Synagogue is the reputed tomb of the prophet Nahum. The monastery belongs to the Roman Catholic Uniats (Chaldeans).

Third and Fourth Sundays after Easter.

Fifth Sunday after Easter. Mar Adai "the Apostle, one of the Seventy, the Converter of the East. He first converted Abgarus the black king of Urhai (Edessa)." The legend of his

---

[1] See above, page 341.

[2] In allusion to the salutation, "Light to your dead." See above, page 107.

mission and of the correspondence between our Lord and Abgarus is given in the "Teaching of Adai" which has been translated into English. The Greek form of Adai is Thaddaeus, and this saint has often been confused with the Apostle, whose name in Syriac is Tadai. (For a full account, see Smith and Wace, D.C.B., *s.v.* Thaddaeus.)

Ascension Day.

Sunday after Ascension.

The seven weeks from Easter to Pentecost is called the Shawu'a of the Resurrection.

Whitsunday ("Pentecost").

At Pentecost begins the Shawu'a of the Apostles (fifty days); and the first Sunday after Pentecost is called the Second of the Apostles.

Wednesday after Pentecost. "On this day was the first Eucharist celebrated by James the Lord's brother. St. Mary first received, then the Apostles."

Friday after Pentecost. Friday of Gold (Acts iii.).

Seventh Friday after Pentecost (and in old times also the preceding Wednesday), The "Seventy Apostles."

Seventh Sunday after Pentecost, the Twelve Apostles. This is also the first Sunday of the Shawu'a (seven weeks) of summer. Also called Nusardil. On this day the Syrians sprinkle one another with water.

First Friday of Summer (eighth after Pentecost). Mar Sergis (Sergius). But in some places this is observed on the preceding Sunday.

Second Friday of Summer (ninth after Pentecost). Mar Mari, pupil of Mar Adai.

Sixth Friday of Summer (thirteenth after Pentecost). Mar Shimun Barseba'i, ninth Catholicos of the East and martyr, A.D. 314 to 330 or 326 to 344 (date uncertain). He died on Good Friday (see April 15). His name means "son of a dyer." (Assem., B. O. vol. iii. pt. 1, p. 611.) Otherwise called, in English, Simeon Bar Saboë.

The Shawu'a of Elia (seven Sundays) follows that of summer; the last four Sundays being also counted after Holy Cross Day (Sept. 13). See below.

Third Friday of Elia (sixteenth after Pentecost). Memorial of Elijah the Tishbite.

Four Sundays of Mar Mushi (St. Moses) follow the Shawu'a of Elia, and then four Sundays of the Hallowing of the Church, which terminate the cycle. Each of these seasons is called for convenience a Shawu'a. The first Sunday of the Hallowing of the Church is also called *Ma'alta* or Entrance; on this day the Syrians move from the summer chapel to the nave of the church for their daily prayers. In this Shawu'a the services speak chiefly of the constitution of the church. Albiruni (A.D. 973–1048), in his "Chronology of Ancient Nations," p. 306 (qu. in Smith and Wace, "Dict. Christ. Biog.," *s.v.* "Nestorianism"), says that on Ma'alta they wandered from the nave to the roofs in memory of the return of the Israelites to Jerusalem.

Third Friday of the Church. Mar Ogin.

Old Style.

January 1. Mar Shalita (obsolete; see September 19).
January 24. St. George's companions, martyrs (obsolete).
March. First Wednesday. St. George, martyr.
April 15.[1] Mar Shimun Barseba'i, Catholicos (obsolete).
April 24 (*sic*). St. George, martyr. A great festival.
April 27. St. Christopher, martyr, and St. George (obsolete).
May. First Tuesday. Sons of Shmuni (2 Macc. vii.). Universally observed.
May 15. St. Mary.
July 3. St. Thomas, who "was pierced with a lance in India. His body is at Urhai (Edessa), having been brought there by the merchant Khabin." A great festival.
July 15. St. Cyriac ("Mar Quriaqus, whom Halinns killed in Persia, and Diuliti his mother"). Ruinart, in his "Acta Martyrum Sincera" (p. 477), says that St. Cirycus and Julitta died at Tarsus about 305, A.D. The Greeks keep their festival on this day, but the Latins on June 16.
July 29. St. Peter and St. Paul (obsolete).
August 1. Fast of St. Mary begins (fifteen days).
August "is the month of the sons of Shmuni" (this is obsolete).
August 6. Transfiguration ("Revelation;" also called "The Ascension of our Lord on Mount Tabor").

---

[1] In Smith's "Dict. Christ. Biog.," given as April 17.

August 10. Mar Shalita (obsolete; see September 19).
August 15. St. Mary.
September 1. Raban Hurmizd of Shiraz. "On this day, after his death, he opened the eyes of a blind man" (obsolete).
September 8. Nativity of St Mary. "Also the memorial of Yunakhir and Khana (Hannah) her parents."
September 13 (*sic*). Feast of the Cross.
September 19. Mar Shalita, patron saint of the patriarchal church at Qudshanis, disciple of Mar Ogin.
October. First Monday. St. George.
October. First Wednesday. Mar Tiadorus (Theodore) the Interpreter (obsolete).
October 1. Khnania (Ananias), "who baptized Paul; he was the first metropolitan of Damascus" (obsolete).
October 2. Mar Papa, Catholicos (*cir.* 300, A.D., Assem., *ubi supra*) (obsolete).
October 4. The eight (*sic*) boys, *i.e.* sleepers, of Ephesus. The day is obsolete, but the Syrians often relate their story.
October 12. Three hundred martyrs at Shigar (obsolete).
October 13. St. John the Evangelist (obsolete).
October 25. Raban Pithiun, martyr. There is a very old church dedicated to him on the mountain side above the Tkhuma valley in Turkey, which is much resorted to on this day. He was the opponent of "the Magi (astrologers), the sons of error." (Martyrs Anthem for Saturday evening.)
November 1. St. Cyprian (obsolete).
November 15. Mar Audishu (Ebedjesus). There were several fathers of this name. Perhaps the celebrated author of the "Pearl," *cir.* 1298, A.D., is here commemorated. He was metropolitan of Nisibis and Armenia.
November 17. Mar Agnátis (Ignatius), "disciple of the sons of thunder." St. George. St. Basil (all obsolete).
November 19. Mar Yaqu Mpasqa (St. James the mutilated). So called because his limbs were cut off one by one.
November 22. Diodorus, Bishop of Tarsus, and twelve thousand Martyrs (obsolete).
December 22. Mar Quriaqus (St. Cyriac).

NOTE.—The fourth Sunday of Elia must always be the first after the Festival of the Cross (September 13), and if necessary the other Sundays of Elia must be changed. Excepting only that if Holy Cross Day fall in the week before the first Sunday of Elia, then the first Sunday retains its place and on the following Sunday the service of the fourth Sunday of Elia is used.

If Easter fall late, all or some of the Sundays of Mar Mushi are omitted; and, apparently, if it fall as late as possible, the last Sunday of Elia also. If Easter fall on the earliest possible day, the fifth and fourth Sundays of Elia will have to be interchanged so as to follow the rule given above. But this arrangement is not explicitly ordered.

To find Easter.[1]

RULE 1. The cycle of the moon is found by adding 12 to the year and deducting 1800. Divide by 19, and the remainder is the cycle. *Examples:*—1815, cycle 8; 1826, cycle 19; 1891, cycle 8.

RULE 2. Having found the cycle of the moon look in the table for the date written against it, and Easter is the following Sunday. [The dates are Old Style; to translate into New Style, add 12 days.]

Table.

1. April 2.	11. April 12.
2. March 22.	12. March 31.
3. April 10.	13. March 21.
4. March 30.	14. April 9.
5. April 18.	15. March 29.
6. April 7.	16. April 17.
7. March 27.	17. April 5.
8. April 15.	18. March 25.
9. April 4.	19. April 13.
10. March 24.	

Example:—1891, cycle 8, Easter Day, April 21 (Old Style), May 3 (New Style).

[1] From the Greek Σύνοψις ἱερά.

INDEX.

ABBOTT, Mr. Consul-General, 127
Abduction, 78, 126
Abdurrahman Beg, 26
Abgarus, 348
Absolution, 202, 248, 265
Abuse worse than a blow, 131
Adai, Mar, 3, 247, 303, 348
—— Sheikh, 46
Advent, 346
Affinity, Table of, 146
Age of marriage, 142
Ahmed Beg, 24
Ahriman, 115
Albiruni, 331, 350
Alighting before a Mussulman, 125
Alqosh (Elkosh), 323, 348
Amadia, 46
Amir-i-Nizam, 111
Angels, orders of, 181, 184
'Anidha, 233, 340
Antidoron, 209, 249, 260
Antioch, 336
Arabian Nights, 320
Ararat, 9
Arbela, 193
Archdeacons, 182
Ardishai, 165, 196
Armenia, 193
Armenians, 77, 137
Arrack, 74
Artushi Kurds, 28
Ascension Day, 335
Asceticism, 316
Ashiret, the name, 10

Ashitha, 34, 38, 205
Ass, five-legged, 206
Assyria, 8, 9, 97, 193
Assyrian, the name, 6, 8
Astronomy lesson, 175
Audishu, Mar, 7, 8, 265, 303, 337, 348, 351
Auraham, Mar, 16, 195
Awa, Mar, 226, 239, 347
Azerbaijan, 9

BABYLON, Patriarch of, 5
Badger, Dr., 7, 46, 151, 190, 203, 247, 266, 277, 285, 286, 298
Bail, dangers of, 128
Baita or "house," 39, 51
Balakhana, balcony, 53
Balal the fool, 46
Baptism, 267, sqq.
Baqchiqal'a, 338
Bar Hebraeus, 283
Barandus river, 77
Bas, 29, 31, 44, 195
Basil, St, 546, 351
Bastinado, 136
Bathing, 79, 340
Bazaar at Urmi, 60
Beards, 97
"Beautiful pen," 165, 171
Bedr Khan Beg, 10
Bedsteads, 48
"Before and after," 217, sqq., 232
Bells, 210, 213, 297
Bema, 202, 254, 292
Benedicite, 231
Berwer, 45, 195, 298

2 A

INDEX.

Betrothal, 143, *sqq.*
Bible, the Syrian, 163, 252, *sqq.*, 320
Bishops' duties, 198
Bith Garmai, 193
Bith Sluk, 193
"Blessing," 106, 133
Blood money, 129
Bookbinding, 180
Booths, 71
Bradust, 77
Bread, 40, 85
Breakfast, 17, 49
Breaking-up, 176
Bribing, 26, 108, 128, 132, 167
Bridges, 31, 62, 64
Bright, Dr., 311, 313
Buffaloes, 66, 80, 128
Burakha, 233
Burial Service, 233, 279, *sqq.*
Busra (Bussorah), 193
Butter, 87, 88
Butter Stone, 44

CANDLES, 90, 217, 235
Canon of Scripture, 321
"Canons" in the Liturgy, 255
Carnival, 175
Carpets, 52
Carshunic, 323
Catholicos. *See* Patriarch.
Cemeteries, 282
Ceremonial defilement, 138, 314, 341
Chalcedon, 200
Chaldean, the name, 6, 8
Chaldean Uniats, 5, 78, 348
Chaldee astrology, 7
Character, Syriac, 172
———, Syrian, 326
Charms, 321
Cheese, 88
Cherubic Hymn, 257
Chess, 19
Children's dress, 92, 161
——— communion, 260
China, missions in, 5, 193, 194
Chorepiscopi, 182, 210
Christmas, 243, 331, 341, 346
Christopher St., 350

Churches, plan of, 290, *sqq.*
Churchwardens, 33
Clan feeling, 29
Clergy, orders of, 181, *sqq.*
Coffins, 280
Collects, 216, 225
Communicatio idiomatum, 307, 308
Communion, Holy, 243, *sqq.*
——— at funerals, 284
——— of the people, 259
——— of clergy, 261
Compline, 233, 342
Composition on Syrian customs, 148
Condolences, 107, 283, 333
Confession, 265
Confessors, the, 348
Confirmation, 271
Consecration of churches, 303
Constantine and Helena, 205, 335
Cottage in a vineyard, 71
Council of patriarch, 15
Creed, Nicene, 256
Cross, sign of, 215, 236, 248, 336
———, festival of, 244, 335
Crowning, order of, 151, 272
Cuckoos, 82
Curfew, 106
Cyriac, St. (Mar Quriaqus), 303, 338, 350, 351
Cyril, St., 312

DAILY service, 212, *sqq.*
Damascus, 193
Dancing, 333
——— on tight-rope, 155, 334
Daughters-in-law, 156
Deacons, 181, 207, 209, 255, 276
Deaconesses, 210, 277
Degaluh, 115
Devotion to B. V. M., 238
Digamy, 157, 203
Digdin, 40
Diminutives, 198, 325
Diodorus of Tarsus, 307, 351
Dipping in the dish, 103
Divorce, 98, 137, 157

INDEX.

Diz or Dizin, 29, 195, 299
Diza, 26, 299
Dogs, 314
Doors, 57, 297
Doorkeepers, 210
Doorways, 50
Doubling letters, 3
Dowi, 88
Dowry, 155
Dress in Persia, 90, 148
—— in Kurdistan, 94
—— of clergy, 203
"Drunken Europeans," 65
Duri, 45, 195, 298

EARNEST money, 140
East, praying towards, 235
Easter, 330, 345, 348
——, to find, 352
"Eating sticks," 136
Edessa (Urhai), 322, 348, 350
Ejaculations of deacons, 208, 255
Election of patriarchs (ancient), 187
Elements, preparation of, 249
Elia, Mar, 5, 331, 341, 349
Eloping, 156
Elymais or Elam, 188, 190, 193
Ephesus, Council of, 305, *sqq.*
——, sleepers of, 351
Ephrem, St., 185, 229, 307
Epiphany, 243, 247, 334, 346
Estrangela, 172
Evensong, 215, *sqq.*
Excommunication, 191, 202
Execution outside the gate, 135
Exhortations, 209
Exorcists, 210
Expulsion of catechumens, 256
Externals, regard for, 316

FALSEHOOD, 326
Fan and shovel, 76
Farcing psalms, etc., 215, *sqq.*
Fars, 193
Fasts, 340, *sqq.*
Fasting Communion, 343
Feasts, 102, 334
February, 329

Festivals, depending on Easter, 330
—— of our Lord, 331
Fields built up, 34
Fikri Pasha, 24
Fireworks, 114
"Firstborn," the, 252
Firstfruits, 199
Fishing, 76
Fleeing, 173
Floors in Tiari, 43
Food, Syrian, 105, 149, 342
Friday mosque, the, 60
Frontier troubles, 21, 136
Fruit, 74
Fuel, 69, 87

GABRIEL, Archangel, 348
Gagoran, 299
Games, 171
Gauriel, Mar, 112, 196
Gavilan, 77, 196
Gawar, 26, 135, 299
George, St., 60, 303, 337, 350, 351
Geza, 233
Girls at school, 176
Giving a sop, 103
Giving in marriage, 144
Glass, 58
Gloria in excelsis, 230
Godparents, 147, 273
God save the Queen, 113
Good Friday, 348
Gospel, the one, 252
Gourds, 43
Governor's duties, a, 131
Gramqayi, 193
Grant, Dr. Asahel, 277, 336
Grapes, 43, 72
Gravestones, 288
Greek doctors, 247, 347
—— words in Syriac, 245
—— kings, 157

HAGGLING, 61
Hakkiari government, 23
Halil Pasha, 23
Hedges of vineyards, 71
Herat, 193

Herki Kurds, 28
High Schools, 164
Highwaymen, 135, 155
Hindustan, 193
Hipzillah Beg, 13
Honey, 87
Hoopoes, 81
Horses, 64
Hospitality, 83, 100
Houses, 38, sqq., 49, sqq.
Housetops, 54
Huc, M., 19, 177, 319, 332
Hulala, 227
Hurmizd, 115, 277, 348, 351

IGNATIUS, St., 217, 351
Incense, 230
Independence of Seleucia, 4, 190
Infant communion, 260
Inheritance, laws of, 140
Intercessions, 237, sqq.
Invocation in Liturgy, 258
—— at Baptism, 269, 270
—— of Saints, 239
Irrigation, 67, 72
Isaak of Ishbad, 247, 309
Ishuyaw, Mar, 45, 195
Iyal, 274, 297

JACOBITES, 6, 283
James, St., 346
——, the mutilated, 352
Jebel Judi, 74
Jester, the patriarchal, 29
Jews, the two, 120
Jilu, 29, 44, 195, 249
John Baptist, St., 247, 320
Jonah, 347
Joseph, St., in European hat, 60
Julamerk, 12, 23
Julitta, 350
Justice in Kurdistan, 25, 27
—— in Persia, 126, sqq.
——, sense of, 134

KALENDAR, the, 328, sqq., 346, sqq.
Kashkul, 221, 232, 346
Kermi, natural bridge at, 34
Khananis, 22, 299

Khnana, 143, 151
Khnania, Mar, 348, 351
Khnanishu, Mar. See Matran.
Khudhra, 229, 232
Khulwan or Khalakh, 193
Kissing the cross, 215, 236, 336
—— the hand, 99, 215, 221
Kneeling, 237, 257
Knitting the bridechamber, 152
Kochanis. See Qudshanis.
Kokha or Kokhaya, 124
Kuhi, 7, 188
Kurasta, 233

LAKHUMARA, 219, 233, 268, 275
Lamps, 90
—— at weddings, 153
Landlord system, 121
Layard, Sir H., 8, 44, 46
Lay baptism, 276
Learning by heart, 165, 209
Leaven, the holy, 248
Lections, system of, 251
—— at baptism, 268
—— at funerals, 282
Lectionaries 233, 252
Lent. See Fasts.
Letters, 114
Life without clocks, 17
Lights, 234
Litanies 182, 184, 208, 254
Liturgies, the three, 245
Lobster salad, 314
Locks, 57
Lodge in garden of cucumbers, 71
Lord's Prayer, how said, 216

MA'ALTA, 350
Magi, 55, 301
Malabar, liturgy of, 246
Malaria, 70
Meliks, 13, 45
Mar, the title, 307
Mar Bishu, 195, 295
Mari, Mar, 3, 247, 303, 349
Mariam, Mart, 55, 301, 334, 341, 346, 350, 351
Marriage service, 151, 233
Marriages, Christian, 142, sqq.

INDEX.

Marriages, Mussulman, 153
——, early, 157, 167
——, clerical, 203
Martyrs, 222
Masta, 37, 87
Master and servant, 117
Matai, Mar, 283
Matran, 20, 22, 192, 195
Maundy Thursday, 244, 247, 248, 346, 347
Melons, 44, 71
Memorials of departed, 287
Mergawar, 77, 195
Merv, 193
Method, want of, 172
Metropolitans, list of, 193
Metropolitan. *See* Matran.
Mid-lent, 345
Mills, 69
Mira, Kurdish, 24
Modakhel, 61
Monasteries, 211, 234
Monks, 157, 342
Monophysites, 313
Months, blessing of, 329
Morning service, 227, 228
Mosaic law, 315
Mosquitoes, 42
Mosul, 5, 31, 193, 323
Mountains and plains, 168
Mushi, Mar, 11, 331, 350
Music, 105
Mussulmans and Christians, 139, 147
Mysteries, the, 249

Names, 277
Natur kursi, 187
Nazar, Sheikh, 46
Nazarites, 187
Nazla river, 77, 196
Neale, Dr., 190, 285
Nersai, Mar, 347
Nestorius, 4, 150, 245, 248, 305, *sqq.*, 347
Nestorianism, 306, *sqq.*
New or Red Sunday, 346, 348
Night service, 227, 228
Nimrod, Shamasha, 16
Nineveh, 55

Ninevites, Rogation of, 243, 247, 341, 347
Nisibis, 193
Noah's vineyard, 74
Nusardil, 337, 349

Obeidullah, Sheikh, 21, 28
Offering sheep by roadside, 112
Ogin, Mar, 350
Oil in baptism, 269
Open, Sesame, 320
Oppressions, 23, 130
Ordinal, 233
Ordination of bishops, 182
——, age of, 201
Original sin, 285
Oxen muzzled, 75
Ovens, 40, 41, 51

Painting the eyes, 149
Palm Sunday, 348
Palu, 345
Papa, Mar, 351
Parables, 319
Paris (Fars), 193
Parseeism, 114
Partridges, Asiatic, 82
Pastoral staff, 262
Patriarch of the East, 5, 12, *sqq.*, 195
—— of Babylon, 5
—— designate, 16, 195
Patriarch's difficulty, a, 33
—— titles, 185
—— duties, 188
Patriarchates, number of, 189
Passover. *See* Maundy Thursday.
Peace (salutation), 106
—— kiss of, 215, 255, 273, 287
Pearl, the, 265, 351
Periaduti, 182, 210
Perkins, Dr., 163, 326
Persian language, 123, 163, 170
Perspective, ideas of, 59
Peshwaz, 110, *sqq.*
Peter-Paul, 347, 350
Pictures, 59, 236
Pigs, 314
Pilgrims, 81, 206

INDEX.

Pipes, 52
Pison, 11
Pithiun, Mar, 351
Ploughing, 67
Poem on the three birds, 116
Poll tax, 122, 205
Prath of Maishan, 193
Prayers, daily, 212, *sqq*.
——, private, 49
Precedence of bishops, 198
Presents, 108
Prices, 66
Priests' duties, 202
Priests, number of, 205
"Priesthood," the name, 185
Printing, 179
Procession, wedding, 149
——, to meet strangers, 109
Psalter, 218, 240
Public security, 135
Punishing criminals, 135
—— whole families, 318
Punishments, school, 169

QUAILS, 80
Qudshanis, 10, 11, 18, 146, 152, 195, 249, 291, 329, 344, 347, 351
Quriaqus. *See* Cyriac.

RABAN Yonan, 19
Rabbi, the name, 92
Rags and patches, 96
Ramazan, 55
Rams as gravestones, 289
Rayat, the name, 10
Readers, 181
Reading upside down, 59, 217
Reservation, 261
Reviving old oases, 128
Riddles, 320
Rifles of Kurds, 38
Rivers of Urmi plain, 169, 196
Roads, 30, 63
Robe of honour, 133
Roofs, 48, 53
Rosaries, 105
Russia, begging in, 137, 179, 206
——, Syrian villages in, 138
Russian generosity, 206

SABBATH, the great, 348
Sacristans, 13, 210, 249, 295
Saints' days, 331
Salabekan, 35
Salmas plain, 77
Salutations, 30, 103, 106
Samarcand, 193
Sancta sanctis, 270
Sanctuary of churches, 292, 304
Sa-uchbulak, 78
Saurishu, Mar, 195, 286, 303, 347
Sawa, Mar, 301
Schools, 160, *sqq*.
Sebaste, martyrs of, 347
Seleucia-Ctesiphon, 4, 190
Semantron, 210, 213, 251
Sergis, Mar, 195, 302, 349
Sermon on the Eucharist, 264
Servility, absence of, 120
Sewing, 177
Shabrgard, 193
Shalita, Mar, 11, 290, 303, 350, 351
Sham, 193
Shamsdin, 21, 195, 295
Shapatnaya, 160
Shaving, 97
Shawu'i, 332, 350, *sqq*.
Shell-fish, 314
Shepherds and salt, 77
Shian Agha, 13
Shigar, martyrs at, 352
Shimei's curses, 132
Shimun, Mar. *See* Patriarch.
——, Barseba'i, 183, 200, 244, 338, 350, 351
Shkhinta (Shechinah), 295
Shmuni, sons of, 239, 337, 350
Shoes, 149, 214
Shurayi, 219, *sqq*.
Siamidha, 233
Sick, laying on of hands on, 202
Signing and breaking at Eucharist, 258
—— sick children, 275
Singing, 217
Siryuki, 40
Sliwa, Mar, 195

INDEX. 359

Smoking, 52, 104
Snow, travelling in, 80
Solduz, 196
Solomon and hoopoes, 81
Soma, 344
Spinning and weaving, 90
Sponsors, 147, 273
Stained glass, 58
Standing at prayer, 236
Stephen, St., 307, 347
Stewards, 210
Stoles, 226
Stools in Tiari, 42
Stores for winter, 89
Storks, 81
Straw for building, 53
Subdeacons, 181, 209
Succession to patriarchate and episcopate, 186, 194, 197
Sunday, 339
Superghan, 165, 196, 338
Supna, 45
Surnames, 279
Sursum Corda, 256
Swaddling, 274
Syriac, 163, 165, 322
Syrian, the name, 6, 7
—— doctors, 7, 347
Synods, 191, 199

TABRIZ, 79, 109
Takhsa, 173, 232, 243, 265, 343, 345
Tal, 29, 44, 195, 303, 335
Tamerlane or Timur, 5
Taxes, 27, 122
Tea and coffee, 17, 89, 332
Teacher and pupil, 120, 161
Temperature of Urmi, 82
Tenure of houses and vineyards, 122, sqq.
Tergawar, 77, 195
Termani, 303
Thaddæus, 350
Theodore the Interpreter, 245, 307, 347, 351
Theotokos, 307, 310
Thomas, St., 3, 79, 244, 337, 350
——, Christians of, 246
Threshing-floor, 75

Tiari, 10, 29, sqq., 95, 152, 187, 195, 205, 214, 283, 295, 301, 323, 330
Tis, 195, 298
Tkhuma, 10, 29 sqq., 187, 195, 205, 295, 352
Tobacco, 72
Tonsure, 204
Tortoises, 314
Tournament, a, 18
Trades, 137, 179
Transfiguration, 350
Translation of bishops, 183
Travelling in Persia, 82
Trousseau, a bride's, 146
Truth, 133
Turkish language, 123, 163, 170
Types of face, 44

UKEI, 45, 195
Unction, 248, 269, 272
Urmi, the name, 10, 114
—— plain, 65, 77, 255, 323
——, Sea of, 78
——, town of, 55, sqq.
Usury, 139

VALI Ahd, the, 109
Van, 18, 45
Veils, 93
Vestments, 226, 261
Village festivals, 333
—— houses, 51
—— schools, 163
Vines in Tiari, 43
Vineyards, 71
Virgins, Rogation of, 347

WAGES, 56, 65
Waltu, 29, 195
Washing bodies of dead, 281
—— after funerals, 284
Weapons, 38, 95, 215
Weeping at funerals, 280
Werda, 233
Wills, 141
Windows, 49, 58
Wine, 73, 250
Winnowing, 76
Wolves, 48

Women in Kurdistan, 35
—— in Persia, 85
——, position of, 98, sqq.
——, dress of, 92
Words of Institution, 257
Writing, 165, 171

YASHMAQ, 94
Yawalaha, Mar, 46
Year, beginning of, 328

Yezidis, 46
Yonan, Mar, 45, 195, 196
Yukhanan, Mar, 195, 296
—— Bar Zobi, 247

ZAB, Zawa, 11, 31, sqq., 306
Zaya, Mar, 44, 346
Zoroaster, 114, 338
Zozan, 37
Zuhma, 37, 38, 345

SYRIAC WORKS PUBLISHED AT THE MISSION PRESS, URMI.

(*To be had at the S.P.C.K. depôt, and at the office of the "Assyrian Mission," 7, Dean's Yard, Westminster.*)

1. The *Takhsa*, Part I., containing the three Liturgies, Baptismal Service, and Short Festival Anthems, in red and black, 4to. Price 21s. in sheets, 25s. bound.

2. The *Takhsa*, Part II., containing the Collects, Occasional Prayers, Offices for the Preparation of the Elements, for the Consecration of Churches, etc., and Benedictions, in red and black, 4to. *Nearly ready.*

3. The *Marriage Service*. *In the press.*

4. The *Lectionary*, giving all the proper lections from the *Khudhra*. 8vo. Price 5s.

5. A *Grammar of Classical Syriac*, with the explanations in the vernacular. Founded partly on the Eastern copies of Bar Hebraeus and on Bar Zobi, and giving the Eastern Syrian traditions from which the Jacobite grammars in many cases differ. 8vo. Price 10s. 6d.

6. A *Grammar of Vernacular Syriac*, with an analytical spelling-book, giving a comparison of the various dialects; the explanations in the vernacular. 8vo. Price 10s. 6d.

7. A *Larger Catechism*, in the vernacular. 8vo.

8. A *Shorter Catechism* for elementary schools. 8vo. Price 2s. 6d.

9. A *Vocabulary of Verbs* now in use in the different districts, with their meanings in English; with a short *English Grammar* prefixed (the explanations in vernacular Syriac). Small 4to. Price 5s.

10. The *Psalter*, as divided by the Eastern Syrians.

11. An *Easy Ecclesiastical History* of the First Four Centuries, in the vernacular. Price 2s. 6d.

The press has also issued for local use a Register of Births, Marriages, and Deaths, etc., and two short and easy spelling-books.

The Service-books mentioned above are all in classical Syriac.

PUBLICATIONS

OF THE

Society for Promoting Christian Knowledge.

Star Atlas.

Gives all the stars from 1 to 6·5 magnitude between the North Pole and 34° South Declination, and all Nebulæ and Star Clusters, which are visible in telescopes of moderate power. Translated and adapted from the German of Dr. KLEIN, by the Rev. E. McCLURE, M.A. Imp. 4to. With 18 Charts and 80 pages illustrative letterpress. Cloth boards, 7s. 6d.

The Face of the Deep.

A Devotional Commentary on the Apocalypse. By CHRISTINA G. ROSSETTI. Demy 8vo. Cloth boards, 7s. 6d.

History of India.

From the Earliest Times to the Present Day. By Captain L. J. TROTTER. With eight page Woodcuts and numerous smaller Woodcuts. A new and revised edition. Post 8vo. Cloth boards, 6s.

Beauty in Common Things.

Illustrated by twelve Drawings from Nature. By Mrs. J. W. WHYMPER. Printed in Colours. Demy 4to. Cloth boards, 7s. 6d.

The Fern Portfolio.

By FRANCIS GEORGE HEATH. With fifteen Plates, elaborately drawn, life size, exquisitely coloured from Nature, and accompanied by descriptive texts: all the species of British Ferns, which comprise a large proportion of the Ferns of America, and many other parts of the World. Elegantly bound in cloth, 8s.

Scenes in the East.

Consisting of twelve Coloured Photographic Views of Places mentioned in the Bible, beautifully executed, with descriptive letterpress. By the Rev. CANON TRISTRAM, Author of "The Land of Israel," etc. 4to. Cloth, bevelled boards, gilt edges, 6s.

Sinai and Jerusalem; or, Scenes from Bible Lands.

Consisting of Coloured Photographic Views of Places mentioned in the Bible, including a Panoramic View of Jerusalem with descriptive letterpress. By the Rev. F. W. HOLLAND, M.A. Demy 4to. Cloth, bevelled boards, gilt edges, 6s.

Bible Places; or, The Topography of the Holy Land.

A succinct account of all the Places, Rivers, and Mountains of the Land of Israel mentioned in the Bible, so far as they have been identified; together with their modern names and historical references. By the Rev. CANON TRISTRAM. With Map. Crown 8vo. Cloth boards, 4s.

The Land of Israel.

A Journal of Travel in Palestine, undertaken with special reference to its Physical Character. By the Rev. CANON TRISTRAM. Fourth edition, revised. With Maps and many Illustrations. Large Post 8vo. Cloth boards, 10s. 6d.

The Natural History of the Bible.

By the Rev. CANON TRISTRAM, Author of "Bible Places," etc. With numerous Woodcuts. Crown 8vo. Cloth boards, 5s.

A History of the Jewish Nation.

From the Earliest Times to the Present Day. By the late E. H. PALMER, M.A., Author of "The Desert of the Exodus," etc. With Map of Palestine and numerous Illustrations. Crown 8vo. Cloth boards, 4s.

Pictorial Architecture of the British Isles.

By the Rev. H. H. BISHOP. With about 150 Illustrations. Royal 4to. Cloth boards, 4s.

Pictorial Architecture of Greece and Italy.

By the Rev. H. H. BISHOP. With numerous Engravings. Royal 4to. Cloth boards, 5s.

Pictorial Geography of the British Isles.

By MARY E. PALGRAVE. With numerous Engravings. Royal 4to. Cloth boards, 5s.

British Birds in their Haunts.

Being a popular Account of the Birds which have been observed in the British Isles; their Haunts and Habits; their systematic, common, and provincial Names; together with a Synopsis of Genera; and a brief Summary of Specific Characters. By the late Rev. C. A. JOHNS, B.A., F.L.S. Post 8vo. Cloth boards, 6s.

Flowers of the Field.

By the late Rev. C. A. JOHNS, B.A., F.L.S. With numerous Woodcuts. Crown 8vo. Cloth boards, 5s.

The Forest Trees of Britain.
By the late Rev. C. A. JOHNS, B.A., F.L.S. With 150 Woodcuts. Post 8vo. Cloth boards, 5s.

Freaks and Marvels of Plant Life; or, Curiosities of Vegetation.
By M. C. COOKE, M.A., LL.D. With numerous Illustrations. Post 8vo. Cloth boards, 6s.

Toilers in the Sea.
By M. C. COOKE, M.A., LL.D. With numerous Illustrations. Post 8vo. Cloth boards, 5s.

A Chapter of English Church History.
Being the Minutes of the S.P.C.K. for the years 1698-1703. Together with Abstracts of Correspondents' Letters during part of the same period. Edited by the Rev. E. McCLURE, M.A., Editorial Secretary of the S.P.C.K. Demy 8vo. With a Woodcut. Cloth boards, 5s.

Turning Points of English Church History.
By the Rev. EDWARD L. CUTTS. Crown 8vo. Cloth boards, 3s. 6d.

Turning Points of General Church History.
By the Rev. EDWARD L. CUTTS. Crown 8vo. Cloth boards, 5s.

Africa, seen through its Explorers.
By CHARLES H. EDEN, Esq. With Map and several Illustrations. Crown 8vo. Cloth boards, 5s.

Australia's Heroes.

Being a slight Sketch of the most prominent amongst the band of gallant men who devoted their lives and energies to the cause of Science, and the development of the Fifth Continent. By C. H. EDEN, Esq. With Map. Crown 8vo. Cloth boards, 3s. 6d.

Wellington; or, The Public and Private Life of Arthur, First Duke of Wellington.

As told by himself, his comrades, and his intimate friends. By G. LATHOM BROWNE. With Portraits, etc. Crown 8vo. Cloth boards, 5s.

Christians under the Crescent in Asia.

By the Rev. EDWARD L. CUTTS, B.A., Author of "Turning Points of Church History," etc. With numerous Illustrations. Post 8vo. Cloth boards, 5s.

Some Heroes of Travel; or, Chapters from the History of Geographical Discovery and Enterprise.

Compiled and re-written by the late W. H. DAVENPORT ADAMS, Author of "Great English Churchmen," etc. With Map. Crown 8vo. Cloth boards, 5s.

The Fifth Continent, with the Adjacent Islands.

Being an Account of Australia, Tasmania, and New Guinea, with Statistical Information to the latest date. By C. H. EDEN, Esq. With Map. Crown 8vo. Cloth boards, 5s.

Frozen Asia: a Sketch of Modern Siberia.

By CHARLES H. EDEN, Esq., Author of "Australia's Heroes," etc. With Map. Crown 8vo. Cloth boards, 5s.

Heroes of the Arctic and their Adventures.

By FREDERICK WHYMPER, Esq., Author of "Travels in Alaska." With Map, eight full-page and numerous small Woodcuts. Crown 8vo. Cloth boards, 3s. 6d.

China.

By Professor ROBERT K. DOUGLAS, of the British Museum. With Map, and eight full-page Illustrations and several Vignettes. Post 8vo. Cloth boards, 5s.

Russia: Past and Present.

Adapted from the German of Lankenau and Oelnitz. By Mrs. CHESTER. With Map and three full-page Woodcuts and Vignettes. Post 8vo. Cloth boards, 5s.

LONDON:
NORTHUMBERLAND AVENUE, CHARING CROSS, W.C.;
43, QUEEN VICTORIA STREET, E.C.
BRIGHTON: 135, NORTH STREET.

www.ingramcontent.com/pod-product-compliance
Lightning Source LLC
Chambersburg PA
CBHW022333230426
43664CB00040B/472